OXFORD INTENSIVE ENGLISH COURS

TEACHER'S BOOK

DAVID BOLTON
MARY BOWEN
CLIVE OXENDEN
LEN PETERSON

Oxford University Press
1989

Oxford University Press,
Walton Street, Oxford OX2 6DP

Oxford New York Toronto Melbourne Auckland
Petaling Jaya Singapore Hong Kong Tokyo
Delhi Bombay Madras Calcutta Karachi
Nairobi Dar es Salaam Cape Town

and associated companies in
Berlin Ibadan

Oxford is a trade mark of Oxford University Press

ISBN 0 19 432355 2

Typeset by Pentacor Ltd, High Wycombe, Bucks
Printed in Hong Kong

The publishers would like to thank the following photographic libraries
for their permission to reproduce photographs:

Britain On View, Hutchison Library, Impact Photos, Rex Features,
Telecom Technology Showcases London.

and the following for their time and assistance:

Midland Bank Plc.; Oxford Academy Language School; Radio Taxis;
Rymans; Salisburys – Handbags Ltd; Samuel H. Plc, Jewellers;
Sylvester Furniture; Watson A. & Sons Ltd, Menswear.

Illustrations by:

Kate Charlesworth, Dave Cockcroft, Susannah English, Conny Jude,
Maggie Ling, Andrew MacConville, Mohsen John Modaberi, RDH Artists,
Christine Roche, Nick Sharratt, Paul Thomas.

Location and studio photography by:

Cathy Blackie, Rob Judges, Mark Mason.

The authors would like to thank staff at International Homestay
Programme, Bromley, and at The British Institute, Valencia, for their help
and co-operation.

CONTENTS

The word *OK* is used all over the world, but nobody really knows where it comes from. These are just a few theories —there are many more. You can take your pick.

- Andrew Jackson, a president of the USA, always wrote 'orl kerrect' on documents.

- *OK* was used as an election slogan in 1840 by Martin van Buren, another American president. One of his nicknames was 'Old Kinderhook', and his supporters formed an OK club.

- *OK* comes from the Haitian port *Aux Cayes* which was famous for its rum. American sailors called the rum *OK*, and then used the word for everything else they liked in Haiti.

- The word comes from the West African languages Ewe and Wolof where *kay* means 'good'. The word was used by slaves brought to the USA.

- Teachers used *OK* on very good exam papers as an abreviation for the Latin *omnes korrectes*.

- The Finnish word *oikea* means 'correct'.

- The Choctaw Indians in Alabama and Mississippi have a word *okeh* which means 'it is so'.

- The Greek words *ola kala* mean 'everything is good'.

- A famous Indian chief, Old Keokuk, used his initials when he signed documents.

INTRODUCTION

Who is *OK* for?

OK is intended primarily for teenagers on short courses of 3–4 weeks.

Book 1 assumes students will already have learnt English for 1 or 2 years.
Book 2 assumes 2 or 3 years of English.
Book 3 assumes 3 or 4 years of English.
Book 4 assumes 4 or 5 years of English.

What are the components of *OK*?

The Student's Book

This contains twelve units. Each unit is divided into three sections or lessons.

Lesson 1 concentrates on practising basic grammar in lively and interesting contexts based on the experiences of a young foreign student in England.

Lesson 2 concentrates on the kind of useful and practical phrases and vocabulary students need in everyday situations, for example when shopping, when eating with an English-speaking family, etc.

Lesson 3 contains a variety of games, activities and tasks. Although there is a strong element of fun, the activities are also designed to improve the students' ability to understand, pronounce and speak English.

A special feature of this section is the 'Now you are here' exercises which include mini-projects, tasks and questionnaires for the use of students who are on courses in Great Britain and Ireland. They are designed to encourage students to speak English to native speakers and to learn more about the country they are staying in. In this way they also practise and consolidate language they have just learnt in class.

It is important to remember that it is not necessary to spend exactly the same amount of time on all three sections. Teachers and students can choose which of the section(s) they want to spend more time on, according to their interests and needs.

The Workbook

This is for use either in class or for students to use on their own, outside class. It consists of follow-up and extension material. The Workbook is optional and the Student's Book can be used on its own.

The answers to the Workbook exercises are included in the back of the book but they can be removed, if necessary.

The Cassette

This contains all the dialogues in the Student's Book as well as exercises for listening comprehension and pronunciation practice.

The Teacher's Book

This contains:

- a complete syllabus
- a description of the course
- hints and guidance on classroom techniques
- instructions for all the exercises and activities
- tapescripts
- an answer key to Student's Book exercises
- a test for placing students at the right level
- progress tests.

Placement test

There is a placement test which should be used at the beginning of the course. It is designed to help teachers/course organizers to divide students into classes/groups according to their level of English. See page 105 for more details.

Progress tests

There are progress tests for use after every four units (i.e. after units 4, 8 and 12.) See page 105 for more details.

1 The role of the teacher

- Make clear from the start that you are in charge. Friendly but firm is the best rule.

- Learn students' names as quickly as possible.

- Try to create a relaxed but positive learning atmosphere.

- Always have a clear idea of what you want to do in a class and what you want the students to learn. Always make a short lesson plan to guide you.

- Give students as much chance as you can to speak in English. The best classes are often when the teacher says very little. *You* don't need the practice, *they* do.

- Try to avoid being always the focus of attention—don't dominate the class. Keep in the background whenever you can, especially when students are working in pairs or groups.

2 Organizing the classroom

- If you can move the chairs, a semi-circle around the blackboard is ideal.

- Make sure all the students can see the board.

- Make sure students can quickly and easily move to pair or group work.

3 Motivation and encouragement

- Praise and encourage students as much as possible, without patronising them.

- Give students confidence and make them feel they are really making progress.

- If you give homework, make sure you correct it.

- At the beginning of each lesson revise what you did the day before. Give students a chance to show how much they remember.

- Encourage students to practise and improve their English as much as possible outside class, by talking to native speakers, reading, watching television, etc.

4 Learning a language

If you described the rules of cricket to foreigners who didn't know the game, they would not immediately be able to play it well. They would need to watch it being played, practise it and develop the necessary skills. The same is true of learning a language. It is not enough to know the rules, you must be able to put them into practice.

Speaking
Students must be given every opportunity to speak English. In *OK* there are a variety of activities, some controlled, others freer, designed to get students talking. Whenever possible get students to talk about things which are meaningful to them—themselves, their family, their country, etc. Try to let conversation arise naturally rather than force it or programme it into the lesson.

Listening
Listening is a skill which needs a lot of practice. English is especially difficult to understand because unstressed words are 'swallowed' or spoken quickly.

Students need to be given plenty of opportunity to listen to conversations and to just try to get the gist of what is being said without worrying about having to understand all of it. Improving listening comprehension takes time and students need to be encouraged to feel they are making progress. In *OK* there are exercises to practise 'gist listening' as well as exercises in which students are asked to listen for specific information and disregard what is irrelevant.

Reading
Reading provides reinforcement of language learnt and helps to consolidate and build vocabulary. As well as reading texts in *OK*, students should be encouraged to read magazines, comics, newspapers, signs, etc.

Writing
Writing reinforces new language which has already been heard and spoken. It gives students a chance to clarify their ideas, gives the teacher important feedback on students' errors and often provides students with a welcome break after intensive oral practice.

Many of the exercises in *OK* can be used for written consolidation. It is inadvisable to give students unguided or uncontrolled writing tasks at this early stage, since they will only make a lot of mistakes and be discouraged.

GENERAL HINTS FOR TEACHERS

5 Presenting new language

Most of the new language in *OK* Student's Book 1 is presented to the student in the form of dialogues. This language may be completely new to some students but familiar to others. Generally it is a good idea to try to present the new language to the class in a clear and memorable way yourself before using the textbook. To do this you can use blackboard drawings, magazine pictures (to present *like/don't like*, for example), the classroom furniture, students themselves (to present *prepositions of place*, for example) or a mime (to introduce the idea of somebody asking for directions), etc.

In each unit we have made suggestions for presenting the new language. These are only *suggestions*. Don't hesitate to use your own ideas.

6 Using the taped dialogues

We have suggested a standard method of exploiting the taped dialogues in *OK*. Don't feel that you are bound to follow this method unit after unit. Don't be afraid to experiment. The important points to remember are:

- use the taped conversations as a model, if possible, for students to imitate
- try to exploit the visual element of the photo stories
- get students to role play the situations
- try to let the controlled oral practice (repetition of the dialogue, etc.) lead on to a freer stage where students use the new language to talk about their own experiences.

7 Transfer

Whenever possible move away from the fictitious world of the textbook to the students' own lives and experiences. For example, if you are practising the past tense, ask students to tell you what they *really* did last night. It is important that they are able to 'transfer' what they are learning to express their own ideas and opinions.

8 Choral repetition

As a general rule, language should be first heard, then spoken. When learning a new word or phrase students need a lot of practice at 'getting their tongue round it', catching and imitating the pronunciation. To do this students usually need to hear and repeat the same word or phrase several times.

Repetition by the student after the teacher is an extremely useful technique. Choral repetition (all the class repeating together) maximizes the time available for practice. Also students, shy ones especially, feel more secure when repeating in chorus. Choral repetition can be used whenever new language is being introduced and practised.

A common method would be:

- give a model twice or three times, e.g. *Can you tell me the way to the station, please?*
- use a natural intonation, not exaggerated or stilted
- indicate with a clear gesture that the class should repeat all together
- say the phrase again and get the whole class to repeat
- quickly get individual students to say the sentence (or word) to check their pronunciation. If they are having trouble, go back to the 'chorus' and give everybody another chance to say it.

9 Pair and group work

Many activities in *OK* are designed for pair or group work. It is often the most efficient and natural way of practising language. If students work simultaneously in pairs, for example, they get more chance to practise the new language than if they have to wait their turn in a whole class activity. Similarly, if students work in groups or teams, the opportunity for speaking is increased. Also, students often feel more at ease working in pairs or groups—they feel less exposed than when they talk in front of the whole class.

Here are some general hints for pair and group work.

- Try to arrange the class so that students are already sitting in pairs or can form pairs very quickly.

- Change the pairing of students frequently. If students are sitting in lines, simply moving one student from one end of the line to the other will change the pairs.

- Sometimes, especially in mixed ability classes, better students can be paired with weaker ones.

- Get students to form pairs and groups as quickly and quietly as possible. It is a good idea to keep the same groups/teams in the same position in the class for several days running and to name or number them.

- Make sure students change roles when they work in pairs. Pairs who finish quickly can repeat the activity or change partners with another pair who have finished.

- Don't worry about the increase in noise level. Try to get students to speak more quietly than usual when they are working in pairs or groups.

- Invent a clear signal when you want to end pair or group work, for example a sharp clap of the hands.

- When students are working in pairs or groups, try to keep a 'low profile'. Move around quietly, listening and encouraging. Interrupt only if really necessary.

10 Teaching vocabulary

There are many ways of explaining the meaning of a new word:

- miming, for example 'cold', 'angry', 'to hit', 'slowly', 'below'
- giving the opposite, for example 'rude', the opposite of 'polite'
- drawing on the blackboard, for example 'bridge', 'candle'
- giving a synonym, for example 'begin' = 'start'
- giving an explanation, for example 'exhausted' *When you are very very tired you are 'exhausted'*.
- using a 'visual aid' such as a magazine picture, for example a fridge
- using students as 'visual aids'

  Example:
  'curly' – point to a student with curly hair
  'high heels' – point to a student wearing high heels
  'between' – point to a student who is 'between' two others.

Make sure students know how to pronounce any new words. Let them say the word(s) after you and get them to mark where the stress falls, like this: tele<u>vi</u>sion.

Make sure they copy the new words down correctly.

Let students use a dictionary in class, but preferably only as a back-up to your teaching.

11 Pacing your lessons

- Don't simply plod through all the exercises and activities at the same speed. Vary the pace and activity to maintain your students' interest and motivation. For example, after a period of intensive oral practice students could 'rest' with a short written exercise.

- Be sensitive to the mood of the class. If you see they are flagging or getting bored, don't be afraid to cut short an activity and play a game to liven them up again.

- Vary the type of activity, for example, whole class/pair work/group work/individual work.

- Get students moving around as much as possible— playing games, acting out situations, etc.

12 Giving instructions

- Speak clearly but avoid speaking too slowly or in a stilted, unnatural way.

- Make sure that you have the attention of the whole class when you are explaining a new activity and that everybody knows exactly what they have to do, especially when they are working in pairs or groups.

  Always get one pair of students (or you and a student) to demonstrate the activity to the class; don't go through the *whole* exercise.

- If the activity is going wrong, don't be afraid to stop it, re-explain it and start again.

13 Asking questions

Forming questions in English is difficult and students need plenty of practice. Make sure your students get practice in asking questions and not just in answering yours.

When you ask a question the general rule is: question first, then the name of a student to answer it. If you give the name first, everybody else switches off.

- Don't ask questions in a fixed order around the class. If students don't know who is going to be asked the next question they will concentrate far more.

- Don't be afraid to let all the students answer a question all at once sometimes.

14 Correcting students

- Be sensitive with your corrections. If you correct harshly or too often, students will not dare to say anything.

- The time when you should correct most is when you are helping students to pronounce new words and phrases.

- When students are working in pairs or groups it is best not to interrupt too often to correct but to listen unobtrusively, note mistakes and deal with them later.

GENERAL HINTS FOR THE TEACHER

- Be especially careful not to overcorrect in the freer stage of a lesson when students are making an effort to use the new language to express their own ideas.

- Don't embarrass a student by making him/her the centre of attention and focusing on the mistake.

- If students make a mistake, indicate with a gesture or facial expression that something is wrong. Give them a chance to correct the error. If they can't, get another student to correct it. Then go back to the student who originally made the mistake.

15 Pronunciation

- Don't aim too high. Most foreign students will never lose their accents. The important thing is that they can be understood.

- Encourage students to use a friendly, lively intonation. This can be taught at the listening and repetition stage when students copy your intonation or that on the cassette. Remember that a flat intonation, with no movement in the voice, can make a student sound bored or unfriendly.

- Get students to learn where new words have their stress, for example photograph, important. Mark the stress on new words or get students to tell you where it is.

- Give plenty of praise and encouragement.

16 Use of the students' own language

If students all speak the same language and you also speak it, try to use it as little as possible. Occasionally, it may be useful to explain a tricky grammar point, but it is better if students listen to English as much as possible. Obviously in a class of mixed nationalities (even if one language group predominates) only English should be used.

17 Using contractions

In normal spoken English contracted or short forms are almost always used, for example I don't smoke (not I do not smoke) and I'm tired (not I am tired).

- Students, therefore, should be taught to always use contractions in spoken English. Nothing makes a foreigner sound more 'foreign' than speaking without contractions.

- Uncontracted forms are used in formal written English, for example in a letter to a bank manager (not usually in a

letter to a friend).

- Contracted forms are used in OK. Keep correcting students if they don't use them in spoken English (a concertina gesture with the hands is useful for this).

18 Now you are here

English language lessons in the students' own country are, by their very nature, artificial—far removed from reality. In contrast, from the moment they get off the boat or plane in the UK, students are often painfully aware of the inadequacy of the English they've learned in their country. They can neither understand what they hear nor say what they mean when, for example, they have to introduce themselves to their host family, ask for more potatoes at mealtimes, ask the way to the sports centre or cash a travellers cheque. As a result students on courses in the UK will, perhaps for the first time, be highly motivated. They have a unique opportunity to learn in the classroom and then immediately put into practice the language they have just learnt as soon as they walk out of the door. It is up to the teacher to exploit this fact and, with the help of this book, make lessons as relevant as possible to their learning needs.

In the 'Now you're here' section of the third lessons, students are encouraged to speak to British people, outside the classroom, about various aspects of British life and customs. By doing this they will not only practise their English but also broaden and deepen their knowledge of all aspects of Britain. It is important that you prepare students well for these activities and that you teach them a polite introductory phrase to use such as, Could I ask you a few questions, please?

Students should also be encouraged to watch television, listen to the radio, read newspapers and magazines, go to the cinema and so on—in other words, to immerse themselves as much as possible in the country, its language and its culture.

19 Writing in the book

Many exercises in the Student's Book require students to fill in gaps, complete tables or write down information that they hear on the cassette. Where there is not enough space to write in the book (or where you don't want students to do this), give students time to copy any grids, etc. on to separate pieces of paper.

20 Ice-breakers

Please _don't_ start teaching before you've read these suggested 'ice-breakers'!

Perhaps the most important function of the first lesson with a new class is for students to get to know you and each other. So don't use the course book for at least the first 15 minutes. Concentrate instead on creating a happy working atmosphere with your class. Get them to look and smile at each other, and get them interested in each other. This is not a waste of time. If from the start your students are relaxed, happy and interested, both your teaching and their learning will be easier and more enjoyable.

How can you do this? Here are some ideas for 'breaking the ice'.

Ball game
You can use a ping-pong ball, or a ball of screwed up paper.

● Get students to stand in a circle. You must join in too. Say your name and throw the ball to a student. He/She must say his/her name and throw the ball to another student, and so on. Immediately students will start looking at each other and so establish eye-contact.

● When you think they know each other's names, change the game. Now throw the ball to a student and say _his/her_ name, and so on.

Mimed introductions
● Students work in pairs. They must not know anything about their partner except his/her name.

● Ask them to find out as much as possible about each other in three minutes _without_ speaking or writing. (They can mime or draw but don't tell them this—at least not at first!)

● When the three minutes are up, get them to sit in a circle (or two circles if it is a large class) and tell the others about their partner. The partner can make corrections if necessary.

Having 'broken the ice' with either or both of the above activities, you can now start using the Student's Book itself.

At some stage in the course you may like to draw student's attention to the images on the covers of OK. At each level, these relate to the number of the book. Book one depicts: an ace; a unicycle; a monocle; a winner ('first'); number one (the goalkeeper in a football team); a hole in one (a golfing term); a queue ('single file'); a one-way sign.

UNIT	LESSON 1	LESSON 2	LESSON 3
	GRAMMAR IN ACTION	**ENGLISH IN SITUATIONS**	**FUN WITH ENGLISH**
1 PAGES 6–11	*to be* possessive adjectives apostrophe 's' genitive	introductions greetings countries and nationalities apologizing saying goodbye	*Further practice in:* pronunciation listening vocabulary reading finding out about the UK
2 PAGES 12–17	demonstratives plural nouns *here/there* definite article	asking and describing where things/places are thanking and responding to thanks	*Further practice in:* pronunciation listening vocabulary reading finding out about the UK
3 PAGES 18–23	*have got* indefinite articles *a/an* – adjective + noun	the alphabet and spelling asking somebody to repeat something using a payphone and making an international phone call	*Further practice in:* pronunciation listening spelling reading finding out about the UK
4 PAGES 24–29	present simple: incl. *do*-construction	telling the time making requests making offers accepting and refusing food	*Further practice in:* pronunciation listening vocabulary reading finding out about the UK
5 PAGES 30–35	present simple: incl. *do*-construction adverbs of frequency	asking for things asking and talking about the cost of things	*Further practice in:* pronunciation listening vocabulary spelling reading finding out about the UK
6 PAGES 36–41	*can/can't*	talking about rules and obligations	*Further practice in:* pronunciation listening vocabulary reading finding out about the UK

UNIT	LESSON 1 GRAMMAR IN ACTION	LESSON 2 ENGLISH IN SITUATIONS	LESSON 3 FUN WITH ENGLISH
7 PAGES 42–47	present continuous for present time	using the telephone taking messages on the telephone	*Further practice in:* pronunciation listening vocabulary reading finding out about the UK
8 PAGES 48–53	*there is/are* *some/any*	inviting making offers accepting/refusing invitations and offers apologizing and making excuses	*Further practice in:* pronunciation listening vocabulary spelling reading finding out about the UK
9 PAGES 54–59	past simple: regular verbs *was/were*	making arrangements making suggestions making excuses	*Further practice in:* pronunciation listening vocabulary reading finding out about the UK
10 PAGES 60–65	past simple: irregular verbs	buying clothes – talking about sizes and colours	*Further practice in:* pronunciation listening vocabulary reading finding out about the UK
11 PAGES 66–71	comparatives/superlatives	asking permission giving/refusing permission talking about dates	*Further practice in:* pronunciation listening vocabulary reading finding out about the UK
12 PAGES 72–77	future: *going to*	saying goodbye revision of various functions	London picture quiz UK quiz

UNIT ONE · LESSON ONE

GRAMMAR IN ACTION

First meeting

Dominique is a French boy. He is sixteen. He is in England for the first time. He is on an English language course

6

GRAMMAR IN ACTION

Grammar summary

- the verb *to be*
- possessive adjectives (*my/your/his/her/its/our/your/ their*)
- the apostrophe *'s* (genitive)

- You could begin the first lesson like this:

  Teacher (T) *My name's Alison. What's your name?*
  (pointing to student)
  Student I (S1) *My name's Martin.*
  Student 2 (S2) *My name's Steffi.*

  Make sure students use contracted/short forms (*My name's Martin*, not *My name is Martin*).

  Say *My name is Alison* and then *My name's Alison*, so students can hear that one sounds 'foreign', the other sounds English.

  Write the two sentences on the board if necessary.

- Students go round the class asking and answering the question *What's your name?* They write down the names they find out.

- Demonstrate the difference between 'his' and 'her' by pointing at individual students and saying:
  His name's Martin.
  Her name's Steffi.

- One student at a time stands up, points and says quickly:
  His name's Martin.
  Her name's Steffi. etc.

  When a student makes a mistake or can't remember a name, another student continues.

First meeting

Notes and possible problems

- Always insist that students use contracted/short forms when they speak (*I'm, she's, it isn't*, etc.). You can use gestures to remind them when they use full/ uncontracted forms. Point out that in written English the full/uncontracted form is more normal. (See the introduction to the dialogue: *Dominique is a French boy.*)

- Make sure that students understand the difference between the apostrophe *'s* (genitive) and the short form of *is*.

Example:
Dominique's a boy's name = Dominique is the name of a boy.

- Mr and Mrs Bond, Miss Fox

  Explain that Mr and Mrs are used with the surname when you talk to adults. They cannot be used on their own, without a name afterwards. Explain that Miss is used with the surname when you talk to an unmarried woman, and can be used on its own. Students may see Ms. Explain that this is used about both married and unmarried women.

Presentation of the dialogue

- Describe the background to the dialogue 'First meeting'. Tell students:

  Dominique's a French student. He's 16. He's in England for the first time. He's on an English language course.

- Pre-teach/check the following words and phrases (by demonstration, drawings, mime, explanation, translation, etc.). Write the words and phrases on the blackboard.

  language course   of course   I'm sorry   rude
  Nice to meet you   bag   over there   heavy

- Students repeat individually or all together the words/ phrases on the board.

- Students listen to the dialogue on the cassette with books closed.

- Ask easy comprehension questions, like these:

  Is Dominique English?
  Is Dominique a boy or a girl?
  Are Mr and Mrs Bond French?
  Are Dominique's bags heavy?

- Students listen to the dialogue again, with books open at p.6.

- Form groups of four students. Students choose one part each (Dominique, Mr Bond, Mrs Bond, Miss Fox) and practise the dialogue.

  Two or three groups can come to the front of the class and act out the dialogue *from memory* (with the teacher's help if necessary).

  Don't insist that the lines are exactly the same as those in the book. Students should be encouraged to improvise.

Exercises

I Questions and answers

Notes and possible problems

- Point out that you can't shorten/contract positive short answers.

  Example:
  Yes it is. not *Yes, it's.*

- One of the purposes of this exercise is to encourage students to use short answers, like *Yes, I am.* or *No, they aren't.* A simple *Yes/No* can sound rude, and a full sentence answer like *Yes, I'm French.* or *No, they aren't English.* sounds heavy or too formal.

- Students can check each other's answers to a) in pairs.

- Check that students don't look at the answers when they do b). Make sure they change roles so they both practise asking and answering the questions.

2 You and Dominique

- Give some examples comparing yourself with Dominique first. Then get some examples from students in which they compare themselves with Dominique.

a Students write sentences individually.

b They can compare their sentences in pairs before reading them out to the rest of the class.

3 Find out

Notes and possible problems

- In a weak class, students can suggest the questions and the teacher can write them on the board.

- 'first name' is sometimes called 'Christian name' or 'forename'. Similarly 'surname' is sometimes 'family name'.

- Focus attention on the question *How old are you?* as this question cannot be translated directly into Latin languages. Point out the use of the verb *to be* not the verb *to have*.

- The two possible answers to the question *How old are you?* are *I'm 15.* or *I'm 15 years old.* not *I'm 15 years.*

- Teach students the words *Sorry?* or *Pardon?* if they don't hear or understand the first time.

4 Memory game

- If a student makes a mistake or hesitates too long, another student takes over.

5 What's missing?

Notes and possible problems

- Point out that *you* can refer to one or more people.

- Students may confuse *his* and *her* because they are the same in some European languages.

  Point out that *its* as in *The dog ate its food* is not the same as *it's* which is short for *it is*.

- First teach the remaining possessive adjectives: *its, our, your* (plural), *their* using students in the class and their names.

- Elicit similar sentences from the students so that all the possessive adjectives are practised.

- Students fill in the missing words, and then check each other's answers.

6 Whose is it?

Notes and possible problems

- Before doing the exercise, teach the apostrophe *'s* (genitive).

  Hold up various things belonging to students in the class and say, for example:

  This is Luc's book.
  This is Katarina's pen.
  These are Antonio's glasses.

  Write on the board:
  Luc's book
  Katarina's pen
  Antonio's glasses

- Point out that the apostrophe *'s* means that these things belong to these students. (In many European languages, you express the same idea with 'This is the book of Luc', 'These are the glasses of Antonio', etc. but this is incorrect in English.)

I Questions and answers

a Match the questions on the left with the answers on the right.

Example: I – f

1 Is Mr Bond French?
2 Is Dominique on an English language course?
3 Is Mrs Bond rude to Dominique?
4 Are Mr and Mrs Bond English?
5 Is Mrs Bond's first name Sue?
6 Is Miss Fox a student?
7 Are Dominique's bags heavy?
8 Is Dominique's surname Fox?

a) No, they aren't.
b) Yes, it is.
c) Yes, they are.
d) No, it isn't.
e) Yes, he is.
f) No, he isn't.
g) No, she isn't.
h) No, she isn't.

b Work in pairs. Student A asks the same questions. Student B answers them without looking at the answers above. Change roles.

2 You and Dominique

In what ways are you different from Dominique?

a Write sentences like this:

Dominique's French but I'm not. I'm Italian.
Dominique's tall but I'm not. I'm quite short.

b Read out your answers in class.

3 Find out

a What are the questions to get the following information?

	First name	Surname	Age	Nationality	Town	First time in England
Student 1						
Student 2						
Student 3						

Examples:
What's your first name?
How old are you?

b Move round the class and ask three students the questions. Fill in the form.

4 Memory game

a The teacher points at a student in the class (student A). That student stands up. Other students in the class say what they can remember about him/her.

Example:
B *His name's Paul.*
C *He's 15.*
D *He's from Menton.*

b The teacher points at another student and the game continues in the same way.

5 What's missing?

I	.....my.....
....	our
it	....
....	his
they	....
....	her
you	....

6 Whose is it?

a Each student gives the teacher one thing.

Examples:
a comb, a key, a lipstick, a watch

b The teacher holds up one thing at a time and asks 'Whose is it?'

c Students answer 'It's Mario's' or 'It's Julia's', etc. (You must **not** answer if the thing is yours!)

Grammar summary: page 82

1 Introductions

a 🗣 Practise this dialogue in pairs.

A *Hello. I'm Sue.*
B *Hello. My name's Dominique.*

b Now practise with the other students in the class. Use your own names.

c Practise the following dialogue in groups of three.
Use your own names. Take it in turn to be A, B and C.

A *(Dominique), this is (Steve).*
B *Hello, (Dominique). Nice to meet you.*
C *Hello, (Steve).*

Note: You may hear older people say 'How do you do?' The answer is 'How do you do?'

2 Greetings

a 🗣 Practise this dialogue in pairs.

A <u>Hello.</u> How are you?
B <u>Fine,</u> thanks.

b Now use these words instead of the underlined words.

A	B
(Good) morning	Very well
(Good) afternoon	All right
(Good) evening	Not too bad
Hi	OK

3 Countries and nationalities

Look at the map below.

Per Eklund
Swedish

Juan and Luis Gomez
Spanish

Paola Pavoni
Italian

Hans Bauer
Swiss

Danielle Ricard and Claire Farge
French

Karen Olsen
Danish

ENGLISH IN SITUATIONS

Students practise
• introducing themselves and other people
• greeting people
• talking about countries and nationalities
• saying they're sorry
• saying goodbye

1 Introductions

Notes and possible problems

- *Hello.* This is sometimes spelt 'hallo' or 'hullo'.

- *I'm (Sue) / My name's (Dominique).* You can introduce yourself in either of these two ways. They mean the same.

- *Nice to meet you.* An alternative would be *Pleased to meet you.*

- Point out that *How do you do?* does not mean *How are you? How do you do?* is formal and not often used by young people nowadays.

a Start by saying to student A *Hello. I'm (Alison).* Student A should then answer *Hello. My name's (Dieter).* Student A should then do the same with student B, and so on.

b Students can move around the class as much as they like and greet as many people as possible.

c After practising in groups of three, ask one group to come to the front of the class and act out the conversation.

2 Greetings

Notes and possible problems

- *Hi.* This is often used nowadays as an alternative to *Hello.*

- Students are sometimes unsure when to use *Good morning / afternoon / evening.* This is an approximate guide:

  Good morning – until lunchtime
  Good afternoon – until 6 o'clock
  Good evening – until bedtime

- *Good morning / Good afternoon / Good evening* are often shortened to *Morning / Afternoon / Evening.* They are less often used than in other European languages. *Hello / Hi* are used instead.

- *Good day* exists but is hardly ever used as a greeting.

- Point out that *Good night* is not used as a greeting as in other languages but is only used when someone is going to bed.

- Another possible answer to the question *How are you?* is *I'm not very well.*

b Demonstrate with a student in front of the class how the substitution dialogue works.

Get students to go round the class using any of the greetings and responses.

You can also take the dialogue a stage further.

Example:
A *Hello. How are you?*
B *Fine, thanks. And you? (How are you?)*
A *Oh, not too bad.*

Note that A usually uses a different answer from B.

3 Countries and nationalities

Notes and possible problems

- Students may confuse nationality and country.

  Example:
  I'm from German / I'm Germany.

- Note that 'from' in the question *Where's Danielle from?* is stressed or emphasized. In the answer *She's from France,* 'from' is unstressed or weak.

a Look at the map and start by asking student A *Where's Danielle from?* Student A answers *She's from France* or *From France.*

Student A then asks student B another question about the people on the map.

Example:
Where are Juan and Luis from?

Students work in pairs, asking and answering questions in the same way.

b Start by asking student A *Is Hans Swiss?* Get a full answer from student A (*Yes, he is.*). Student A then asks student B about one of the other people on the map.

Students then work in pairs, asking and answering in the same way.

C As a follow-up, the teacher can ask questions like these:

Where's Per Eklund from?
What nationality is Hans Bauer?

Students must answer without looking at the book.

4 Where am I from?

Notes and possible problems

- The English names of cities are often different from their original ones.

  Example:
  Wien = Vienna, Napoli = Naples.

  Help students with the English names if necessary.

- To get a point, students must answer with a full sentence.

- Write up on the board any country / nationality / language word not in the book already.

  Example:
  Brazil / Brazilian / Portuguese.

- If students find it difficult to think of cities, the teacher can hand them pieces of paper with the names of other cities on them.

  Example:
  Paris Stockholm Miami Manchester Copenhagen
  Brussels Barcelona Milan Tokyo Beijing
  Moscow Rio de Janeiro Geneva Munich
  Amsterdam Lisbon

5 ▤ What's missing?

- If students are not used to listening to English, tell them not to panic if they don't understand every word. What they hear on the cassette, contains a lot of irrelevant information. They only have to listen for the important, relevant information.

- Tell students to look at the table in the book. Explain that they are going to hear six people talking about their age / country / nationality. With a weak class, copy the grid on to the board and write in your own name on the left. Then tell the class about yourself.

  Example:
  I'm Alison Spencer. I'm 24 years old, and I'm from London in the south-east of England. I'm English, of course.

  Then tell the class to fill in your information.

- Play the cassette once. Students listen without writing anything.

- Play the cassette again. This time, pause after each speaker, and give the students time to fill in the missing information.

- Students give each other their answers to correct.

- Ask students questions like *How old is Ria Muhren?* and fill in the answers in the table on the board. Students mark each other's answers right or wrong.

- Play the cassette again if there is disagreement about any of the answers.

6 ▤ Saying you're sorry

Notes and possible problems

- *I'm sorry.* and *Sorry.* are both acceptable.

- *That's all right / That's OK.* are standard responses to the apology *I'm sorry.*

  Some students may know other responses, for example, *Never mind.* or *It doesn't matter.* Give them these phrases if you think that they will not be confused by too many alternatives.

  All right, is sometimes written *Alright,* especially in American English.

a Before the pairwork, go round the class pretending to tread on students' feet, knocking their pencils on to the floor or bumping into them. Apologize by saying, *I'm sorry.* and get students to respond *That's all right / That's OK.*

b Give the groups 2–3 minutes to think up their reasons for apologizing. After today, insist that students apologize in the correct way (if they are late, for example).

7 ▤ Saying goodbye

Notes and possible problems

- *Goodbye* is more formal than the other forms.

b After practising with one other student, students can go round the class saying goodbye to as many people as possible, using the different ways of saying goodbye and responding.

a Work in pairs. Ask and answer questions like these about countries.

Examples:
A *Where's Danielle from?*
B *She's from France.*

A *Where are Juan and Luis from?*
B *They're from Spain.*

b Now ask about nationalities in the same way.

Examples:
A *Is Hans Swiss?*
B *Yes, he is.*

A *Is Per Danish?*
B *No, he isn't. He's Swedish.*

A *Are Juan and Luis French?*
B *No, they aren't. They're Spanish.*

c Write sentences about the people on the map.

Examples:
Paola's Italian.
Danielle and Claire are from France.
Hans isn't from Germany. He's from Switzerland.

4 Where am I from?

Form two teams (A and B). Each team prepares a list of cities from different countries.
One student in team A then says, for example: 'I'm from Athens.' The students in team B must then say 'You're Greek', or 'You're from Greece' to get a point. Team A gets a point if team B can't answer or if the answer is wrong. One student in team B then says the name of another city, and so on.

5 What's missing?

Listen and fill in the missing information.

Name	Age	Country	Nationality
Ria Muhren			
Hans Beck			
Estelle Verrier			
Manuel Santos			
Maki Tadeshi			
Miguel Salazar			

6 Saying you're sorry

a Practise these conversations in pairs.

A *I'm sorry he's so rude.*
B *That's all right.*

A *I'm sorry I'm late.*
B *That's OK.*

b In two groups, A and B, think of different reasons for saying 'I'm sorry . . .'
One student from group A then apologizes, and a student from group B responds.
One student from team B then apologizes, and a student from team A responds, and so on.

7 Saying goodbye

a Practise this conversation in pairs. Take it in turn to be A and B.

A *Bye.*
B *Bye. See you tomorrow.*

b Now use these words instead.

A	B
Goodbye	soon
Bye-bye	on Monday
Cheerio	next week

Summary of English in situations

- introducing yourself and other people
- greeting people
- talking about countries and nationalities
- saying you're sorry
- saying goodbye

1 Sound right

a Find pairs of words which rhyme.

Example:
no – so

what	there
are	too
for	not
my	car
where	your
you	SO
NO	I

b Form two teams. The teacher writes words from the two lists on the blackboard. The teams take it in turn to add words to the lists. The words *must* rhyme but you must *not* write words from the other team's list.

The team with the longest list is the winner.

c Now practise pronouncing the groups of rhyming words on the blackboard.

2 Listen to this

Listen to the following short conversations. Where do they take place? Write the correct number under each picture. Listen to the example first.

a ....

e ....

b ....

f ....

c ....

d ....

3 Work on words

Find the opposites. Match the words on the left with their opposites on the right.

Example:
yes – no

boy	light
YES	polite
first	horrible
good	tall
Mr	evening
here	goodbye
nice	woman
husband	there
rude	wife
hello	last
heavy	bad
short	late
early	NO
man	Mrs
morning	girl

10

I ▣ Sound right

Notes and possible problems

- The aim of the exercise is to make clear that, unfortunately, words which are spelt in a similar way are often pronounced differently. Similarly, words with different spellings can rhyme.

- Before looking at the exercises, give students examples of pairs of words which rhyme although they have different spellings.

  Example:
  one – son   two – blue   your – for

  Then give examples of pairs of words which have similar spelling but which do not rhyme.

  Example:
  do – no   your – our   where – here

a After students have written their answers, write the correct pairs up on the board. Students then practise the pronunciation of the words individually or all together.

b Students must know the meaning of the words they write. Set a time limit of 3 minutes, and then change the word at the top of the lists.

c After each round, practise pronouncing the words on the two lists.

2 ▣ Listen to this

- Play the example twice to give students confidence.

- Play the exercise through once without stopping. Students do not write anything.

- Play it again, stopping after each conversation. Give students enough time to write their answers.

- Play it through a third time, if necessary, so that students can check their answers.

- Students change books, and correct each other's answers.

- Ask students where each conversation took place.

- Ask students which word(s) helped them to get the right answer.

  Example:
  conversation f – *Dire Straits / album / cassette.*

3 Work on words

- Teach the question *What's the opposite of . . . ?*

- Students can check their answers in pairs, taking it in turns to ask and answer. The student who answers must not look in the book.

  Example:
  A *What's the opposite of 'here'?*
  B *There.*   **B** *What's the opposite of 'last'?*
  A *First.* etc.

4 Play games in English

Who are you?

- Students should think of their own questions apart from those in the book, for example *Are you tall?/Are you good-looking?/Are you old?*

- Write up new, useful vocabulary on the board.

- Students can also practise questions in the third person singular by asking *Is he/she . . .?*

5 Read and think

- In a weak class, copy the figures on to the board. Read out the first instruction and ask a student to come up to the board and follow the instruction. The rest of the class can help him/her, if necessary.

- Students can compare and check their answers in pairs.

6 Now you're here

British money

- Point out that the old one and two shilling coins are now worth 5p and 10p respectively.

- 'Pence' is often abbreviated to 'p'.

- Point out that, for example, £5.20 is usually said *five pound(s) twenty* or just *five twenty*. 'Pence' or 'p' is not necessary here.

Extra activity

Give each student a fairly large piece of paper. On this they write down ten facts about themselves using only a few words.

Example:
three
swimming and ice-skating
blue
Rome
Mario and Helena
cats
Australia
Dire Straits
April
15

They pin the pieces of paper to their fronts. Working in pairs, students have to try to find the right questions to fit these answers.

When they have both finished, each student can tell the rest of the class something new/interesting/unusual about his/her partner.

---

4 Play games in English

Who are you?

a One student at a time thinks of a famous person.

The other students ask him/her questions like this:
Are you alive/dead?
Are you a man/a woman?
Are you English/American? etc.
Are you a politician/film star/pop singer? etc.

The student can only answer 'Yes, I am' or 'No, I'm not'.

b The student who gets the right answer then thinks of another famous person and the rest of the class ask him/her questions.

5 Read and think

Look at these words.

circle   triangle   square   cross   line

Now follow these instructions.

1 Write your first name on the line under the big square.
2 Put a cross in the small circle if you're not English.
3 Put a square in the big circle if you're a student.
4 Write your surname in the big square on the right.
5 Put a small cross on top of the big square if you're a girl.
6 Put a cross in the top triangle if you're fourteen.
7 Put a circle in the bottom triangle if you're in England for the first time.
8 Put a cross in the square on the left if you're on an English language course.
9 Put a small circle under the small square on the right if you're a boy.

6 Now you're here

British money

a Learn the value of these British coins.

b Take out your British money. Work in pairs. Student A puts some money on the desk. Student B says how much there is. Change roles.

UNIT TWO
LESSON ONE

GRAMMAR IN ACTION

🖼 Dominique's room

These bags are heavy!

This is the bathroom in here.

Oh yes.

Um . . . where's the toilet?

Oh, the loo! That's the loo over there.

That's our bedroom . . . and this is your room.

Oh, it's very nice . . . um . . . and it's quite big.

That's the wardrobe there and these drawers are for your clothes.

Right, thanks.

I'm sorry about all the flowers, and the doll . . . But Dominique is a girl's name.

That's all right, Mrs Bond. I like flowers too.

I   Right or wrong?

Tick (✓) the correct answer.

	Right	Wrong
1 Dominique's bags are heavy.	✓	☐
2 The bathroom's downstairs.	☐	☐
3 The toilet's in the bathroom.	☐	☐
4 'Loo' is another word for 'toilet'.	☐	☐
5 Dominique's bedroom's quite small.	☐	☐
6 There's a wardrobe in the bathroom.	☐	☐
7 A wardrobe's for books.	☐	☐
8 The drawers are for Dominique's clothes.	☐	☐
9 Dominique's a boy's name and a girl's name.	☐	☐

Grammar summary
• demonstratives (*this*/*these*, *that*/*those*)
• plural nouns (*flowers*, etc.)
• the definite article

📰 Dominique's room

Notes and possible problems

- *This* (singular) and *these* (plural) are used for people or things which are near you. *That* (singular) and *those* (plural) are used about people or things not near you.

- Students in Britain need to recognize *loo* as a commonly used colloquial word for *toilet*.

- *over there* (photograph 3) Remind students that *there* is the opposite of *here*. *Over there* is used when the object you are pointing at is out of reach.

- *It's quite big.* (photograph 4) Students may have difficulty understanding the meaning of *quite* (see pre-teaching of vocabulary).

Presentation of the dialogue

Here are some suggestions for teaching/checking grammar and vocabulary.

- Teach the demonstratives if necessary. Use classroom objects (pens, books), and students, etc.

  Pick up a book and say *This is a book*. Put another book on a desk, point to it from a distance and say *That's a book*. Repeat the demonstration using two girls instead of two books.

  Pick up two pens and say *These are pens*. Put two pens on a desk, point to them from a distance and say *Those are pens*.

  Repeat the demonstration using boys instead of pens.

  Give students practice in pronouncing the sentences and write them up on the board.

  Check students understand the difference between the four demonstratives.

- *It's quite big.* You could demonstrate with a drawing showing that *quite big* is between *small* and *big*.

- Tell students they are going to hear a conversation in which Mr and Mrs Bond and Dominique arrive home, and Mrs Bond shows Dominique his room and the rest of the house. Students have their books closed.

- Write on the board:

  bedroom
  bathroom
  loo

  Ask students to copy the words and then number them 1, 2, 3 according to the order in which they hear them.

- Play the dialogue once or twice and give students time to number the three words.

- Check their answers.

- Students open their books at page 12. Play the dialogue again in small sections. Stop after each section and explain/check the meaning of words and phrases.

- Play the dialogue again right through. Students listen with books closed.

- Students repeat the dialogue sentence by sentence after the teacher (or after the cassette).

- Make sure students repeat with a natural, lively intonation. Concentrate, if necessary, on the correct pronunciation of *this* and *these* which students may confuse.

- In pairs, students practise the dialogue between Dominique and Mrs Bond, taking it in turns to take both parts.

- Choose one or two pairs to act out the dialogue in front of the class from memory (with help from you and the class if necessary). Don't insist that the lines are exactly the same as those in the book. Students should be encouraged to improvise.

Exercises

I Right or wrong?

- Teach students the phrases *That's right*/*That's wrong* and give practice in pronouncing them.

- Students work individually and then check their answers in pairs.

- Get students to correct the sentences which are wrong.

2 Where are they?

- Students look at the picture and study the new vocabulary.

- Practise pronouncing the new vocabulary (choral repetition).

- Practise the questions *Where 's/are . . .?* and the house and furniture vocabulary as below.

- Students will have problems remembering to use the singular and plural of the verb *to be* correctly. Insist on the contraction *Where's . . .?* with singular words.

- Point out that the definite article in English (the) is the same with both singular and plural words.

- Use single word prompts to practise the questions.

  Example:
  Teacher *sofa*
  Class   *Where's the sofa?*
  Teacher *beds*
  Class   *Where are the beds?* etc.

- Ask the class a few questions yourself with *Where's/are?*

  Example:
  Where's the sofa? It's in the sitting room.

- Students work in pairs. Student A asks the questions, student B answers them. Then change roles.

- Get one pair of students to demonstrate the activity to the class first.

Extra activity: Crazy houses

Draw a very simple plan of a house on the board: sitting-room and kitchen upstairs, bedroom and bathroom downstairs. Students copy the house.

They choose eight items of furniture from the list in Exercise 2 and draw two items of furniture in each room of the house, putting them in rooms where they are not usually found. They then draw an identical plan—but without the furniture.

Working in pairs, and without looking at each other's plans, A finds out about B's house and fills in the information like this:

B *television*
A *Where's the television?*
B *It's in the bathroom.*

(continued)

A then draws a picture of the television in the bathroom. When A has drawn the eight pieces of furniture, they change roles and B finds out about A's house. Finally they can compare their plans to check they are the same.

3 Make changes

- This exercise checks that students can use the demonstratives correctly. It can be done either as a writing exercise or orally.

- Students work individually or in pairs and then check each other's answers.

4 Your home

a Give students enough time to draw their plans.

b Focus attention on the example.

- Give practice in asking the question *What's this room?*

- Get one pair of students to demonstrate the activity to the class first.

- Students exchange their plans and ask and answer questions.

c Give students enough time to draw in the furniture.

- Practise the question *What are these?*

- Students exchange plans again and ask and answer questions about them.

Extra activity: Odd one out

Divide the class into 2 teams (or 4 if the class is large). Get them to make up their own Odd One Out game using the vocabulary from this lesson.

Example:
sofa armchair table   (table is the odd one out)

The teams make up at least 6 sets of words.

Each team takes it in turns to ask the other team(s) to find the 'odd word out'. They score one point for the correct answer and an extra point if they can explain why it is odd. For example, you usually sit on a sofa or in an armchair, but not on a table.

---

2 Where are they?

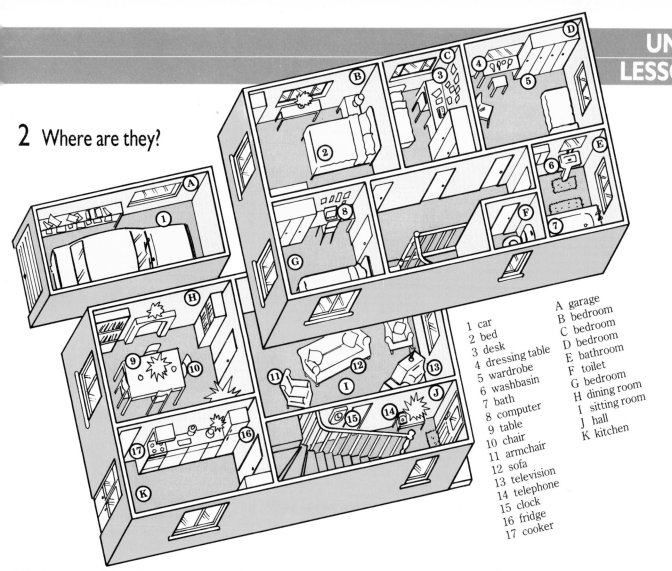

1 car
2 bed
3 desk
4 dressing table
5 wardrobe
6 washbasin
7 bath
8 computer
9 table
10 chair
11 armchair
12 sofa
13 television
14 telephone
15 clock
16 fridge
17 cooker

A garage
B bedroom
C bedroom
D bedroom
E bathroom
F toilet
G bedroom
H dining room
I sitting room
J hall
K kitchen

Work in pairs. Ask and answer questions about the Bonds' house.

Examples:
A *Where's the fridge?*
B *It's in the kitchen.*

A *Where are the armchairs?*
B *They're in the sitting room.*

3 Make changes

Change these sentences from singular to plural.

Example:
This chair's heavy.
These chairs are heavy.

1 That's our bedroom.
2 This drawer's full.
3 This room's a bedroom.
4 That bedroom's big.
5 That's Dominique's bag.
6 This is her book.

4 Your home

a Draw a plan of the house or flat you're living in in Britain, or your house or flat at home, like this:

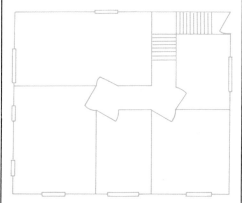

b Work in pairs. Give your plan to another student. Student A points to one room on student B's plan and asks:

A *What's this room?*
B *That's the sitting room.*

c Add some furniture to your plans, like this:

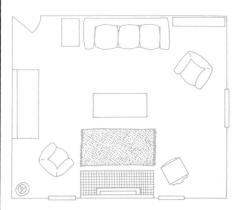

d Ask each other questions like this:

A *What are these?*
B *They're armchairs.*

Grammar summary: page 82

1 Where are they?

Picture A

a Fill in the gaps, using words and phrases from the box below.

Example:
The computer's on the desk.

1 The cassettes are . . . the drawer.
2 The Walkman's . . . the desk.
3 The Amstrad's . . . the Walkman.
4 The posters are . . . the desk.
5 The small table's . . . the window.
6 The clothes are . . . the floor.
7 The stereo's . . . the desk.
8 The stereo's . . . the wardrobe.
9 The lamp's . . . the corner.
10 The records are . . . the stereo.

```
in . . .
on . . .
next to . . .
on the right/left of . . .
above/below . . .
```

b Ask the person next to you about the picture above.

Examples:
Where's the lamp?
Where are the clothes?

2 What's different?

a Work in pairs. Student A looks at the picture in exercise 1 (picture A). Student B looks at picture B on page 78.

Now try to find the differences between the two pictures. Ask questions like: *Where's the Walkman?*

There are six differences between the pictures.

b Write down what the differences are.

Example:
In picture A the clothes are on the floor, but in picture B they are on the bed.

Asking for directions

Dominique *Excuse me. Where's the post office, please?*
English woman *It's opposite the ABC Cinema, between the Midland Bank and the chemist's.*
Dominique *Thanks very much.*
English woman *You're welcome.*

3 Where are they?

Look at the map at the top of page 15. Write complete sentences using the words and phrases below.

Example:
The post office is opposite the ABC Cinema.

1 ....
2 ....
3 ....
4 ....
5 ....
6 ....
7 ....
8 ....
9 ....
10 ....

```
opposite
between
next to
on the corner of
in . . .
on the right/left of . .
```

- asking and describing where things / places are
- thanking and responding to thanks

1 Where are they?

- Before starting the exercise, check that students know the prepositions in the box. This can be done by demonstration, changing the position of objects (e.g. a pen or book) or by referring to the position of students or classroom furniture.

  Examples:
  T   *Where's Joanne?*
  S1 *She's next to José.*
  T   *Where's the poster?*
  S2 *It's on the wall.*

- Students work individually or in pairs and fill in the gaps.
- Students check their answers and practise pronouncing the sentences.

2 What's different?

a Get one pair of students to demonstrate the activity to the class first.

b Students write down the differences individually.

- Ask students for the differences orally.

Note: Make sure students do not 'cheat' when they are doing this activity.

📼 Asking for directions

- Students have their books closed. Play the dialogue on the cassette.
- Ask where Dominique and the woman are and what Dominique is asking.
- Play the dialogue again. Students listen and repeat.
- Draw students' attention to the politeness words / phrases *Excuse me, please / Thanks very much / You're welcome.*

- Tell students that *excuse me* does not mean *I'm sorry* or *pardon.* It is used to attract somebody's attention or if somebody is in your way.

- Teach students that probably the most common response to *Thank you.* among young people nowadays is *You're welcome.* It is now British English, not just American English. Common alternatives are *That's all right,* or *That's OK.* Students may also hear *Not at all.* but this is becoming less common.

- Books open at page 14. Play the dialogue one more time.

3 Where are they?

- Focus attention on the map on page 15 and the box containing prepositions (page 14).

- Ask students questions like *Where's the bus station?* to get *It's next to the X,* etc. Continue asking until all the prepositions have been used at least once.

- Tell students to fill in the gaps, and check students' answers.

- Practise pronouncing the sentences.

4 Ask and answer

a Get one pair of students to demonstrate the activity to the class first.

● Students work in pairs, taking it in turns to ask and answer questions.

b Take the opportunity to tell students where important places/buildings in your town/area are. Draw a map on the board if necessary.

● The students may have genuine questions they want to ask about where things in the town are.

Example:
Where's the cinema? Where are the tennis courts?

You can answer their questions or perhaps other students can.

Extra activity

This is suitable for homework.

Make sure each student has a map of the town. Give them a list of things/places/shops, etc. to mark on the map, for example the statue of Queen Victoria, Tesco, the Odeon cinema, Lloyds Bank, JR's disco, etc.

To find out where these things are they will either have to walk round the town or ask a local person to help them. Get them to report on their findings next day.

---

5 Complete the maps

Note: This is an 'information gap' exercise where students A and B have different information. They must question each other to fill in the gaps in their information, i.e. student A has the information B requires and vice versa. In this kind of exercise the students have a real reason for asking each other questions.

● Divide the class into pairs (A and B). Student B turns to page 78.

● Get one pair of students to demonstrate the activity to the class first.

● Students A and B take it in turns to ask and answer questions in order to fill in their own missing information.

Note: Make sure students write in the missing information. Don't allow students to 'cheat' by looking at their partner's information.

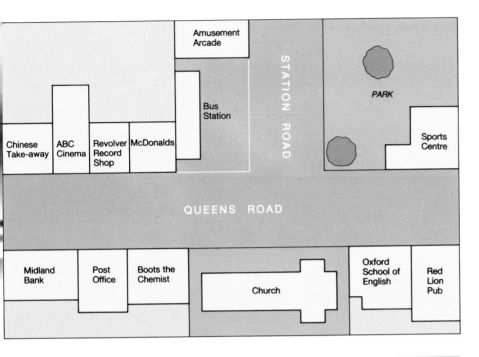

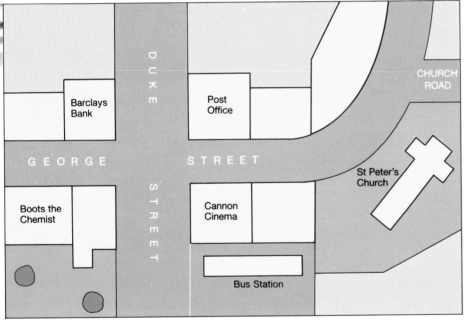

4 Ask and answer

a Work in pairs. Look at the map. Student A asks where a building or place is. Student B describes where it is. Then student B asks about another building or place, and student A answers.

Example:

A *Excuse me. Where's the bus station, please?*

B *It's on the corner of Queens Road and Station Road.*

A *Thanks very much.*

B *That's OK./You're welcome.*

b Ask and answer in the same way, using buildings and places in the town where you are.

5 Complete the maps

Work in pairs. Student A looks at the map opposite. Student B looks at the map on page 78.

Student A

You want to know where these places are:

1 Ashton Park
2 the Pizza Hut
3 Shades disco
4 the Queen's Head pub
5 the Bombay Indian take-away
6 C & A

Ask questions and fill in the information that Student B gives you.

Summary of English in situations
• asking and describing where things are
• asking where places are
• thanking and responding to thanks

1 Sound right

a Which word does *not* rhym with the other two?

Example:
is (trees) his
The answer is 'trees' because it doesn't rhyme with 'is' and 'his'.

1 this   these   please
2 here   there   we're
3 where   near   pair
4 quite   right   quiet
5 or   four   hour
6 your   for   our
7 I'm   him   time
8 all   shall   call

b Now practise saying the sets of words above.

2 Work on words

What's the missing word? All the words are in units 1 and 2.

Example:
England/English   France/*French*

1 a husband/Mr   a wife/...
2 I/my   we/...
3 he/his   she/...
4 this/here   that/...
5 14/fourteen   40/...
6 hello/hi   OK/...
7 right/left   above/...
8 Wednesday/a day   March/...
9 O/a circle   □/...
10 —/a line   x/...
11 books/a bookcase   clothes/...
12 Steve/first name   Bond/...
13 all right/OK   cheerio/...
14 west/east   north/...
15 to drink/thirsty   to eat/...
16 Britain/a country   Hastings/...
17 Italy/Italian   Spain/...
18 Monday/today   Tuesday/...
19 1,000 m/1 km   100p/...
20 a car/cars   a bus/...

3 Listen to this

Listen to three short conversations. They all take place at the station. Follow the directions which you hear and draw lines on the map. Where does each person want to go to?

The first person wants to go to . . .
The second person wants to go to . . .
The third person wants to go to . . .

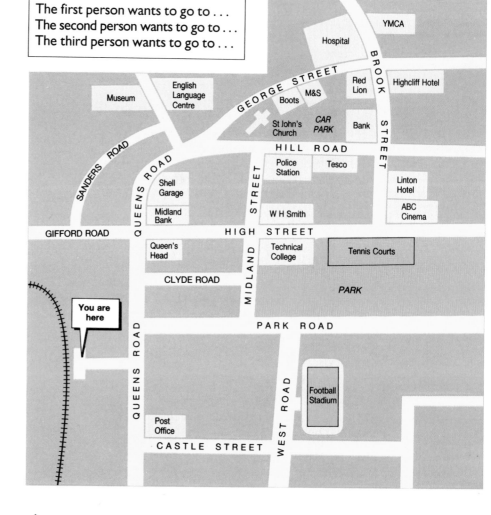

4 Read and think

There are eight people at a table. Read these clues and then write down who is who.

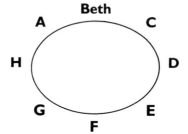

Tim is between Mark and Di.
Liz is opposite Di.
Nick is between Liz and Di.
Beth is between Kim and Liz.
Tim is opposite Beth.
Mark is on Tim's left.
Sue is on Kim's right.

A =   F =
C =   G =
D =   H =
E =

1 🔊 Sound right

- The purpose of the exercise is to make students aware that they must not rely on the spelling of a word as a guide to pronunciation.

a Students work in pairs to find the words which don't rhyme.

- Check their answers.

b Practise pronouncing all the words, chorally and individually. Put some extra life into pronunciation practice by keeping a good rhythm going.

You could even sing the words! These go very well to the tune of 'Frère Jacques': first you sing each group of words and then the students repeat them.

2 Work on words

- Make sure students understand how the exercise works.

- Students work in pairs to find the missing words.

- Check their answers.

- Which pair has the most right answers?

3 🔊 Listen to this

- Make sure students understand what they have to do.

- Play the exercise through once, stopping briefly after each conversation. Students don't write anything.

- Play it again. Give students enough time to write their answers after each conversation.

- Play the cassette through a third time, without stopping, so that students can check their answers.

- Students exchange books and correct each other's answers.

- Read out similar directions to a particular place / building on the map. Students follow the directions and write down their destination.

- Students work in pairs, giving each other directions and following them on the map.

4 Read and think

- This is a kind of brainteaser which also practises detailed reading comprehension and revises prepositions of place.

- Students work individually or in pairs to identify the eight people.

- Students check their answers.

- As a follow-up, students can cover up the sentences below the picture and ask each other questions.

Example:
A *Where's Liz?*
B *She's opposite Di.*
B *Who's between Kim and Liz?*
A *Ben.*

5 Play games in English

Make a word

- The number of students in each team can be four or six depending on the number of students in the class.

- Give out five pieces of paper (preferably A4 size) to each group.

- Give students 2 minutes to choose their letters.

- If there are four students in each team, one student can hold up two letters.

- Keep a record of the score.

- Play several rounds of the game.

6 Now you're here

British signs

- Give students a few minutes in pairs or groups to decide what the signs mean.

- Tell students to ask a British person the meaning of the signs they don't know.

- Tell students to 'collect' other similar signs.

- Students write or draw their signs on the board and the rest of the class guess what they mean and where you usually see them.

Extra activity: Miming signs

Prepare some slips of paper with signs written on them, for example *No smoking, Keep off the grass, No Entry*, etc.

Give these out to pairs of students. They must prepare a mime to demonstrate their sign.

The rest of the class must guess what it is.

Things you buy

Note: Many European students will be surprised that film, make-up and toothpaste can all be bought in a chemist's.

- The 's in *chemist's* is an abbreviation of *chemist's shop* (i.e. the shop of the chemist). Nowadays the final 's is often left out—*chemist*, or the apostrophe is omitted—*chemists*.

- Make sure students know what sort of shops they are.

a Students work in pairs.

- Students check each other's answers.

b Ask for students' suggestions.

Extra activity

Divide the class into two teams. Each team make a list of items and the shops where they can be bought. (You may need to help them with shop names.)

Team A say the name of an item (for example *shampoo*). Team B must say where you buy it (a chemist's). Then Team B ask Team A, and so on.

For the purposes of this game 'supermarket' is not allowed!

---

5 Play games in English

Make a word

Form teams of five students.
Each team writes five different letters on five large pieces of paper.
Each student holds one letter.
The team stand in a line and make as many words as they can in two minutes.
A two-letter word gets 2 points, a three-letter word 3 points, etc.
The team with the most points is the winner.

6 Now you're here

British signs

What do these signs mean?
Where do you usually see them?
Ask a British person if necessary.

Things you buy

a Match the things on the left with the shops on the right where you can buy them.

aspirins
a newspaper
bananas   a chemist's
stamps
toothpaste
sweets   a newsagent's
a film
a magazine
suncream   a post office
apples
postcards
oranges   a greengrocer's
make-up

b Now think of other things you can buy at a chemist's, a newsagent's and a greengrocer's.

UNIT THREE
LESSON ONE

GRAMMAR IN ACTION

Rob meets Dominique

Half an hour later

Rob How old are you?

Dominique I'm sixteen. How about you?

Rob I'm fifteen.

Dominique Have you got any brothers or sisters?

Rob Yes, I've got a sister. She's at a friend's house at the moment.

Dominique What's she like?

Rob She's OK, but she's got a terrible temper!

Dominique You're lucky! You've got a computer.

Rob Yes, it's an Amstrad. But I've only got a few games.

Dominique Have you got a moped?

Rob A moped? No, I haven't. Have you?

Dominique Yes, I've got a 50 cc Honda.

Rob *You're* lucky! I've only got an old bike!

1 Questions and answers

a Match the questions on the left with the answers on the right.

Example: 1 – d

1 Have Mr and Mrs Bond got some bad news for Rob?
2 Has Rob got a bike?
3 Has Dominique got a computer?
4 Has Rob's sister got a terrible temper?
5 Have Mr and Mrs Bond got three children?
6 Has Rob's sister got two brothers?
7 Has Dominique's bedroom got a wardrobe?

a) Yes, he has.
b) No, they haven't.
c) Yes, it has.
d) Yes, they have.
e) No, he hasn't.
f) Yes, she has.
g) No, she hasn't.

b Work in pairs. Student A asks the same questions, Student B answers them without looking at the answers above. Change roles.

18

Grammar summary

- *have (got)*
- the indefinite articles (*a/an*)
- adjective + noun

🎧 Rob meets Dominique

Notes and possible problems

- Students have problems remembering to use *got* in *Have you got a . . . ?*, *I've got . . .*, etc. Point out that *Have you a sister?* is not natural English. *Have you got a . . . ? I've got*, *She's got*, etc. is the most common form in British English.

- *brothers and sisters* (line 6) In some languages the equivalent word for 'brother' can include boys and girls. Point out that in English you have to ask *Have you got any brothers or sisters?* not simply *Have you got any brothers?*

- *What's she like?* (line 9) Students may confuse this question with *What does she like?* or *What does she look like?* The question refers to a person's personality or character.

Presentation of the dialogue

Here are some suggestions for teaching/checking grammar and vocabulary.

- To teach *Have you got . . . ?* draw a cat and/or dog or bike/car on the board. Then go round the class asking *Have you got a cat?* getting them to answer with a short answer. Then get students to ask the question and others to answer it. Finally write up the question and the answers on the board.

- The indefinite article *a* is used before words starting with *u* only if the *u* is pronounced as if it were a consonant, for example the *u* in university is pronounced like *y*, so it is preceded by the definite article *a*, not *an*.

  As a check, write the following words and phrases on the board and ask the class to put *a* or *an* before them:

  apple, car, easy question, egg, ugly man, French girl, interesting book, European country, unusual name.

  Check answers and practise pronunciation. Make sure students pronounce both *a* and *an* very weakly.

  Also teach/check the words and phrases below and any others you think necessary (see page vii). Practise pronunciation.

  a bike   a moped   you're lucky   a terrible temper

- Tell students what the dialogue is about (books closed).

- Write the following questions on the board:

  How old's Dominique?
  How old's Rob?
  Has Rob got any brothers or sisters?
  Has Rob got a computer?

- Play the cassette once or twice and give students time to write their answers and then check them.

- Students open their books. Play the dialogue again in small sections. Stop after each section and explain/check the meaning of words and phrases.

- Students repeat the dialogue sentence by sentence after the teacher (or after the cassette).

- Students practise the conversation between Rob and Dominique in pairs, changing roles.

- Choose one or two pairs to act out the dialogue in front of the class from memory (with help from you and the class if necessary).

Grammar

- *Have* changes to *has* in the third person singular.

- *got* cannot be used in short answers. So, for example, you can't answer *Yes, I've got.*

- Do not emphasize or stress the word *got*. It should be said as quickly as possible.

- *the French girl* Point out that adjectives in English usually come before, not after the noun, and that they don't have different forms but stay the same with masculine and feminine, singular and plural nouns.

Exercises

I Questions and answers

a Students work individually to match questions and answers.

b Students work in pairs asking and answering. Make sure they change roles and that the student who is answering has the answers covered or the book closed.

2   What have you got?

a   Students fill in the boxes with personal information.

b   Practise the question for all the words in the list by giving word prompts.

Example:
T   *a moped*
S1   *Have you got a moped?*
T   *an alarm clock*
S2   *Have you got an alarm clock?*

- Get one pair to demonstrate the activity to the class.

- Students work in pairs asking and answering and filling in their partner's information.

c   Ask two or three students to read out one or two of their sentences.

3   What are they?

a   Ask two or three questions yourself.

- Get one pair to demonstrate the activity to the class.

- Students work in pairs asking and answering alternately.

b   Give students time to write down one or two questions.

Example:
What's vodka?
It's a Russian drink.

- Check students' answers paying particular attention to the pronunciation of *a* and *an*. If there are still problems with this, give students some more examples of them.

4   The things you've got

a   Help with vocabulary if necessary by giving them the English words for some of the things in your pocket/bag.

b   Get one pair to demonstrate the activity to the class.

- Students work in pairs asking and answering alternately. For variety, make sure they work with a different partner from the previous exercise.

5   Quick questions

- Ask students what the questions will be in each case.

Note: If you want to find a student who hasn't got a brother you still ask the same question: *Have you got a brother?*

- Show how the example works by moving around the class asking different students *Have you got a sister?* until you get the answer *No, I haven't.* Then mime writing down the name of that person.

- Make sure students have space to move about in. Push back the desks and chairs if necessary.

6   Tell a lie

- Check students understand *a lie*.

a   Write four statements about yourself (with *have got*) and ask students to guess which of the four is a lie.

- Give students time to write their own sentences.

b   Ask a number of students (according to the time available) to read out their sentences. The class decide which of the four statements is a lie.

Extra activity

This could be done for homework.

Sometimes the British and their houses must seem different or even odd to foreign students. Ask the class to think about their host families and their houses. What have they got (or haven't got) that the students think is unusual or interesting?

Example:
The house hasn't got shutters.
They've got a bath but they haven't got a shower.
They've got three dogs, two cats, six chickens and a goat.

If the exercise is done for homework, students can report back next day.

---

2 What have you got?

a Fill in the box with information about yourself.

		You	Your partner (B)
Have you got	a brother?		
	a sister?		
	a bike?		
	a moped?		
	a computer?		
	a radio?		
	an alarm clock?		

b Ask another student (B) about the things he/she's got and fill in the box.

Examples:
You *Have you got a brother?*
B   *Yes, I have.*
You *Have you got a bike?*
B   *No, I haven't.*

c Write five sentences about yourself and student B.

Examples:
I've got a bike but I haven't got a moped.
Pia's got a brother but she hasn't got a sister.

3 What are they?

a Work in pairs. Student A chooses a word from the list and asks, for example:
What's an Amstrad?
Student B answers with an adjective of nationality, like this:
It's a British computer.

Mercedes Benz	cricket	champagne
Rio de Janeiro	Hastings	SAAB
Oldsmobile	Bombay	koala bear
Coca Cola	vodka	Juventus
Alfa Romeo	Pentax	Toyota
Valencia	Lyon	Milan

b Write down some other things from different countries. Ask each other about them.

4 The things you've got

a Make a list of the things you've got in your pockets or bag.

Examples:
a comb, a pen, a passport, a wallet

b Talk to the student next to you. Find out what you've *both* got.

Example:
A *Have you got a comb in your bag?*
B *Yes, I have.*
A *I have, too.*

5 Quick questions

Go round the class asking questions. Find a student who:

	Name
hasn't got a brother	
has got a Walkman	
hasn't got a Japanese watch	
has got a tennis racket	
hasn't got a camera	
has got an umbrella	

Ask questions like this:
Have you got a brother?
The winner is the student who collects six names first.

6 Tell a lie

a Write four sentences about your brothers/sisters/the things you've got. Three sentences must be true, one must be a lie.

Example:
I've got one brother.
I haven't got a sister.
I've got a bike.
I haven't got a moped.

b Read your four sentences to the class. They must guess which one is a lie.

Grammar summary: page 82

1 The alphabet

Listen and repeat the letters of the alphabet.

2 What's the word?

Write down the letters you hear. What words do they make?

Example:
B-O-Y   Boy

1 ....
2 ....
3 ....
4 ....
5 ....
6 ....
7 ....
8 ....
9 ....
10 ....

3 Act it out

Practise the following dialogue in pairs, using your own address in Britain.
Say 'Sorry?' if you don't understand what your partner says. Change roles.

Spelling in English

Dominique *Mrs Bond, what's your full address?*
Mrs Bond *9, Cornwallis Gardens.*
Dominique *Sorry?*
Mrs Bond *9, Cornwallis Gardens.*
Dominique *How do you spell Cornwallis?*
Mrs Bond *C-O-R-N-W-A-L-L-I-S.*
Dominique *And what's your postcode?*
Mrs Bond *TN34 6JW.*

4 Spelling game

Form two teams. Ask each other how to spell English words.

5 How to use a payphone

Match the following instructions with the pictures, and fill in the blanks next to the pictures.

- Don't forget to take your unused coins back.
- Put in your money.
- Pick up the receiver and listen for the dialling tone.
- Dial the number you want.
- Speak when somebody answers.
- Have your money ready (10p, 50p, £1).

How do you spell clothes?

c-l-o...

20

ENGLISH IN SITUATIONS

Students practise

- spelling in English
- asking people to repeat things
- using a payphone
- making an international phone call

🎧 Spelling in English

- Play the dialogue once.
- Ask students who is talking and what they are talking about.
- Play the dialogue one more time.

1 🎧 The alphabet

- Practise the alphabet quickly round the class. Write up on the board the letters which give problems, usually the vowels, and consonants like G, H, J, R, W, Y.

2 🎧 What's the word . . . ?

- Play the tape two or three times. Give students time to write their answers. Use the pause button if necessary.
- Give more practise by spelling out other words.

3 Act it out

- Get the students to repeat the dialogue line by line.
- Students practise in pairs, substituting details of their own address in Britain.

4 Spelling game

- Give the teams a few minutes to think of some words (preferably words from earlier units). Don't allow obscure words.
- Keep a record of the score.

Extra activity: The alphabet in pairs

Students play in pairs or small groups. Each pair choose a letter of the alphabet e.g. L. The student who says this letter according to the following rules is the winner.

Students take it in turns to say one or two letters of the alphabet, but no more.

Example:
S1 *A*
S2 *BC*
S1 *DE*
S2 *F*
S1 *GH*
S2 *I*
S1 *JK*
S2 *L*

In this case player 2 wins as he/she was the one who said L. Change the winning letter and don't always start with A. In this way all the letters of the alphabet can be practised.

Extra activity: Missing vowels

Write short sentences on the board with the vowels missing.

Example:
DmnqsFrnchstdnt
Bsthscndlttrfthlphbt

(Answers: Dominique is a French student
    B is the second letter of the alphabet.)

Students can work individually or in pairs to decipher the sentences and spell the words out loud.

You can include sentences relating to the units covered so far in the book, familiar expressions or song titles.

5 How to use a payphone

- Focus attention on the pictures.
- Students work in pairs to match the instructions to the correct pictures.
- Each pair should agree on the correct order.

6   How to make an international call

- Point out that you can phone direct to most countries in the world from a British payphone. It is also much cheaper for students to ring direct from a payphone than to make a 'reverse charge' call.

- If students don't know their country or city code, point out that this information is given in the telephone book under International Calls. If possible, take a phone book into class to show them. The country codes are also shown in most phone boxes.

- Exercises 5 and 6 can be made more realistic if you can actually take the class to a nearby payphone and give a demonstration.

- Tell students where and how they can buy phonecards as these are becoming more and more commonly used.

- Point out that in phone numbers *0* is pronounced *oh*, not *zero* (as in the USA). When two numbers are the same (for example 445566), we say *double four, double five, double six*.

Extra activity: Practising phone numbers

On the board write: *home number*
                          best friend's number
                          host family's number

The students copy this and write down the appropriate numbers. Working in pairs, A then asks B *What's your home number?* etc. and writes down the numbers. They then change roles.

When they have finished asking and answering, they can check their answers are correct.

1 ....

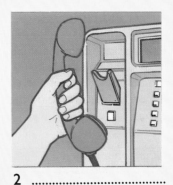

2 ....

3 ....

4 ....

5 ....

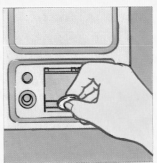

6 ....

6 How to make an international phone call

1 Dial 010.
2 Then dial the code for your country.
Examples:
France 33, Italy 39, Japan 81, Brazil 55, West Germany 49

3 Now dial the code for the town or city you want *without* the first number.
Examples:
Stockholm 8, Madrid 1
4 Finally, dial the number of the person you want to speak to.

Now write down the full number of your family or a friend if you want to phone them from Britain.

Summary of English in situations

- spelling
- asking someone to repeat something
- using a payphone and making an international phone call

010 International code	34 Country code (Spain)	1 City code (Madrid)	4476807 Number of family, friend, etc.

1 Sound right

a 🖥 Listen to these pairs of words. What is the difference in pronunciation between the words on the left and the words on the right?

this	these
it	eat
hit	heat
sit	seat
fill	feel
live	leave
ship	sheep
will	wheel

b Now listen again and repeat the words.

c Choose six of the words above. Write them in boxes, like this:

sit	feel	ship
it	seat	live

d Listen to the teacher when he/she reads out words from the two lists above. Cross out your words when you hear them, like this:

~~sit~~	~~feel~~	~~ship~~
~~it~~	~~seat~~	~~live~~

e When all your words are crossed out, shout BINGO!

2 Work on words

Odd one out

Which of the four sums has a different answer?

3 Listen to this

🖥 Listen to the conversations. Which conversation goes with which picture?

a . . .

b . . .

c . . .

d . . .

e . . .

f . . .

A	1 eleven – three	B	1 seven + twelve	C	1 three × five	D	1 eighty-four ÷ three
	2 four × two		2 twenty-one – two		2 thirteen + two		2 forty – twelve
	3 sixty-four ÷ eight		3 three × six		3 sixty ÷ four		3 fourteen + fifteen
	4 six + three		4 fifty-seven ÷ three		4 twenty – six		4 seven × four

FUN WITH ENGLISH

1 🖭 Sound right

Most foreign students have difficulty with the sound [ɪ] as in *hit* and the sound [i :] as in *heat*.

a Let students repeat the words after the cassette. Use the pause button if necessary. Students should make the short [ɪ] sound as short as possible and the long [i :] sound as long
as possible. Making a serious face for the short sounds and a bright, smiling face for the long sounds will help them. (Point out the photographer's phrase: "Say 'cheese'"!)

e Practise shouting the word *Bingo*. Call out each word twice. Keep a record of the words you call out and check the winning student's card. It is very likely he / she will have made a mistake. Play the game several times.

2 Work on words

Odd one out

- Teach the spoken equivalents of the mathematical symbols:

  $+$ = *plus* or *and*
  $-$ = *minus*
  $\times$ = *times*
  $\div$ = *divided by*
  $=$ = *equals*

- Give your own example on the board and ask students for the answers orally. Ask which one is different.

- Students work in pairs. When checking the answers insist that each sum is done orally so as to practise saying numbers.

- Students can write their own questions and test them on each other.

3 🖭 Listen to this

- Play the example twice to give students confidence.

- Play the exercise once through without stopping. Students do not write anything.

- Play it again, stopping after each conversation. Give students enough time to write their answers.

- Play it through a third time, if necessary, so that students can check their answers.

- Students exchange books and correct each other's answers.

- Ask students which word(s) helped them to get the right answer.

  Example:
  conversation e – *stamp / post office*.

- If there is time, practise repeating the short dialogues in chorus.

Extra activity: Spoof

For practice with smaller numbers this is great fun.

Groups of five to seven students sit or stand in a circle. Each student has three matches. Without letting the others see, they put a number of matches (or none) in their right hands and put their left hands (containing the unused matches, if any) behind their backs. In turn the students guess the total number of matches the group have in their right hands. Each guess must be different.

When everyone has guessed, each person opens his / her right hand to show how many matches he / she has. Count them. The student who guessed correctly is 'out'.

Continue until one student is left. He or she is, in fact, the 'loser' and has to sing a song, recite a poem, do a dance, buy everyone a drink or whatever the group decides.

4 Read and think

Who's who?

- Teach/Revise the following words using blackboard drawings or students in the class.

  He's (quite) | *tall/short.*
                 | *thin/fat.*

  He's got | *long/short/straight/curly hair.*
             | *a beard/a moustache.*

  He's bald.

- Students practise pronouncing the words and phrases and copy them from the board.

a and **b** Students work in pairs.

C Ask two or three students to read out their descriptions. The rest of the class can guess who the people are.

5 Play games in English

Hangman

- Play the game first with you choosing a word from a previous lesson.

- Insist on correct pronunciation of letters, especially the vowels A, E, I, O, U.

- Let all students call out a letter in turn.

- Another line is drawn for each wrong guess.

- The winner thinks of a word and goes to the board.

- This game can also be played in pairs.

6 Now you're here

a Students ask you the questions.

- Students ask each other the questions.

- Tell students to ask a British person the same questions after class and make notes of their answers.

b Students tell the rest of the class about their most interesting answers the next day.

4 Read and think

Who's who?

a Read these descriptions of four men.

b Match the descriptions with the pictures below.

A's about thirty. He's quite tall and thin. He's got straight black hair. It's quite long. He's got a moustache.

B's about forty. He's not very tall, but he's quite heavy. He's got curly black hair, and a beard.

C's about thirty-five. He wears glasses. He's got brown hair but he hasn't got much of it left – he's almost bald. He's of medium height and build.

D's about forty-five. He's got short grey hair and a grey moustache. He wears glasses. He's short and fat.

C Now write a similar description of a person you know.

5 Play games in English

Hangman

One student thinks of an English word. He/she writes a dash (–) on the board for each letter of the word.

Example:
COMPUTER = _ _ _ _ _ _ _ _

The other students then say one letter at a time. If the letter is in the word, the student at the board fills in the letter(s).

If the letter is not in the word, the student at the board draws one line of this picture:

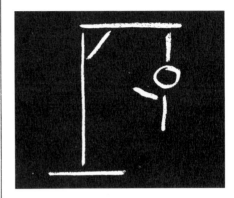

Students' right letters so far:
_ o _ _ u t _ _

Students' wrong letters so far:
s i a b n h w d

The students must try to guess the word before the man is 'hanged'.

6 Now you're here

a Ask a British person these questions and note down his/her answers.
You can practise the questions in class first.

- Have you got a passport? (How old is it?)
- Have you got a computer? (What kind is it?)
- Have you got any brothers or sisters? (What are their names?)
- Have you got a relative in a different country? (Which country is he/she in?)
- Have you got an old Beatles or Elvis Presley record? (Which one/s?)
- Have you got an English dictionary? (How big is it?)
- Have you got a typewriter? (What kind is it?)
- Have you got a boat? (Where is it?)
- Have you got a bicycle? (What make is it?)

b Compare the answers you get with other students' answers.

UNIT FOUR
LESSON ONE

Do you like it?

Dominique What's this record?
Debbie It's Razzmataz.
Dominique What does that mean?
Debbie It doesn't mean anything. Do you like it?
Dominique It's all right.
Debbie What do you mean 'It's all right'? It's fantastic!!
Dominique Is it?
Debbie Yes, and Rob likes it too.
Dominique Does he?
Debbie Yes, he's got the record. What kind of music do you like, Dominique?
Dominique I like French music.
Debbie What do you mean, 'French music'?
Dominique Pop music with French singers and French words.
Debbie Do you have pop music in France?
Dominique Huh – of course we do. I've got a cassette in my room. Do you want to hear it?
Debbie Um . . . not now . . . um . . . I haven't got time.

1 Questions and answers

a Complete the questions and answers with *do/does/don't* or *doesn't*.

Example:
Does Debbie like pop music? Yes, she does.

1 . . . Debbie like Razzmataz?   Yes, she . . .
2 . . . Razzmataz mean 'fantastic'?   No, it . . .
3 . . . Debbie and Rob like pop music?   Yes, they . . .
4 . . . Dominique think Razzmataz is fantastic?   No, he . . .
5 . . . Dominique like French music?   Yes, he . . .
6 . . . Debbie and Rob know any French pop songs?   No, they . . .
7 . . . Debbie want to listen to Dominique's cassette? No, she . . .

b Work in pairs. Student A asks the questions. Student B answers them without looking in the book.

Grammar summary

- the present simple tense (the verb *to like*)
- the 'do construction' (*Do you like coffee?* / *I don't like coffee.*)

📺 Do you like it?

Notes and possible problems

- The *do* construction is probably the biggest problem for elementary students. It needs to be constantly practised and revised.

- *Do you like it?* (line 4) Point out that *it* is absolutely necessary and that the question *Do you like?* is not correct English.

- *It's all right* (line 6) is a neutral answer. An alternative expression is *It's OK.*

- *It doesn't mean anything* (line 4) Point out that only one negative is possible in English. *It doesn't mean nothing.* is wrong.

Presentation of the dialogue

- Take some pictures of well-known pop singers and groups into class. Before starting work on the dialogue, stick the pictures up around the room.

- Here are some suggestions for teaching / checking grammar and vocabulary.

  Write on the board the following list of drinks: *coffee, tea, Seven Up, Coca Cola, beer, wine*

  Ask individual students questions: *Do you like beer / wine / tea?* etc. and get them to answer *Yes, I do / No, I don't / It's OK.*

  Prompt pairs of students at random to ask and answer.

  Write up the question and answers and practise pronouncing them.

- Focus students' attention especially on the third person singular (the *-s* ending in the affirmative, the *does* in the interrogative and the *doesn't* in the negative). Give the students this list to help them remember:

  He likes pop music.
  Does he like pop music?
  No, he doesn't.

- Write on the board two or three common words from other languages, for example, *Bonjour, Adios, Jawohl.*

Ask the class *What does Bonjour mean?* and repeat the question with the other words.

Write up the questions and answers and underline the 3rd person singular *s*.

- Pre-teach new vocabulary and set the scene for the dialogue (books closed).

- Write up these questions on the board:

  What does Razzmataz mean?
  Does Rob like Razzmataz?
  What kind of music does Dominique like?
  Does Debbie want to hear Dominique's cassette?

- Play the dialogue once or twice and give students time to write their answers.

- Students check each other's answers.

- Students open their books. Play the dialogue again in short sections. Stop after each section and explain / check the meaning of words and phrases if necessary. Students listen and repeat.

- Students practise the dialogue in pairs, taking it in turns to take the parts of Dominique and Debbie.

- Choose two or three pairs to act out the dialogue in front of the class from memory (with help if necessary).

Exercises

1 Questions and answers

a Students work individually or in pairs, referring to grammar on page 83 if necessary.

- Check their answers.

b Students practise saying the questions and answers.

Note: Be careful not to stress *do* and *does* in the question form.

- Get one pair to demonstrate the activity to the class first.

- Student A tests student B who has his / her book closed. They then change roles.

2 Do you like . . . ?

- Take in pictures of objects and people doing things (horses, hamburgers, someone skiing, etc.). Ask questions about them and elicit appropriate answers. Get the students to ask each other questions based on the pictures. Then go on to the exercise.

Note: The verb *to like* is usually followed by the *-ing* form of a verb (the gerund), for example *I like playing computer games.*

a Students fill in their own answers.

b Practise the question and answer. Choose students at random to ask you the questions. Reply using a positive, negative or neutral answer.

- Get one pair of students to demonstrate the activity first.

- Students work in pairs. Student A asks student B and notes down his/her answers. They then change roles.

  c and **d** are writing exercises to check they have really understood the structure. Be careful that students don't forget the *s* in the third person singular.

- Get some students to read out their sentences.

3 A survey

- Introduce the topic with a photograph, song, or by quickly telling the class your own favourite groups/ singers.

a Agree on the list of five and write them on the board.

- Divide the class into groups.

b Get one group to demonstrate the activity to the class first.

- If you feel your class can manage it, add some more adjectives:

  fantastic   wonderful   brilliant   terrific   superb   great all right   OK   not bad   terrible   awful   dreadful horrible.

c Students can first work out who is the most popular among their own group and then among the class as a whole.

4 Likes and dislikes

This is another information gap exercise (see page T15) which practises questions and short answers in the 3rd person singular. Make sure that student B turns immediately to page 78 and doesn't 'cheat' by looking at the boxed information about Paul on page 25.

5 What does it mean?

- Make up a nonsense word, for example, *'Samitogooloo'*. Say it. Repeat it. You'll get puzzled looks. Pretend to go out. Wave. Say *Samitogooloo*. Then ask the class *What does Samitogooloo mean?* Elicit the answer that it means 'goodbye'. Tell them that it means 'goodbye' in Mongolia, Greenland, Tibet or wherever. Make up a few more funny-sounding words for 'stand up', 'sit down', 'come here', etc. Then move on to the exercise.

a Practise the question and answer in the example.

- Keep a record of the score.

b Give the teams time to think of some words and phrases. Make sure they are not too difficult.

2 Do you like . . .?

a Fill in your answers to the questions in the table.

√ = Yes, I do.
x = No, I don't.
o = It's/They're OK.

b Work in pairs. Ask and answer questions like this:

You *Do you like pop music?*
A *Yes, I do.*

c Write four sentences about yourself.

Examples:
I like hamburgers.
I don't like the winter.

d Write four sentences about Student A.

Examples:
He/She likes football.
He/She thinks this town is OK.

		You	A
Do you like	dancing?		
	football?		
	playing computer games?		
	hamburgers?		
	English coffee?		
	tea?		
	the winter?		
	this town?		
	learning English?		

3 A survey

a Write down the names of five pop groups/singers who all the class know.

b Form groups. Ask each other, 'Do you like . . .?'
Answer like this:

Yes, they're (he's/she's) fantastic.
(3 points)

Yes, they're (he's/she's) good.
(2 points)

They're (He's/She's) all right.
(1 point)

No, they're (he's/she's) terrible.
(0 point)

One student in each group writes down the points and adds up the total.

c Work out which is the most popular group or the most popular singer.

4 Likes and dislikes

a Work in pairs. Student A looks at the information about Paul. Student B looks at the information about Carmen on page 78.

b Student A asks questions about the Spanish girl like this:

A *Does she like English pop music?*
B *Yes, she does.*

Student A fills in the missing information about her.

c Change roles. Student B asks questions about Paul.

Paul

English pop music: YES
English food: YES
Spanish food: NO
English weather: NO

Carmen

English pop music: . . .
English food: . . .
Spanish food: . . .
English weather: . . .

5 What does it mean?

a Form two teams. Team A asks team B questions like this about the words/phrases in the box. Choose only words or phrases you know:

A *What does 'auf wiedersehen' mean?*
B *It means 'goodbye' in German.*
(1 point)

B *What does 'arrivederci' mean?*
A *It means 'come here' in Portuguese.*
(0 points)

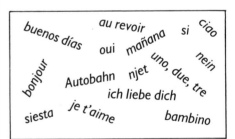

buenos días   au revoir   si   ciao
bonjour   oui   mañana   nein
Autobahn   njet   uno, due, tre
ich liebe dich
siesta   je t'aime   bambino

b Think of other foreign words or phrases. Ask the other team what they mean, in the same way.

Grammar summary: page 83

Telling the time

Debbie *What's the time?*
Dominique *Sorry?*
Debbie *What time is it?*
Dominique *It's five to five.*
Debbie *Oh no!*
Dominique *What's the matter?*
Debbie *Can you turn on the radio, please?*
Dominique *Why?*
Debbie *I want to listen to the new Top 40.*
Dominique *Pardon?*
Debbie *The Top 40—you know, this week's charts.*
Dominique *I'm sorry, I don't understand.*
Debbie *Oh, you're hopeless, Dominique! I haven't got time to explain. Just turn on the radio, quick!*

1 Times

Listen to these times and write them down.

Example:
Twenty past five = 5.20

1 ....
2 ....
3 ....
4 ....
5 ....
6 ....
7 ....
8 ....
9 ....
10 ....

2 What's the time?

Work in pairs. Take turns to ask and say what time it is.

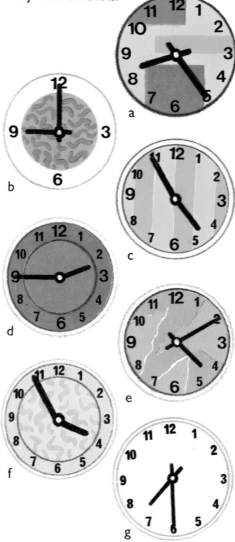

3 Dominique's timetable

 9.00 – 10.00 'Grammar in action'
10.00 – 10.15 Break
10.15 – 11.15 'English in situations'
11.15 – 11.30 Break
11.30 – 12.30 'Fun with English'

Now ask each other when Dominique's lessons start and end.

Example:
A *What time does 'Grammar in action' start?*
B *It starts at nine (o'clock).*

4 What's missing?

Work in pairs. Student A looks at the list of programmes on Radio 1 on this page. Student B looks at the list of programmes on page 79. Ask each other questions, and fill in the missing information on your page.

Example:
What time does Adrian John's show start.

TUESDAY

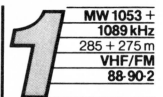

MW 1053 +
1089 kHz
285 + 275 m
VHF/FM
88-90-2

VHF/FM Stereo between 10.0pm and 12 midnight
News on the half hour from 6.30am until 8.30pm, then 10.0 and 12 midnight

[ ] **Adrian John**

7.0 Simon Mayo
with the **Breakfast Show**. Just before 8.0, an exclusive preview of the new Top 40.

9.30 [ ]

11.0 The Radio 1 Roadshow

with **Mike Read** at Portobello Beach, Edinburgh

[ ] **Newsbeat**
with **Frank Partridge**

12.45 Gary Davies
with this week's Top 40

3.0 [ ]

5.30 Newsbeat
with **Frank Partridge**

[ ] **Peter Powell**
At 6.30 Peter reviews the new Top 40 singles.

7.30 Robbie Vincent
with special guests

10.0-12.0 [ ]

Students practise

- asking and telling the time
- asking and saying what time things start and finish
- accepting and refusing offers of food
- making polite requests at mealtimes

🎦 Telling the time

Notes and possible problems

- Both questions *What's the time?* and *What time is it?* have been included in the dialogue for recognition. It is probably better to practise only one of them.

- Point out that *minutes* is only used for numbers which are not multiples of 5, for example, *two minutes past three, nine minutes to eleven.*

- *Five, ten, twenty-five* are said without minutes, for example *ten to seven, twenty past five.*

- Be careful with the pronunciation of *half* (the 'l' is not pronounced) and the weak *to* in *It's five to six.*

- Notice also that *a* in *a quarter to,* etc. is given only a very weak stress and can be left out completely.

- Students will also hear *six twenty, nine forty-five.* This way of telling the time is not practised here.

Presentation of the dialogue

- A cardboard clock with moveable hands would be extremely useful for this lesson.

- Introduce the dialogue explaining where it takes place and who is speaking.

- Ask students to listen for the following points. Write these questions on the board:

  What's the time?
  What's on the radio?
  Does Dominique understand?

- Play the dialogue, twice if necessary, and elicit answers to the questions.

- Play the first four lines again. Ask students what questions Debbie asks and elicit the two forms *What's the time?* and *What time is it?*

- Books open. Play the dialogue again. Students listen and repeat line by line.

- Students read the dialogue in pairs and then change roles.

Write about ten different times on the blackboard. Point to a time on the board and then to one student. He/she then says, for example, *It's ten to eleven.*

Exercises

1 🎦 Times

- This is a kind of dictation. Students have to write the time in numbers, not in words, for example 6.20, 8.35, etc.

- Play the exercise at least twice and give students time to write their answers.

2 What's the time?

- Focus attention on the clock faces.

- Ask the class *What's the time?* for one or two of the pictures.

- Students work in pairs. A points at a clock face and B answers. They then change roles.

3 Dominique's timetable

- If necessary, substitute the names of the lessons and the times students start and finish on their course to make the exercise more realistic.

4 What's missing?

- Divide the class into pairs (As and Bs). Tell students B to turn to page 79. Students A and B ask and answer alternately to find out the missing information.

- Get one pair of students to demonstrate the activity to the class first.

- Students write in the missing information without 'cheating' by looking at their partner's information.

📼 What to say at mealtimes

- Before dealing with the dialogue, take the opportunity of letting students talk a little about English food and the meals their host families provide. They may have strong opinions!

  Write on the board:
  breakfast
  lunch
  dinner

  Elicit the following questions and write them on the board:

  What do you have / eat for breakfast in your country?
  What do you have in England?
  Do you like English breakfasts?

  In pairs students ask and answer similar questions about all the meals.

  Get two or three pairs to report back to the class. With luck there may be some amusing stories.

- Now look at the dialogue.

- Emphasize the importance of saying *Yes, please / No, thank you.* when you are offered food or drink. Although it seems strange to foreigners, simply to answer *Yes* or *No.* sounds rude in English.

- *Could you pass the salt, please?* is a slightly more formal alternative to *Can you pass . . . ?*

- *No thanks, I'm full* has been included as a polite way of declining an offer of more food.

- You could take the opportunity to teach *Thank you, that was very nice / lovely.* as a way of expressing appreciation after a meal.

- Listen to the dialogue once, all the way through.

- Students listen and repeat the dialogue, line by line.

5 Can you . . . please?

- Focus attention on the first picture and the example.

- Practise the question and answer with choral and individual repetition.

- Use mime to demonstrate the actions for the other pictures, for example *turn on, tidy.*

- Students work in pairs, alternately asking and answering.

6 Would you like . . . ?

a Students ask and answer in pairs using the items in the picture as prompts. Make sure they change roles.

b They continue in the same way using items they think of themselves.

Note: If students ask why *some* and not *any* is used in the question *Would you like some ice cream?* (*any* is usually used in questions) explain that *some* is used in questions when we make an *offer*.

Follow-up

Insist that at their next meal with their host families students must use *Can you pass . . . ?*, *Would you like . . . ?*, and, of course, *please* and *thank you.* Tell them you'll check up next day!

5 Can you . . . please?

Work in pairs. Ask and answer like this:

pass

A *Can you pass the salt, please?*
B *Yes, all right. / OK.*

2 open

3 shut

4 turn

What to say at mealtimes

Dominique *Can you pass the salt, please, Rob?*
Rob *Yes, here you are.*
Mrs Bond *Do you like it, Dominique?*
Dominique *Er . . . yes, it's very nice.*

(Five minutes later)

Mrs Bond *Would you like some more, Dominique?*
Dominique *No thanks, Mrs Bond, I'm full.*
Mrs Bond *Do you want some ice-cream?*
Dominique *Yes, please.*

5 answer

6 tidy

---

6 Would you like . . .?

a Work in pairs. Ask and answer questions like this:

Would you like some ice-cream?
Yes, please. / No, thank you.

meat	a pear
peas	an apple
gravy	sprouts

b Ask and answer questions in the same way. Use your own ideas.

Example:
Would you like some ketchup?

Summary of English in situations

- telling the time
- making requests
- making offers
- accepting and refusing food

27

1 Sound right

a 🎧 Listen to these pairs of words. What is the difference in pronunciation between the words on the left and the words on the right?

cat	cut
hat	hut
match	much
cap	cup
bat	but
ran	run
sang	sung

b Now listen again and repeat the words.

c Now tick (✓) the words you hear.

1 but ☐		2 ran ☐	
bat ☐		run ☐	
3 cat ☐		4 much ☐	
cut ☐		match ☐	
5 cup ☐		6 sung ☐	
cap ☐		sang ☐	
7 hat ☐			
hut ☐			

d Work in pairs. Student A writes down seven of the words from the lists above. He/she then reads them out to student B.
Student B writes them down.
Student A and B compare their two lists. Change roles.

2 Listen to this

🎧 Listen to the three interviews.
Fill in the missing information in the table below with one of these symbols: ✓ o x

✓ = he/she likes it
o = he/she thinks it's OK
x = he/she doesn't like it

	✓	o	x

	Pop music	Football	Modern fashion
Gary Carter			
Sandra Brent			
Charles Wentworth-Smythe			

3 Play games in English

Word tennis

Form two teams. The teacher chooses a category, for example:
food, transport, relatives, sport, weather.

Team A calls out one word in the category. Team B must say another word in the same category in only five seconds. The game goes on until one team can't think of another word in that category.

1 🔊 Sound right

- The aim of the exercise is to practise pronouncing the sound [æ] as in *bat* and the sound [ʌ] as in *but*.

a The sound [æ] is very difficult to pronounce for many foreign students. Encourage them to open their mouths as much as possible. A bright, smiling face for *cap* and a serious expression—with facial muscles relaxed—for *cup* might help.

b Play the list of words twice. Students repeat the words with the correct vowel sound.

c Play the cassette. Students tick the words they hear. Play it again, stopping after each pair of words for students to check their answers. They compare their answers in pairs.

d This is a kind of word dictation. Choose two or three words yourself and read them out twice to give students the idea. Students note them down.

2 🔊 Listen to this

Note: Explain that students should not panic if they don't understand everything they hear. They only have to complete the table. A lot of redundant language has been added to get students used to listening for 'gist' or general meaning.

- There is no example so explain carefully what the students have to do.

- Play the interviews through once without stopping. Students do not write anything.

- Play them again, stopping after each interview. Give students enough time to fill in their answers.

- Play the cassette through a third time, so that students can check their answers.

- Students exchange books and correct each other's answers.

- Students can say which word or phrase helped them to get the right answer.

- If students are interested, explain some of the new vocabulary they hear on the tape.

3 Play games in English

Word tennis

- Write the chosen category on the board.

- Write down the words underneath as the teams call them out.

- If a team can't think of a word, 'count them out' 5–4–3–2–1.

- Play several rounds of the game.

- After the game, students can practise pronouncing the word lists on the board. Make sure they understand what the words mean.

4 Work on words

a Students work in pairs or groups.

● Ask pairs or groups to read out which word is different.

b Encourage students to try to explain why the word is different. But remember, in many cases it is difficult to explain with their level of English. Encourage them to 'get the message across'.

Extra activity
In small groups students make up their own 'Odd one out' exercise, with at least five questions, to ask the rest of the class.

5 Read and think

● Students read the story in pairs and decide the best caption (d) was the original caption).

● Ask pairs of students to act out the story.

● Get the class to retell the story with their books closed. Prompt with single words if they can't remember.

Follow-up:

A lot of jokes are about a customer and a waiter in a restaurant. For homework, get students either to make up one such joke or get one from a British person.

They can retell their joke(s) the next day.

6 Now you're here

a Students can ask you the questions first and then each other.

b Students tell the rest of the class their most interesting answers the next day.

4 Work on words

a What is the odd word out in the following groups of words?

Example:

orange

banana

potato

apple

'Potato' is the odd word out because it is a vegetable. The other three are fruits.

1	French	7	tennis
	Spanish		squash
	Italy		football
	German		badminton
2	husband	8	park
	brother		pub
	sister		church
	father		bank
3	hi	9	record
	cheerio		computer
	goodbye		tape
	bye		cassette
4	ugly	10	chips
	beautiful		hamburger
	attractive		hot dog
	pretty		milk
5	bike	11	OK
	moped		terrible
	motorcycle		fine
	car		all right
6	doctor	12	salt
	dentist		pepper
	student		crisps
	teacher		ketchup

b Now explain why the odd word out is different from the other three.

5 Read and think

Read the story below. What do you think the man says in the last picture? Choose from a) b) c) or d).

A man goes into a restaurant. The waiter is surprised because the man has got boxing gloves on.

The man orders the most expensive things on the menu.

It's difficult for the man to eat and drink with his boxing gloves on.

The man eats an enormous meal, and then drinks a bottle of champagne.

The man finishes his meal, and asks for the bill.

Which is the best answer?

a) 'Because I'm a boxer.'
b) 'Because my hands are cold.'
c) 'Because I can't hold a knife and fork without them.'
d) 'Because I haven't got any money to pay the bill!'

6 Now you're here

a Ask a British person the following questions and note down his/her answers.
You can practise the questions in class first.

- Do you like fish and chips?
- Do you like champagne?
- Do you like cricket?
- Do you like boxing?
- Do you like jogging?
- Do you like pubs?
- Do you like dogs?
- Do you like pop music?
- Do you like classical music?

b Tell other students your most interesting answers.

UNIT FIVE · LESSON ONE

Rob What's your mother like, Dominique?

Dominique She's OK, but she always asks my friends too many questions. She wants to know everything about them. 'Where do you live?' she asks. 'What does your father do?', 'Does your mother work?', and 'Where do you go for your holidays?', and so on and so on. It's so embarrassing!

Debbie What about your father?

Dominique He's all right, but he's got one really terrible habit.

Debbie What does he do?

Dominique He sings!

Debbie What's so terrible about that?

Dominique Well, he doesn't just sing in the bath. He sings when my friends are in the house, and his voice is so bad!

Rob Dad's got a really terrible habit too. He never remembers the names of my friends. But when they come to our house, he doesn't just say 'Hello'. He says 'Hello Peter' when really his name is Paul, or 'Hi Katherine' when her name's Karen.

Debbie Ummm, he sometimes embarrasses me too.

Dominique What does he do?

Debbie He wears jeans, tight jeans. He forgets he's nearly forty, not fourteen!

The problem with parents is . . .

Rob Yes you're right. But what about Mum? Sometimes my friends come round and we talk about pop music. Then Mum comes in. She doesn't know anything about modern music, so she talks about the Beatles and the Rolling Stones instead!

Dominique But does she dance to the music too? My mother does, and that's *really* embarrassing!

I Make true sentences

Make true sentences from the table.

Example:
Debbie's mother likes the Rolling Stones.

Rob's father	(like)	her.
	(sing)	people's names.
Dominique's father	(wear)	a terrible voice.
	(have got)	tight jeans.
Debbie's mother	(dance)	in the bath.
	(forget)	too many questions.
Dominique's mother	(want)	to his records.
	(embarrass)	to know about his friends.
	(ask)	the Rolling Stones.

<table>
<tr><td colspan="2">Grammar summary</td></tr>
</table>

Grammar summary
• Present simple tense including the *do* construction • Adverbs of frequency (*always, often,* etc.)

📻 The problem with parents is . . .

Notes and possible problems

- *What's your mother like?* (line 1) Students may confuse this with *What does your mother like?* or *What does your mother look like?*

- *She's O.K.* (line 3) and *He's all right* (line 13) are neutral answers, i.e. not good, not bad.

- *What does your father do?* (line 15) Point out that this means *What's your father's job / profession?*

- *and so on* (line 10) = etc. (etcetera)

- *just* (line 17) = only

- *come round* (line 35) = come to our house.

Pre-text activity

- If possible, take pictures of your own family into class. Ideally ask students before this lesson to bring family photos with them. Encourage them to show each other their photos, talk freely about them and ask and answer questions. This will provide a natural lead into presenting the dialogue.

Presentation of the dialogue

Here are some suggestions for teaching / checking grammar and vocabulary.

- Write the following on the board:

What's your	mother father brother sister	like?	He's She's	fantastic. (very) nice. O.K. / all right. not very nice. awful / horrible.

Ask a few students questions such as *What's your mother like?* etc. and get them to answer from the alternatives on the right.

Point at two students at random. Student A asks a question from the alternatives on the left and Student B answers.

- Ask students:

What does your	father mother	do?	He's She's	a salesperson. a doctor.

- *embarrassing* Quickly tell a story with a mime to demonstrate the word.

- Teach / Check the following words and any others you think necessary (see page vii):

  sing   dance   forget   habit

- Set the scene for the dialogue. Students listen with books closed. Rob, Dominique and Debbie are sitting in a park talking about their parents.

- Write up the following on the board:

  asks too many questions
  doesn't remember names
  sings
  wears tight jeans
  talks about the Beatles
  dances

  Check students understand the words / phrases.

  Explain that when they listen to the dialogue they must identify if it is the mother or the father who does these things and whose mother and father it is.

  Play the cassette once or twice and give students time to answer the questions.

  Students check their answers.

- Students open their books. Play the dialogue again in small sections. Stop after each section and explain / check the meaning of words and phrases. Students listen and repeat. Concentrate on a lively, natural intonation.

Exercises

I Make true sentences

- Remind students that they must add an s to the verb in the third person singular (i.e. after he / she, Rob's father, etc.).

- Students work individually or in pairs.

- Check their answers.

2 Ask and answer

a Remind students that *does*, not *do*, is used to make questions in the present tense with *he (your father)*, *she (your mother)*, etc. Tell students to look again at the table in the Grammar summary on page 83.

- Practise the question and answer in the example.

- Nominate students at random to ask the question for each sentence (1–8), checking that they use *do* or *does* correctly.

- Students ask and answer the questions in pairs.

b and C In addition you can ask students to write down things their parents always say, for example *You treat this house like a hotel.* or *Your room is like a pigsty.* etc. They compare what they have written.

3 People's habits

a To demonstrate the meaning of adverbs of frequency a table such as the following can be put on the board.

Mon	Tues	Wed	Thurs	Fri	Sat	Sun	
X	X	X	X	X	X	X	always
X		X	X		X	X	often
	X		X				sometimes
				X			hardly ever
							never

Ask questions to make the meanings clear.

Example:
T *Do you brush your teeth in the morning?*
S *Yes.*
T *Every day?*
S *Yes.*
T *You always brush your teeth in the morning.*

T *How often do you watch TV?*
S *I often watch TV.*

T *How often do you eat caviar?*
S *I never eat caviar.*

b and C Make sure students put the adverbs in the right position before the verb.

- Students can think of other habits and ask each other the same question about them, for example *How often do you wash your hair?*

Extra activity: Habits

- Form groups of three to four students.

- Each student writes down one good habit and one bad habit of each member of the group. The sentences must include one of these words: *always, usually, often, sometimes, hardly ever, never.*

  Example:
  She often helps me with my homework.
  She always arrives late.

- Students compare what they have written about each other.

- The most interesting comments can be read out to the class as a whole.

---

4 Girl meets boy

a Ask a pair of students (a boy and a girl) to come to the front of the class and act out the conversation. The boy has to improvise his answers.

b Get students to move around the class as if in a disco, 'chatting each other up' (or if this is not practical, students practise the dialogue in pairs).

- Students improvise as much as they like.

- Make sure students move fairly quickly from one partner to another. Encourage them to move about, sit on desks, to be as natural as possible. Play disco music on a cassette to help create the right sort of atmosphere.

5 Tell a lie

- Check that students remember what a lie is.

- Write four statements on the board about yourself and ask students to guess which of the four is a lie.

a Give students time to write their own sentences.

b They can read out their sentences in small groups. The best 'liars' in each group can try out their lies on the rest of the class.

2 Ask and answer

a Work in pairs. Ask and answer questions.

Example:
mother / like pop music?
A *Does your mother like pop music?*
B *Yes, she does. (No, she doesn't.)*

1 father / sing in the bath?
2 father / wear tight jeans?
3 parents / like pop music?
4 mother / ask too many questions?
5 father / sing badly?
6 mother / dance well?
7 parents / embarrass you?
8 father / forget your friends' names?

b How do your parents embarrass you? Write three sentences about them.

c Compare your sentences in groups. Read out the most interesting examples to the rest of the class.

3 People's habits

a Work in pairs. Student A asks student B questions and fills in the table.

Example:
A *How often do you forget birthdays?*
B *I never forget birthdays.*

How often do you . . .?	always	often	sometimes	hardly ever	never
forget birthdays?					✓
sing in the bath?					
dance?					
go to church?					
wear jeans?					
listen to Beatles' records?					
travel by train?					
go to a disco?					

b Now write sentences like this about your partner:
He / She never forgets birthdays.

c Tell the class about your partner.

Examples:
Claude never forgets birthdays.
He sometimes sings in the bath.

4 Girl meets boy

a Complete the girl's questions for the boy's answers.

Girl	Boy
● What . . .?	My name's Peter.
● Where . . .?	I live here in Hastings.
● How often . . .?	I come here every Saturday.
● What . . .?	I'm a student.
● Which . . .?	I go to East Hill School.
● What music . . .?	I like rock music.
● . . . dance?	Yes, OK.

b Practise the dialogue in pairs, but think of your own answers to the questions.

5 Tell a lie

a Write down four things about yourself. Three must be true and one must be a lie.

b Read out your sentences to the class. They must guess which one is the lie.

Examples:
I never wear jeans.
I like classical music.
My mother's 42.
I often forget birthdays.

Grammar summary: page 83

31

1 How much is this?

a Work in pairs. Point to the pictures and ask each other questions.

Example:
A *How much is this?*
B *It's 27p.*

1

2

3

4

5

b Now do the same with your own English money.

2 The money game

Look at these prices. What is the minimum number of coins you need to buy these things?

Example: *37p*
4 coins – 20p 10p 5p 2p

1 16p   2 23p   3 20p

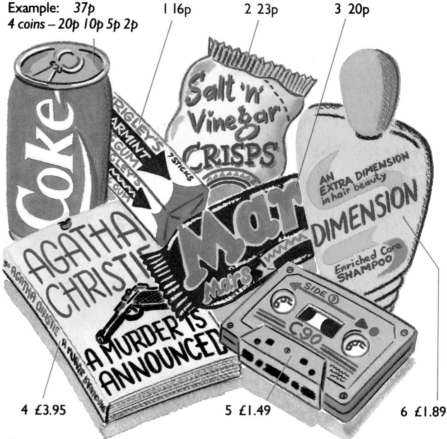

4 £3.95   5 £1.49   6 £1.89

3 How much is it?

Work in pairs. Student A chooses one of the things above and asks how much it is. Student B tells him/her.

Example:
A *How much is a can of Coke, please?*
B *37p.*

4 How much are they?

Work in pairs. Student A asks for two of the things above, student B says how much they cost.

Example:
A *Can I have a can of Coke and a packet of crisps, please?*
B *That's 57p, please.*

5 What's missing?

Listen to this dialogue in a shop. Write down the prices of the things the girl buys, and then the total cost.

1 peanuts   . . . . .
2 bananas   . . . . .
3 milk chocolate . . . . .
4 lemonade   . . . . .

Total: . . . . .

6 What do you need?

Work in pairs. Student A is a customer and wants to buy four things for a picnic. Student B is a shopkeeper and tells student A what the things cost.

<table>
<tr><th>Students practise</th></tr>
</table>

- using English money
- asking for things in a shop
- asking how much things cost in a shop
- changing money/traveller's cheques in a bank

- Ask students to look at the pictures of money. Then ask them to look at the money which they have in their own pockets and purses. In pairs they identify the coins and notes.

1 How much is this?

a Get one pair to demonstrate the activity to the class.

- Repeat so that A and B have asked and answered questions on each picture.

b Do the same activity. This time students take out their own money and show it to each other in different quantities.

2 The money game

- Students work in pairs, checking their answers.

3 How much is it?

- When they have finished, students can ask each other about the prices of the things in the pictures in *their* country.

Example:
A *How much is a paperback in Spain?*
B *It's about 700 pesetas.*
A *How much is that in pounds and pence?*
B *It's about £3.50.*

4 How much are they?

- Emphasize that *Can I have . . . please?* is the most common way of asking for things in a shop, cafe, pub, etc.
- Foreign students often use wrong phrases or expressions such as *Can you give me . . . ?, Give me . . .* or *I want . . .*, which can cause offence.

- Practise saying the question *Can I have . . . please?* with a polite intonation.
- Ask students to suggest what they would say in, for example, a pub *Can I have a Pepsi, please?* or a cafe *Can I have a cup of coffee and a bun, please?*
- Put a list of shops/places on the board:

Example:
*chemist's   newsagent's   greengrocer's   post office
railway station   restaurant*

- Working in pairs or small groups, students think of what they could say in each place.
- They tell the rest of the class some of their suggestions.

5 What's missing?

- Introduce the dialogue. Explain the context.
- Play the dialogue through once without stopping. Students do not write anything.
- Play it again. Give students time to write down their answers.
- Play the dialogue a third time so that students can check their answers.
- Students correct each other's answers.

6 What do you need?

- Write the important phrases from the dialogue on the board.

Example:
*Can I help you?
Can I have . . . ?
Small, medium or large . . . ?*

- Ask students to list items you could buy for a picnic and write them on the blackboard, for example apples, cheese, buns, Coke, etc.
- Get one pair of students to improvise the conversation in front of the class. Use a table as the shop counter.
- Put students in pairs. They practise their conversations, changing roles.
- Choose one or two pairs to act out the conversation in front of the class again.

In a bank

- Introduce the dialogue, explaining the context.

- Books closed. Play the dialogue through once and ask one or two simple questions, for example *Why is the student in the bank?*

- Tell students to listen for two things which they need to do when exchanging traveller's cheques. Play the dialogue again. Elicit answers *show passport, sign the cheques.*

- Tell students that they might also be asked for *a means of identification.*

- *Here you are* is a common expression, used when handing something to somebody.

- *Sorry?* here means *Can you repeat that, please?* Students could also hear *Pardon?*

- *fives* is short for *five pound notes.*

- Books open. Play the cassette once more.

7 Act it out

- Students practise the conversation in pairs, changing roles.

- Choose two or three pairs to act it out in front of the class from memory. (Prompt with words if necessary.)

- Don't insist that the students use the exact words. Encourage improvisation.

8 What's missing?

- As in the previous 'information gap' exercise, careful preparation is needed.

- Give examples of the questions *How much do / does the . . . cost?* Say the price of an item of clothing and tell a student to ask the question.

Note: Students will have problems remembering *do* or *does.*

- Divide the class into As and Bs. Tell the B students to turn to page 79.

- Make sure students write in the missing information but do not 'cheat' by looking at their partner's information.

In a bank

Student *Can I cash these traveller's cheques, please?*
Bank clerk *Yes. Have you got your passport, please?*
Student *Yes, here you are.*
Bank clerk *Can you sign the cheques, please?*
Student *Yes.*
Bank clerk *And can you fill in the date, please?*
Student *What is the date today?*
Bank clerk *It's the 10th. . . . How do you want the money?*
Student *Sorry?*
Bank clerk *Do you want it in fives or tens?*
Student *Fives, please.*

7 Act it out

Practise the dialogue above in pairs. One of you is the student, the other is the bank clerk. You can also use your own ideas.

Summary of English in situations

- asking for things
- asking and talking about the cost of things

8 What's missing?

Work in pairs. Student A looks at the pictures and prices on this page. Student B looks at the pictures and prices on page 79. Ask and answer questions to find out the missing prices.

Examples:
B *How much do the shoes cost?*
A *They cost £35.99.*
  How much does the jacket cost?
B *It costs £49.50.*

1 Sound right

a 🔲 Listen to these words from the dialogue on page 30.

problem	habit
question	remember
everything	forget
holiday	fourteen
embarrassing	forty
terrible	music

b Now listen again. Which syllable (part of the word) do you say most strongly or heavily? Underline that syllable, like this:

<u>pro</u>blem

c Now read the words. Say the syllables you underlined as strongly or heavily as possible.

2 Play games in English

Word chain

Form two teams.
The teacher writes a word in the top left-hand corner of the board (for example: HABIT).
One member of team A adds another word beginning with the last letter of the first word (for example: TERRIBLE). Time limit: 30 seconds. Then one member of team B adds another word beginning with E, and so on.
You get 3 points for a 3-letter word, 4 points for a 4-letter word, etc.

3 Listen to this

a 🔲 Nicola Adams is a friend of Rob's. Listen to what she does every morning. Look at the pictures and fill in the times when she does different things.

1 ....

2 ....

3 ....

4 ....

5 ....

6 ....

b Now write down what Nicola does in each picture.
Use the words in the box.

have breakfast	leave home
catch a bus	get up
have a shower	get dressed

Example:
She gets up at half past seven.

1 ....   4 ....

2 ....   5 ....

3 ....   6 ....

1 🔊 Sound right

- The aim of the exercise is to make students aware of the importance of stressing the right syllable.

- Write on the board the word *student* and mark the stressed syllable like this: <u>stu</u>dent.

- Say the word with heavy stress on the stressed syllable.

- Write up more words and ask where the stress is, for example *difficult, interesting, exam.*

a and b Students work individually and then compare their answers with a partner.

c Students read the words to each other. Ask individuals to read them to the class.

2 Play games in English

Word chain

- Keep a record of the points scored.

- Play the game several times.

- The game can also be played orally, without teams, round the class. If a student cannot think of a word beginning with the last letter of the previous one within 5 seconds, he/she is eliminated from the game.

3 🔊 Listen to this

- A lot of redundant language above the level of the students' English has been deliberately included.

- Teach/check the following words and phrases by drawing, mime, etc.

  alarm clock   to have a shower   to brush your teeth
  to have a shave   bus stop

a Explain that students have to write the time in figures, for example *8.15.*

- Play the exercise through once without stopping. Students do not write anything.

- Play it again, stopping at each pause. Give students enough time to write their answers.

- Play the exercise through a third time so that students can check their answers.

- Students exchange books and correct each other's answers.

b Make sure students use the third person singular form of the verbs *has, catches, leaves, gets.*

Note: verbs which finish in *-ch* or *-sh* add *-es* in the third person singular, present tense, for example *brushes.*

- In pairs, students can ask and answer questions about their own morning routine. They can use the pictures as prompts or make up their own questions if they want to.

  Example:
  What time do you get up?
  Do you have a shower?

4 Read and think

- Students can choose whether to work individually, in pairs or in groups.

- Students will probably find it easier to do both parts of the exercise if they make a grid like this:

likes (√)   *dislikes (X)*

	Adam	Beth	Clare	Linda
chips	X	X	X	√
fish	√	X	√	√
hot dogs	√	X	√	√
hamburgers	X	√	X	X

(Students should fill in the ticks and crosses above, not the teacher.)

5 Work on words

a Students work in pairs, and then check their answers.

b Students work in groups. When they have finished, they can compare their answers with other groups.

6 Now you're here

a Students ask you the questions.

- Students ask each other the questions.

- Tell students to ask a British person the same questions after class and make notes of their answers.

b Students tell the rest of the class about their most interesting answers the next day.

4 Read and think

a Read about which foods these four people like and don't like.

Adam   Beth   Clare   Linda

- Adam likes fish but he doesn't like chips.
- Beth doesn't like fish or hot dogs.
- Clare only likes the same things as Adam.
- Linda likes three things.
- Beth only likes one thing—the thing which Linda doesn't like.
- Clare likes hot dogs.
- Chips aren't the only thing which Adam doesn't like.
- Linda doesn't like hamburgers.

Now answer these questions:

1 Does Adam like hot dogs?
2 Does Clare like chips?
3 Does Linda like fish?
4 Does Beth like hamburgers?
5 Does Clare like fish?
6 Does Linda like hot dogs?
7 Does Adam like hamburgers?
8 Does Beth like chips?

b Look at the picture again and 'give' each person something that he/she likes.

5 Work on words

a Match the verbs on the left with the words on the right.

Example:
You speak English.

You	1 ask	a) a bus
	2 eat	b) jeans
	3 speak	c) a question
	4 wear	d) a hamburger
	5 catch	e) the radio
	6 listen to	f) games
	7 play	g) English
	8 ride	h) a door
	9 read	i) a bike
	10 drink	j) a magazine
	11 open	k) a cheque
	12 cash	l) coffee

b Now think of other words to go with the verbs on the left.

Example:
You listen to a record.

6 Now you're here

a Ask a British person these questions.

- What time do you get up?
- What do you have for breakfast?
- What time do you usually have lunch?
- Where do you have lunch?
- How many cups of tea do you usually drink a day?
- What time do you usually go to bed?
- Which newspaper do you read?
- Which television channel do you watch most?
- Which radio station do you listen to most?
- Where do you usually go on holiday?
- How often do you . . .
    go to the cinema?
    eat in a restaurant?
    go to a pub?
    go to the hairdresser's?
    go abroad?
    go to the dentist's?

b Tell the rest of the class about the most interesting answers.

35

UNIT SIX · LESSON ONE 6

On the beach

Sammy Hey, have you got the time?
Dominique No, I'm sorry, I haven't.
Sammy You're not English, are you?
Dominique Can you hear my accent?
Sammy Yes, of course I can.
Dominique Where am I from? Can you guess?
Sammy Spain?
Dominique No.
Sammy Italy?
Dominique No. Wrong again.
Sammy Are you French?
Dominique Yes, of course I am.
Sammy What a pity.
Dominique Why? What's the problem?
Sammy I can't speak French.
Dominique No problem. I can speak a bit of English.
Sammy But I can't understand your English.
Dominique Can't you?

Sammy Don't worry. I can really. Come on! Let's have a swim.
Dominique No, thanks.
Sammy Why not?
Dominique I can't swim!

1 Questions and answers

a Match the questions on the left with the answers on the right.

Example: 1 – h

1 Is Dominique French?
2 Can he speak English?
3 Can Sammy understand Dominique's English?
4 Is Sammy English?
5 Can Dominique swim?
6 Has Sammy got a watch?
7 Does Sammy speak to Dominique first?
8 Has Dominique got a French accent?

a) Yes, she is.
b) Yes, she does.
c) Yes, he has.
d) Yes, a bit.
e) No, she hasn't.
f) No, he can't.
g) Yes, she can.
h) Yes, he is.

b Work in pairs. Student A asks the same questions. Student B answers them without looking in the book. Change roles.

36

Grammar summary

- can (ability) (*I can swim. Can you swim? I can't swim.*)

📼 On the beach

Notes and possible problems

- *Can* here has the meaning of ability, i.e. 'to swim' or 'I have the ability to swim.' In some languages ability is expressed by the verb to *know*.

- Be careful students do not insert a 'to' between *can* and the following verb, i.e. *I can to swim* is wrong.

- **Note:** *Can* is usually pronounced or stressed weakly in affirmative sentences but strongly in negative sentences. Compare:

  I can swim [kən]
  I can't swim [ka:nt]
  In short affirmative answers like *Yes, I can.* 'can' is stressed and pronounced [kæn].

  Foreign speakers have problems making clear in speech the distinction between *can* and *can't*, i.e. they pronounce the two words in a very similar way. Make them practise pronouncing *can* with a smile and *can't* with a serious face.

- The uncontracted form of *can't* is *cannot* and is written as one word.

- There is no s on the third person singular *he/she/it can*.

- *Have you got the time?* means the same as *What time is it?*

- *What a pity!* (line 15) is a typical response to (not serious) bad news.

Example:
A *I can't come to your party.*
B *Oh, what a pity!*

Students may also hear *What a shame!*

- *a bit of* A common expression meaning 'a little'.

- *Let's . . .* A common expression used when making a suggestion.

Presentation of the dialogue

- Set the scene for the dialogue. Students have their books closed. Dominique is on the beach at Hastings when he meets Sammy.

- Students listen with books closed.

- Write on the board the following questions:

  Has Dominique got the time?
  Can Sammy speak French?
  Can Sammy understand Dominique?
  Can Dominique swim?

  Make sure students understand the questions.

- Play the tape and give students time to answer the questions.

- Students check their answers.

- Students open their books.

- Play the dialogue in small sections. Stop after each section and explain/check the meaning of words/phrases if necessary.

- Students repeat the dialogue sentence by sentence after the teacher (or after the cassette). Concentrate on a lively, natural intonation.

- Students practise the conversation in pairs, taking it in turns to take the parts of Sammy and Dominique.

- Choose one or two pairs to act out the dialogue in front of the class from memory (with help from you and the class if necessary). Don't insist that the lines are exactly the same as those in the book. Students should be encouraged to improvise.

Exercises

I Questions and answers

a Students work individually or in pairs to match questions and answers.

- Students check their answers.

b Make sure that the student who is answering has the answers covered or the book closed.

2 Write it again

a Give students a time limit to write their dialogue. Help with vocabulary and correct where necessary.

b Give students time to rehearse their dialogue.

c Choose two pairs of students to act out their dialogue in front of the class, from memory if possible.

3 Ask a friend

● Make sure that students can pronounce all the verbs correctly.

a Students work in pairs asking answering and noting down their partner's answers.

● Students think of their own verbs and ask each other questions about them.

c Ask some of the students to tell the class two things about their partner, for example *Maria can ski but she can't ride a horse.* Insist on the correct pronunciation of *can*/*can't*.

4 Can they or can't they?

a and b Move around the class yourself, asking questions and noting down names to demonstrate the activity.

c Obviously more information will have been gathered about some students than others.

d Give students time to write their sentences. Help with vocabulary.

● Ask some students to tell the class what they can do.

Extra activity

Write the names of each member of the class on separate sheets of paper and hand them out at random. Make sure that no student receives a paper with his/her own name on it.

On the other side of the paper students must write down as many facts as possible about the person named (using *can* and *can't*).

When students have finished, give each paper a number and stick them all around the walls.   (*continued*)

Students walk around reading the information. They must guess which person is being described on each paper.

Check if their guesses are right or not. Who got the most right?

5 ⊟ Speak to Sammy

● You take the part of Sammy first and ask different students the questions.

● Students work in pairs to complete the dialogue.

● Check their answers. There are usually several possibilities.

● Choose one or two pairs to act out the dialogue in front of the class.

Extra activity: What can you do with them?

Write these words on the board:

a bed   money   a window   a letter   a knife   a ball
paper   a picture   water   food   jeans

Form two teams. Team A chooses a word and says something you can do with it.

Example:
Team A *a bed   You can sleep in a bed.*
Team B *You can sit on a bed.*
Team A *You can jump on it.*
Team B *You can hide under it.*

The game goes on like this until one team can't think of a 'correct' sentence.

They then do the same with the next word *money*, etc.

Variation

In pairs or small groups, students choose an object and write four clues for it.

Example:
You can sit at it. You can hide your money in it. You can listen to it. You can play it.

The answer is *a piano.*

You could introduce a points system. 5 points to the pair /group who guesses correctly after the first clue, 4 points to whoever guesses correctly after the second clue and so on.

2 Write it again

a Work in pairs. Re-write the dialogue between Dominique and Sammy. This time Dominique speaks to Sammy first.
Student A writes what Dominique says first, and then passes it to student B. Student B writes what Sammy says in reply.
Write four or five lines each.
The dialogue you write can be completely different from the one in the book.

b Practise your dialogue together.

c Act it out in class.

3 Ask a friend

a Work in pairs. Look at the pictures and ask and answer questions about them like this:
A *Can you swim?*
B *Yes, I can. / No, I can't. / Yes, I can a bit.*

Choose from the verbs in the box.

swim	type	ski
skateboard	windsurf	drive

b Write sentences about your partner.

Examples:
He / She can play tennis.
He / She can't windsurf.
He / She can skateboard a bit.

c Tell the rest of the class about your partner.

4 Can they or can't they?

a Ask other students in the class the same questions as in exercise 3.
Ask each student only *one* question.

b Write down the names of the students you speak to and their answers, like this.

Examples:
Juan – swim	Yes
Pia – ski	No
Marco – windsurf	No

Continue until you have got three 'Yes' answers and three 'No' answers.

c The teacher names a student in the class. The rest of the class tell the teacher about the student, like this:

Teacher	*Juan.*
Student 1	*He can swim.*
Student 2	*He can't windsurf.*
Student 3	*He can ski.*

d Write down three other things you can do. Then tell the class about them.

5 Speak to Sammy

Complete this dialogue between Sammy and yourself.

Sammy *Have you got the time?*
You ....
Sammy *You're not English, are you?*
You ....
Sammy *Where are you from?*
You ....
Sammy *How much English can you understand?*
You ....
Sammy *How much English can you speak?*
You ....
Sammy *Why are you here in England?*
You ....
Sammy *How long are you here for?*
You ....

Grammar summary: page 83

37

Rules of the house

① You must be on time for meals

② You must come home before 11 o'clock

③ You mustn't smoke in your room .....

④ You mustn't use the telephone without permission

⑤ You must ask permission before you have a bath

⑥ You mustn't play music too loudly

⑦ You mustn't have friends in your room

I The rules of your house

Tick (√) those rules above which are true in your family in Britain or in your family at home. Compare your answers.

2 Can they or can't they?

Listen to these foreign students talking about their English families. Mark the things they can do with a tick (√), and the things they mustn't/can't do with a cross (×).

	come home late?	smoke in his/ her room?	have a bath every day?	have friends in his/her room?
Marco				
Pia				
Martine				
Takao				

3 Can you or can't you?

Ask other students questions about the rules in their houses.

Ask and answer questions like this:
A *Can you come home after 11 o'clock?*
B *No, I can't.*

Mark the answers with a tick (√) for yes or a cross (×) for no.

Can you . . .

be late for meals? ☐
come home after 11 o'clock? ☐
smoke in your room? ☐
use the telephone without permission? ☐
have a bath without permission? ☐
play loud music in your room? ☐
have friends in your room? ☐

4 Mini dialogue

Practise this dialogue in pairs.

A *Can I use the telephone, please?*
B *Yes, of course./No, I'm afraid you can't.*

Now student A should use the words below instead of the underlined words:

have a bath
come home after eleven
smoke in my room
be late for dinner.

Change roles. Practise more dialogues using your own ideas.

Students practise
• talking about what they must and mustn't do
• talking about what they can (are allowed to) and can't do
• asking what words mean

Rules of the house

- Students repeat the rules on the landlord's list in chorus and individually.

- Make sure students understand the vocabulary.

1 The rules of your house

- Do any of the rules apply to the whole class?

- Working individually or in groups students think of other rules which their families at home or in Britain insist on.

2 ▦ Can they or can't they?

- Play the exercise through once without stopping. Students do not write anything.

- Play it again, stopping after each conversation. Give students enough time to write their answers.

- Play the exercise through a third time so that students can check their answers.

- Students exchange books and correct each other's answers.

- Teach any new vocabulary, if there is time.

3 Can you or can't you?

- Students can tell the rest of the class one or two of the things which their partner can or can't do.

- Remember to insist on the weak pronunciation of *can* (/kən/) and strong pronunciation of *can't* (/ka:nt/).

4 Mini dialogue

- Choose pairs of students at random to ask and answer the questions, using the phrases underneath.

- When pairs have practised asking and answering questions using phrases in the book, get them to think of ideas of their own. Put these on the board. Students practise the mini dialogue again using these.

5 Role play

- In pairs or groups let students prepare a short conversation for each of the situations.

- Go around checking and correcting the conversations.

- Each group nominates a pair of students to act out the conversation in front of the class.

- Don't expect too much from students at this level.

6 What do they mean?

- Ask students where they would see these signs — by the road, in a hospital, etc.

- Ask students what the signs mean. Elicit answers using *must* or *mustn't*. Put the answers on the board.

- Students ask and answer in pairs.

- Before you ask them to change roles, rub out the sentences on the board if you think they can manage without them.

7 Find your own sign

- Students may not be able to remember many signs. It will probably be best to give this exercise as homework. Tell students to write down at least five new signs. Discuss them (where you see them, what they mean, etc.) next day.

Extra activity: Write your own notices

In pairs or groups students make up signs appropriate to their classroom or the school.

Example:
English only, please!
No chewing gum under the desks.

The best ideas could be made into real notices and stuck up in appropriate places.

---

5 Role play

Work in pairs. Act out the dialogues in these situations.

6 What do they mean?

Work in pairs. Student A points at a sign or notice and asks, 'What does this mean?' Student B answers.

Example:
A *What does this sign mean?*
B *It means you must queue on this side of the sign.*
          or
You mustn't queue on the other side of the sign.

7 Find your own

Write down more examples of notices or signs you have seen. Ask your teacher or other students in the class, 'What does this mean?'

Summary of English in situations

- talking about rules and obligations

1 Sound right

a How do you pronounce the names of these companies and products in your language?

Coca-Cola	Pan Am
Kodak	Hilton Hotel
Honda	Mercedes Benz
McDonald's	Texaco
Renault	Rolls Royce
Philips	Sanyo
Esso	Pepsi-Cola
Marlboro	Citroën
Avis	Xerox

b 🎧 Now listen to how they sound in English.

c Listen again and repeat. In what ways is the English pronunciation different from yours?

d Work in groups. Think of other international companies / products. Try to pronounce them in an English way. Check your pronunciation with your teacher.

2 Listen to this

a 🎧 Listen to the instructions on the tape and do exactly what the voice tells you to do.

b Work in pairs. Give each other instructions. Use the following verbs and the parts of the body in exercise 3.

open	close	touch
turn	put	pull
shake	stand	fold

3 Work on words

a Choose the right words from the box to label the parts of the body.

arm	head	eye	mouth	foot	stomach	hand
ear	leg	finger	nose	hair	toe	

b Now work in pairs. Student A points to a part of his / her body, and student B says what it is in English.

1 🔊 Sound right

c Students repeat after the tape. The difference between how the words are pronounced in English and in the students' own language will often involve a difference in stress. Ask students to underline the stressed syllables.

d Write on the board the company / product names that the students think of and mark the stress.

2 🔊 Listen to this

● Teach / revise the following verbs if necessary:

touch   pull   shake hands   fold (your arms)

a Use one pair to demonstrate the activity to the rest of the class.

● Play the cassette and pause after each instruction until all students are obeying the instruction.

● Play the cassette a second time, this time without pauses.

b Student continue, making up instructions from the verbs and parts of the body listed.

Note: In contrast to many other languages, parts of the body are accompanied by a possessive adjective, i.e. in English you say *Open your mouth* and not *Open the mouth.*

Extra activity: Simon says

One student gives the others commands (*Simon says, 'Stand up!'; Simon says, 'Jump up and down!'* etc.)

The others should only follow the instructions when the command begins with the words *Simon says.*

Anyone who makes a mistake is 'out'. The game goes on until there is only one person left (the winner).

So that the game does not drag, it's best to write a list of suitable commands up on the board first.

---

3 Work on words

a After the students have labelled the picture, practise pronouncing the words. *Stomach* and *tongue*, especially, cause problems.

b Give students extra 'body' vocabulary if necessary. (It may also be necessary to tell them that certain words are taboo in English.)

● In pairs, students ask each other to touch (safe!) parts of the body.

Example:
Touch your right foot.
Touch your left ear.

● Students also try to tie each other in knots with instructions like these: *Touch your left ear with your right hand and touch your right foot with your left hand*, etc.

4 Read and think

C Students work in pairs putting the correct letters into the speech bubbles.

● Agree on the correct version.

d The class retells the story in the present simple and present continuous tenses. Agree on a suitable sentence/sentences for each picture.

This gives lots of opportunity for intonation practice.

5 Play games in English

Help 'the blind'

● Make sure students know the meaning and pronunciation of the instructions.

● Students give you instructions which you follow (not blindfolded!).

● If space is very limited, clear a space at the front of the class and arrange a series of obstacles there.

● Just for fun, when the last student is having his/her turn, clear all the obstacles away but give instructions as usual.

6 Now you're here

a Students ask you the questions first.

● Students ask each other the questions.

● Tell students to ask a British person the same questions after class and make notes of their answers.

b Students tell the rest of the class about their most interesting answers the next day.

4 Read and think

a Look at this cartoon story.

b Now read what the men say. The sentences are not in the right order.

a) 'HELP!! WATER . . . WATER!!'
b) 'I've got blue ties, red ties, green ties. . . . Which one do you want?'
c) 'I don't believe it! A restaurant – in the middle of the desert!'
d) 'It's so hot. I must find some water.'
e) 'No, I'm sorry. I haven't got any water. But I've got some ties.'
f) 'Have you got any water? I'm very thirsty.'
g) 'Ties? I don't want a tie. I want water!'
h) 'I'm sorry sir. You can't come into this restaurant without a tie!'

c Now decide where each of the sentences goes in the cartoon story. Put the right letter into the speech bubbles.

d Now re-tell the story. Use the verbs in the box if you want to.

crash	survive	look for
meet	ask	say
try	sell	go on
see	speak	tell

5 Play games in English

Help 'the blind'

One student goes out of the room. The other students change the position of the table and chairs in the room. The teacher blindfolds the student outside the room. He/she comes back into the room. The other students give him/her instructions like these:

Go straight on. Stop!

Take one step to the left.

Turn right.

Go forwards (backwards) one step.

The idea is to guide the 'blind' student from one side of the room to the other without touching anything.

6 Now you're here

a Ask a British person these questions and note down his/her answers.

- Can you speak French/German/Spanish? (How well can you speak it/them?)
- Can you swim? (Can you swim butterfly?)
- Can you type? (How many fingers do you use?)
- Can you ride a motorbike?
- Can you play chess? (How well can you play?)
- Can you play the piano? (How well can you play it?)
- Can you ski?
- Can you skate?
- Can you windsurf?
- Can you dance the waltz?
- Can you knit?
- Can you make a cake?

b Tell other students your most interesting answers.

UNIT SEVEN · LESSON ONE

I'm busy

Steve, what are you doing? Can you lay the table, please?

No, I'm sorry, I can't. I'm peeling the potatoes.

Where's Rob?

He's upstairs, in his room.

What's he doing?

He's probably listening to music, as usual.

Well, what about Debbie?

I don't know. Why don't you ask her?

Debbie! What are you doing? Debbie . . . where are you?

I'm in the bathroom. I'm having a shower.

Oh no!

Can I help you?

No, you're busy—you're writing a letter.

No, it's all right.

1 Questions and answers

a Write six questions and answers from the table.

Example:
Is Mr Bond peeling the potatoes? Yes, he is.

Is	Mr Bond Mrs Bond Mr and Mrs Bond	peeling the potatoes? laying the table? writing a letter?	Yes, No,	he she	is (n't).
Are	Debbie Dominique Rob Debbie and Rob	having a shower? listening to music? working?		they	are (n't).

b Work in pairs. Student A asks his/her questions. Student B answers them.

c Student B asks the questions, Student A answers them.

d Think of more questions about what is happening in the pictures. Ask and answer your questions in pairs.

Oh, thank you, Dominique. You *are* kind.

No, I'm not— I'm starving!

42

GRAMMAR IN ACTION

> **Grammar summary**
>
> ● The present continuous for present time (*What are you doing? I'm cleaning the car.*)

▧ I'm busy

Notes and possible problems

● *What are you doing?* The present continuous is used when we talk about what is happening or what people are doing at the moment of speaking.

Example:
Mrs Bond is washing the car at the moment (not *Mrs Bond washes the car at the moment*).

The present simple, in contrast, is used for habitual actions.

Example:
Mrs Bond washes the car every week.

This distinction does not exist in some other languages and typical mistakes are:

I can't come out because I study.
I'm usually waking up every day at 7.00.
I come now, wait for me.

Give students practise in pronouncing the contracted forms, which always cause difficulty (*I'm / he's / she's working*, etc.).

Point out that the short answers are the same as for the present tense verb 'to be' (*Yes, I am / No, he's not.* etc.)

● *I'm starving* (photograph 8). A colloquial expression meaning very hungry.

Presentation of the dialogue

● Mime various activities and ask the students:

What am I doing? to get the answer:
You're opening the door.
You're washing your hair. etc.

Write up some examples and practise pronouncing them.

● Also teach / check the following words and any others you think are necessary (see page vii):

upstairs / downstairs	I'm busy	having a shower
laying the table	starving	you're kind
peel the potatoes	as usual	

● Set the scene for the dialogue. It's lunch time and Mrs Bond wants somebody to lay the table.

● Students listen with their books closed.

● Write the following questions on the board:

What's Rob doing?
What's Debbie doing?
What's Mr Bond doing?
What's Dominique doing?

● Play the cassette once or twice and give students time to answer the questions. Check their answers.

● Play the dialogue again in small sections. Students listen with their books open. Stop after each section and explain/check the meaning of words and phrases if necessary.

● Students repeat the dialogue sentence by sentence after the teacher (or after the cassette). Concentrate on a lively, natural intonation.

● In groups of four students practise the conversation, taking it in turns to take all the parts.

● Choose one or two groups to act out the dialogue in front of the class from memory, (with help from you and the class if necessary). Don't insist that the lines are exactly the same as those in the book. Students should be encouraged to improvise.

> Exercises

1 Questions and answers

a Students work individually or in pairs, writing the questions and the answers.

● Check their answers.

d Give students a time limit to write their questions.

Note: Students will probably have problems with word order. A typical mistake: *Where is writing the letter Dominique?*

● Check students' questions.

● Students ask and answer in pairs.

2 Dominique's postcard

- Get students to talk about the picture and tell you what's happening.

- Ask students for some ideas on how to finish the postcard.
  Example:
  Hope to see you some time.
  Write soon.

- Students individually write the postcard. Help them with vocabulary.

- Get students to correct each other's postcards.

- Ask one or two students to read out their postcards.

Extra activity: Miming game

Students work in groups. One student mimes an activity. The others ask questions to guess what he/she is doing and where.

Example: Student A mimes making a cake.
B *Are you cooking?*
A *Yes, I am.*
B *Are you cooking dinner?*
A *No, I'm not.*
C *Are you making a cake?*
A *Yes, I am.*
D *Are you in the kitchen?*
A *Yes, I am.*

If students are short of ideas, write a few prompts on slips of paper and hand them out.

Example:
laying the table / in the dining room
listening to music / in your bedroom
swimming / in the sea
eating an ice-cream / on the beach

---

3 What about the verbs?

- Before doing the exercise, make certain that students understand the difference between the present continuous and the present simple. Ask a student, for example, *Are you speaking (French)?* (if he/she is French). He/She will probably answer *Yes, I am.* Say *No, you're wrong.* and then ask other students why. Now ask another student *Do you speak (French)?* and get the answer *Yes, I do.*

- Continue in the same way asking questions like:

  Are you brushing your teeth?
  Are you learning maths at school?
  Are you drinking coffee?

- Carry on like this until all students have grasped the important difference between the present continuous and the present simple.

- Students do the exercise individually, and then compare and correct their answers in pairs.

4 Find out

- Go through the questions and make sure students understand them.

- Students ask and answer in pairs.

- Get students to ask you the questions if they want to.

Extra activity: Famous people

If you have pictures of famous people, they can be used now. Show the class the pictures. They must make up two sentences, one using the present simple, one the present continuous.

Example: Ivan Lendel
He plays tennis.
At the moment he's sunbathing.

You could number the pictures and pass them round to the students. Working in pairs or small groups, they write appropriate sentences.

This could also be made into a team game.

---

2 Dominique's postcard

Dominique's got an American pen-
friend. He's writing a postcard to
her. He's describing what's
happening around him, what he's
doing etc. Write the postcard,
using the information in the
picture.

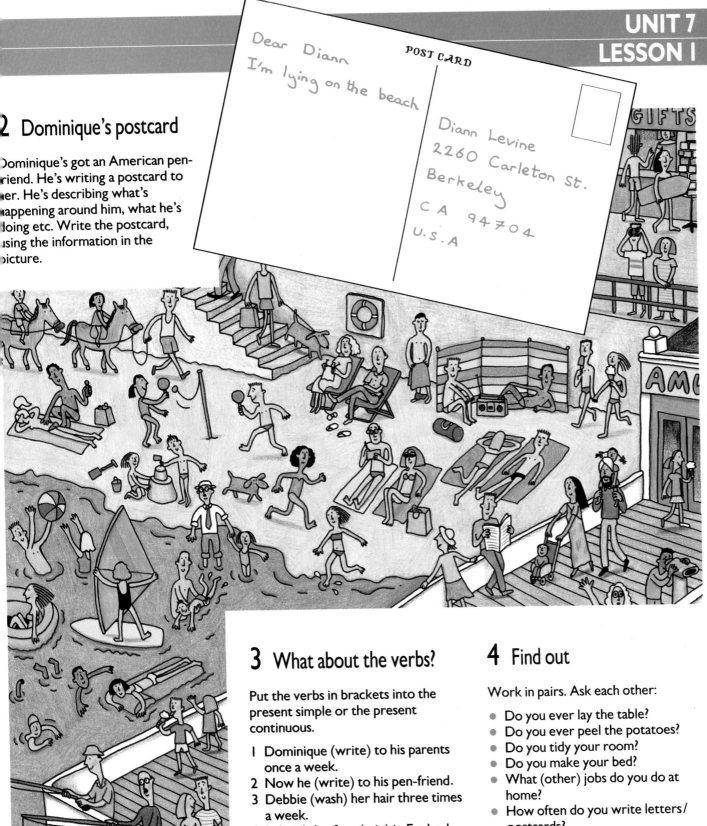

POST CARD

Dear Diann
I'm lying on the beach

Diann Levine
2260 Carleton St.
Berkeley
C A 94704
U.S.A

3 What about the verbs?

Put the verbs in brackets into the
present simple or the present
continuous.

1 Dominique (write) to his parents
   once a week.
2 Now he (write) to his pen-friend.
3 Debbie (wash) her hair three times
   a week.
4 It (rain). It often (rain) in England.
5 I can't answer the phone. I (have) a
   shower.
6 Dominique (speak) quite good
   English, but Rob (not speak) French.
7 What programme you (watch)?
   A Clint Eastwood film.
8 What you (cook)? I (starve)!

4 Find out

Work in pairs. Ask each other:

- Do you ever lay the table?
- Do you ever peel the potatoes?
- Do you tidy your room?
- Do you make your bed?
- What (other) jobs do you do at
  home?
- How often do you write letters/
  postcards?
- How often do you have a shower/
  bath?
- What do you think your mother/
  father/sister/brother is doing now?
- Is it raining?

Grammar summary: page 84

43

What's your telephone number?

Dominique *What's your telephone number, Mrs Bond?*
Mrs Bond *712660.*
Dominique *Sorry, what do you mean – double six?*
Mrs Bond *Six six.*
Dominique *And what does 'oh' mean?*
Mrs Bond *It means zero.*

1 Telephone numbers

Write down the telephone numbers you hear.

1 ....

2 ....

3 ....

4 ....

5 ....

6 ....

2 Quick questions

Go round the class and ask each other, 'What's your telephone number?' Write down the student's name and the number. The winner is the student with the most correct telephone numbers after three minutes.

3 What's missing?

Work in pairs. Student A looks at the page from the Hastings telephone directory on this page. He/She then asks Student B for the missing information.

Example:
A *What's R.M. Bond's telephone number?*
B *Hastings 422952.*

Student B looks at the page from the Hastings telephone directory on page 80 and asks student A for the missing information.

881008	Bond J.R, 1 Surrenden ... Tonbridge 36743 Bone C
210633	Bond Kay, 18 Robertson Ho,Hastings Rd... Tun Wells 22485 Bone C
362786	Bond K, 42 Priory Rd ... Tun Wells 28750 Bone C
712718	Bond K.L, 19 Cavendish Dv ... Bone C
354564	Bond L.A, South Riding,Upper Cumberland Wlk ... Bone
dge 673	Bond L.R, Leighton,Dower Ho Cres,Southborough
s 217591	Bond L.T, Brede 882703 Bone
ells 42819	20 Gresham Wy,Filsham Pk,St. Leonards-o-s ... Hastings 437315 Bone
field 3626	Bond M, Sunnyside,Cackle St ... Heathfield 2679 Bone
-s 212151	Bond M, 2 Quarry Cres ... Tun Wells 33214 Bone
tford 2789	Bond M.A, 7 Holly Clo,Hailsham Rd ... Burwash 883236 Bon
rden 2592	Bond N.C, 4 Earls Rd ... Tun Wells 43297 Bon
nbury 2260	Bond Norman F.G, Linden,Swiffe La,Broad Oak ... Forest Rw 3308 Bor
	Bond N.H, 13 Kendal Pk ... Bor
	Bond N.J, Belnor,Chapel La... Smallfield 2443 Bor
ings 422744	Bond P.D, 2 The Grange ... Otford 4616 Bo
ings 754384	Bond P.E.T, 8 Grange Wy ... Heathfield 2576 Bo
e Gn 830338	Bond P.F, 21a East Hill Fm,Kemsing ... Burwash 882294 Bo
tings 441497	Bond R.A, Unit 14 Waldron Ct Mutton Hall Hill ... Hastings 429077 Bo
tings 429843	Bond R.A, Roseneath,Shrub Rd ... Copthorne 714586 Be
ersham 380	Bond R.C, 166 Sedlescombe Rd Nth,St. Leonards-o-S ... Fairseat 822889 B
gh Gn 884491	Bond R.G, 8 Woodland Clo,Crawley Dwn ... B
mans Pk 403	Bond R.H.C, Five Acres,Oakfarm La ... Sevenoaks 452818
n Wells 34592	Bond R.M, 73 Edmund Rd ... Tonbridge 361242
astings 712533	Bond Robert W, Ashgrove Cott,Gracious La ... Westerham 62567
Hastings 52668	Bond S, 20 Rodney Av ... Edenbridge 862780
Oxted 716714	Bond S.A, 57 Quebec Av ... Hastings 712660
n Wells 510196	Bond S.E, 16 Sunnyside ... Fairseat 823642
Hastings 753684	Bond S.G, 7/39 Cornwallis Gdns ... W Malling 848105
tchingham 451	Bond S.W, 45 Timberbank,Meopham,Gravesend ...
Crowboro 4996	Bond T, 11 Auden Rd,Larkfield ... Tun Wells 41129
tchingham 430	Bond T, 15 The Dene ... Sharpthorne 810721
Oxted 712201	Bond T, 6 Vale Rd,Southborough ...
Hastings 813587	Bond T.C, 2 Warren Cotts,Stonelands,W Hoathly ... E Grinstead 28632
Oxted 717562	Bond T.J, 8 Geary Pl,Westfield ... Hastings 712242
Hawkhurst 2564	Bond T.P, 51 Forest View Rd ... Bexhill-o-s 224220
taplehurst 892438	Bond V.C, 7 Reedswood Rd,St.Leonards-o-s... Tenterden 2658
Sevenoaks 458060	Bond V.F, 1 New Brassey Ct,6,Brassey Rd ...
Uckfield 2569	Bond W, 17 Heather Dv,St. Michaels ... Cranbrook 712311
Buxted 3492	Bond W.F, 16 Keld Dv ... Bexhill-o-s 218416
Crowboro 64110	Bond W.G, Pound Ho,Willsley Pound... Rotherfield 2444
E Grinstead 28890	Bond William.J, 180 Ninfield Rd...
E Grinstead 314599	Bond W.W, Loft Cott 4 New Rd... Paddock Wd 346
Tonbridge 356862	Bondelivery Service Ltd –
Rye 225222	29 Eldon Wy ... Horam Rd 222
Crowboro 2815	Bonding Systems Ltd,Adhesives Mfrs, Vines Cross Rd,Horam ..Paddock Wd 340
Sandhurst 518	Tonbridge 3567
Cooden 4453	Bond's Delivery Service, 29 Eldon Wy ... Tonbridge 3627
Biddenden 291813	Bonds E, 14 Lodge Rd ... Tonbridge 3513
Hastings 751739	Bonds G, 29 College Av ... Oxted 7176
	Bonds R.J, 81 Higham La ... Sevenoaks 4633
Borough Gn 882470	Bone A.N.G, 103 Home Pk,Hurst Gn ... Groombdge
Smallfield 2907	Bone B.J, 14 Hurst Fm Road,Weald ... Newick 2
	Bone C.A, Hamsell Manor Barn,Eridge ... Frittenden
Grinstead 25091	Bone C.A, Fir Tree Cott,Station Rd ... Hadlow 85
	Bone C.A, ... Parsonage Fm ... bridge 35

ENGLISH IN SITUATIONS

Students practise
● saying telephone numbers
● asking for telephone numbers
● speaking on the telephone
● taking and leaving messages on the phone

▨ What's your telephone number?

● Students listen to the complete dialogue and then repeat it, line by line.

● Point out that *0* in telephone numbers is pronounced the same as the letter *O* and not *zero*.

● Double numbers are usually said *double three, double 0,* etc.

● Telephone numbers are never said *seventy–one— twenty–six—sixty,* etc.

1 ▨ Telephone numbers

● Write eight to ten telephone numbers on the board and give students practice in saying them.

Note: When saying a telephone number, pause between the town or area code and the individual's number, for example *0763 (pause) 347781.*

● Play the cassette at least twice.

● Check their answers.

● If further practice is needed, read out more telephone numbers for students to write down.

● Students can read out telephone numbers to each other.

2 Quick questions

● Ask various students their telephone numbers.

● Practise the question *What's your telephone number?/ What's your phone number?*

● Choose pairs of students at random to ask and answer.

● Students play the 'Quick questions' game. Make sure they stand up and move around the class.

● The winner reads out the names and numbers he/she has collected. Students say if they are right or wrong.

● If he/she has made any mistakes, these are subtracted from the total.

3 What's missing?

● Practise the question *What's X's telephone number?,* substituting different names.

● Divide the class into As and Bs. Tell B students to turn to page 80.

● Students A and B ask and answer alternately to find out the missing information.

● Students write in the missing information. Make sure they do not 'cheat' by looking at their partner's book.

ENGLISH IN SITUATIONS

🎙 Speaking on the phone

- Students listen to the dialogue and repeat it line by line.
- Pay special attention to intonation. Keep it lively.

4 Talking on the phone

- Students practise in threes, changing roles.
- Ask one or two groups to come out to the front to act out the dialogue from memory. Prompt them with words if necessary.

🎙 Taking a message

- Students listen and repeat the dialogue.

5 Can I take a message?

- Students practise in pairs, changing roles.
- Ask one or two pairs to come out to the front to act out the dialogue from memory. Prompt them with words if necessary.

6 🎙 Telephone messages

- Play the exercise once through without stopping. Students do not write anything.
- Play it again, stopping after each message. Give students enough time to write their answers.
- Play the exercise through a third time so that students can check their answers.
- Students exchange books and correct each other's answers.
- Check that their answers are correct.

7 Act it out

- Write up the names of the characters in the telephone dialogues.
- Write up some prompts on the board.

Example:
speak / Manolo?   afraid   out   message?

- Ask one pair to act out the conversation in front of the class. The rest of the class prompt.
- In pairs, students act out the same conversation, changing roles.
- Repeat the procedure for the second conversation.

Note: Play the second conversation again before acting it out to refresh the students' memory.

8 What's missing?

- Explain that students are going to work in pairs (A & B) and only B will have the information.
- Practise forming A's questions.
  Where's the concert?
  What time does it start? etc.
- Divide the class into As and Bs.
- Make sure the A students don't 'cheat' by looking at B's information.

Extra activity 1: Look it up

Suitable for homework.

Give students a list of numbers to look up in the local phone book, for example, a cinema, theatre, sports centre, ice rink, railway station, the police, etc.

Check the numbers the next day.

Extra activity 2: Make a phone call

Speaking on the phone in a foreign country and in a foreign language can be very nerve-racking. Give students some real practice.

Each student must take the phone number of one other student. Before the next day's lessons they must phone him/her and either speak to him/her or leave a message.

They can also phone some of the places whose numbers they looked up in 'Extra activity 1' above and find out, for example, the time of the first train to London, how much it costs to go swimming, etc.

They report back on their experiences the next day.

Speaking on the phone

Pam   Hello! 302 6517.
Randy   Hello, can I speak to Sylvie, please?
Pam   Yes, just a minute . . . Sylvie!
Sylvie   Hello!
Randy   Hi, Sylvie. It's Randy.
Sylvie   Oh, hi Randy . . .

4 Talking on the phone

In groups of three, practise the dialogue above. Use your own names and telephone numbers.

Taking a message

Phil   857 0099.
Laura   Hello, can I speak to Mario please?
Phil   No, I'm sorry, he's not in. Can I take a message?
Laura   Yes, can you ask him to ring me tonight?
Phil   OK, who's speaking?
Laura   This is Laura.
Phil   All right, Laura, I'll tell him.
Laura   Thank you. Bye!
Phil   Goodbye.

5 Can I take a message?

Practise the dialogue in pairs. Use your own names and telephone numbers.

6 Telephone messages

Listen to these telephone conversations. Fill in the gaps in the messages.

MANOLO
RING - - - -
          8
- - - HER NUMBER: - - - -

Mitsuko
Rang.
She has 2 tickets
for - - - - - tonight -
starts - - - . Meet
her - - - - - -
          bus station
          - - -

7 Act it out

In pairs, act out the two telephone conversations you heard in exercise 6. Use the messages you wrote to help you. You can also use your own ideas.

8 What's missing?

Work in pairs. Student A looks at the information below. Student B looks at the information on page 80.

Student A

You want to know:

where the concert is   . . . . .
what time it starts   . . . . .
what number bus to take   . . . . .
where to get off the bus   . . . . .
where Tiffany's is.   . . . . .

Student B knows the answers. Ask him/her your questions. Write down the information Student B gives you.

Summary of English in situations

- using the telephone
- taking messages on the telephone

1 Sound right

a 🔊 Listen to these pairs of words.

1 ☐ sin   4 ☐ sank
    ☐ thin   ☐ thank
2 ☐ sink   5 ☐ sort
    ☐ think   ☐ thought
3 ☐ sick   6 ☐ some
    ☐ thick   ☐ thumb

b Listen again and repeat the words.

c Now listen and tick which word you hear.

d Listen to these pairs of words.

thin	tin
three	tree
thank	tank
thick	tick

e Listen and repeat the words.

f Draw six squares and write six of the words from the lists above in them.

Example:

sort	thin	some
tree	tick	thumb

g Listen to your teacher when he/ she reads out words from the lists above. Cross out your words when you hear them.
When all your words are crossed out, shout BINGO!

2 Listen to this

🔊 Look at the picture below.

Now listen to a description of what is happening in the park.
Some of the things you hear are true, some are not true.
Write a tick (√) if the sentence is true, and a cross (×) if it is not true.

1 . . . .   6 . . . .
2 . . . .   7 . . . .
3 . . . .   8 . . . .
4 . . . .   9 . . . .
5 . . . .   10 . . . .

1 🔊 Sound right

- The purpose of the exercise is to give students practice in pronouncing the sound [s] as in *sink* and the sound [θ] as in *think*.

b Give students help by demonstrating that the sound [θ] in 'thin', etc. is made by putting the tongue out and against the top teeth whereas with the [s] sound there is no contact between the tongue and the teeth.

c Play the list of words twice.

d and e Here [θ] as in *think* is compared with [t] as in *tin*.

f and g **Pronunciation bingo**

- Call out the words from the list at random, keeping a record of the ones you have called. When a student calls *Bingo*, check his/her card against the words you have called. It is very likely that students will make mistakes in distinguishing the two sounds.

- Play the game twice.

Extra activity: Tongue twisters
Write up on the board: *Thirty-six sick and thirsty soldiers.* Students repeat the phrase as quickly and correctly as they can. In pairs or small groups students make up their own tongue twisters combining words beginning with *th* or *s*.

2 🔊 Listen to this

- Teach/check the following words and expressions using the picture:

  to have a picnic   *hand in hand*   *a park bench*   *to jog*
  to fish   *a lake*

  Alternatively, ask the students to describe what is happening in the picture. Write up any new words.

- Play the exercise through once without stopping. Students do not write anything.

- Play it again, stopping after each sentence so that students can put their tick or cross.

- Play the exercise through a third time so that students can check their answers.

- Students exchange books and correct each other's answers.

Extra activity
Students work in groups. One student (A) has the book open, the others have their books closed. Student A chooses a word, the others think of a synonym. The first person to say a correct word gets one point. This could also be a team game. You read out the words. One point for the first team to get the right synonym.

3 Read and think

● Practise pronouncing *triangle*, *circle*, etc.

a Students work individually.

To check students' answers draw the same geometrical figures on the board and ask students to give you the same instructions. Follow the instructions, occasionally pretending to make mistakes. Students can compare your drawing on the board with their own.

● If there is time, the teacher can read out a similar list of instructions so that it becomes a listening comprehension exercise.

4 Work on words

● Students can work in pairs or groups.

● Students can try to think of further synonyms for some of the words.

Example:
quick, fast, rapid
to ring, to phone, to call

5 Play games in English

What am I doing?

● Mime one of the actions in the examples and tell students to guess what you're doing.

● Insist that they use a full sentence, for example *You're washing a car*. Shake your head if they are wrong and repeat the mime.

a If students have problems thinking of good mimeable activities, help them by giving them instructions from the following list:

get on a horse   watch a game of tennis   make an omelette
clean a window   cut somebody's hair   wash somebody's hair
lay the table   make a bed

b Insist on full, correct sentences when the students guess.

● Keep the score on the blackboard, one point for each correct guess.

6 Now you're here

a Give students practice in asking the questions but don't give them any of the answers.

● Shy or less able students can work in pairs.

b Compare/check their answers in class the next day.

● Add useful 'local' questions.

Example:
How much does the local evening newspaper cost?
What is the name of the local football team?

3 Read and think

a Follow the instructions below.

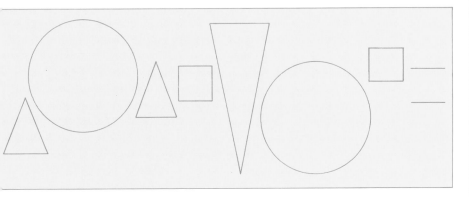

- First, write the number thirteen in the square between two triangles.
- Now draw a straight line under the triangle on the left.
- Then put a cross in the triangle which is on the left of the square with the number thirteen in it.
- Now write your first name in the circle between a triangle and a square.
- After that, join the two parallel lines to make a square.
- Now write today's date in that square.
- Then write your surname in the circle on the left.
- Now draw a small circle in the triangle to the left of the circle with your first name in it.
- Next, draw a line from the top of the triangle on the left to the middle of the line below it.
- Finally, write the answer to this sum in the empty square:
thirteen − three + eighteen ÷ seven × twelve − six

b Work in pairs. Compare your answers.

c Now write your own instructions, like those above. Show them to your partner. He/She follows the instructions.

4 Work on words

Find words in the box on the right which mean the same or almost the same as the words in the box on the left.

Example:
hi   hello

to ring	to talk
all right	to get to
starving	bicycle
right	fantastic
hi	hello
to speak	hungry
to start	OK
to shut	to phone
quick	to close
pardon?	horrible
to arrive	nearly
toilet	large
terrible	until
dad	now
bike	a little
at the moment	fast
too	correct
almost	to begin
you're welcome	sorry?
a bit	not at all
great	father
famous	loo
big	also
to finish	well-known
till	to end

5 Play games in English

What am I doing?

a Form two teams. Think of actions which you can mime.

Examples:
eat spaghetti, watch tennis

b Team A writes an instruction like the examples above, on a piece of paper.
One member of team B reads the instruction, goes to the front of the class and mimes it. His/her team try to guess what he/she is doing. They are only allowed three guesses.

Example:
'What am I doing?'
'You're eating spaghetti.'

c Team B writes an instruction on a piece of paper, and a member of team A mimes it to his/her team, etc.

6 Now you're here

a Find out the answers to these questions.

1 What time do banks open in the morning?
2 What time do pubs close at lunch-time?
3 Which day of the week do the shops in this town close early?
4 What number do you dial if you want to speak to the operator?
5 How much does it cost to send a first class letter in this country?
6 What's the price of a cinema ticket in this town?
7 What's the name of the local evening newspaper?
8 What programme's on BBC1 at nine o'clock tonight?
9 What's the dialling code for Manchester?
10 What's number one in the Top Forty at the moment?

b Compare your answers in class.

UNIT EIGHT
LESSON ONE

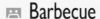 Barbecue

One evening Dominique's language school has a barbecue.

There are a lot of people here. Are there any from your class?

Yes, there are three over there.

Yes, there's some on that table. But are there any hamburgers?

Is there any Coca-Cola?

No, there aren't. There are only sausages left, I'm afraid.

Is there any mustard?

No, I'm afraid there isn't. But there's some ketchup.

Huh . . . ketchup! You have ketchup with everything.

Hello, Dominique. Do you like our English sausages?

Um . . . er . . . they're very different from French sausages.

Dominique, there's a girl over there. She's looking at you.

Oh, it's Sammy.

Hi, Dominique. Would you like to dance?

 Yes, all right.

Two minutes later

Now I know two things you can't do!

What do you mean?

You can't swim *and* you can't dance.

48

<table>
</table>

Grammar summary

- *There is / There are*
- *Is there . . . ? / Are there . . . ?*
- *There isn't / aren't*
- *Some / any*

🎮 Barbecue

Notes and possible problems

- Insist that students make the contraction in *There's . . .* (not *There is*).

- *People* (photograph 1) is a plural word in English unlike some other languages. A typical mistake is *people is*. It is the normal plural of *person*. The word *persons* is only used in official, legal language.

- *Yes, there are three over there* (photograph 1). The two different meanings of *there* may be confused.

- *There are only sausages left* (photograph 3). This is a difficult structure for many students. *left* here means *remaining* but is often confused with *left* (opposite of right).

- *I'm afraid* (photograph 3). Another way of saying *I'm sorry* but confusing for students because of the other meaning of *I'm afraid*, i.e. *I'm frightened*.

- *some* and *any* These words always cause problems for students.

  A basic rule is *some* is used in affirmative / positive sentences.

  Example:
  There's some milk in the fridge.

  any is used in negative sentences and questions.

  Example:
  I haven't got any money. Are there any shops near here?

  The main exception to this rule is that *some* is used in offers or invitations.

  Example:
  Would you like some coffee?

Presentation of the dialogue

Here are some suggestions for teaching / checking grammar and vocabulary.

- *There is some . . .*
  There are some . . .

Draw a fridge or cupboard on the board with various food items (countables and uncountables), for example:

ketchup	sausages	tomatoes
Coca Cola	milk	hamburgers

Label the drawing. Ask *What's in the fridge?* and say *There's some ketchup.* Get students to repeat the answer. Do the same for all the food items and then write up some example sentences.

- *There are only X left.* Ask a few students what the date is. Ask them when they go home / finish the course. Make the calculation and then say *There are only X days left until you go home.* Give another example by calculating the number of minutes left until the end of the lesson.

  Write up the examples. Point out that *left* here has no connection with *left / right*.

- Set the scene for the dialogue. Students have books closed. Dominique's language school is having a barbecue on the beach.

- Write up the following words and ask students to copy them:

chicken	mustard	hamburgers
sausages	ketchup	Coca Cola
Seven Up	coffee	

- Tell students to listen to the conversation on the cassette and to mark (√) for yes and (×) for no if the things above are at the barbecue.

- Play the cassette once or twice and give students time to tick or cross the words.

- Students open their books. Play the dialogue again in small sections. Stop after each section and explain / check the meaning of words and phrases if necessary.

- Students repeat the dialogue sentence by sentence after the teacher (or after the cassette). Concentrate on a lively, natural intonation.

- Students practise the conversation in groups of four, taking it in turns to take the parts of Dominique, Rob, Sammy and Miss Fox.

- Choose one or two groups to act out the dialogue in front of the class from memory (with help from you and the class if necessary). Don't insist that the lines are exactly the same as those in the book. Students should be encouraged to improvise.

Exercises

I Make true sentences

- Remind students that *some* is used in affirmative or positive sentences and *any* is used in negative sentences.

- Tell students to contract *there is* to *there's*.

- Ask students to describe to you orally what *there is / isn't* in the picture.

- Working in pairs or individually, students write sentences describing the picture.

- Check their answers.

2 What's in the picture?

- Ask students questions about the picture and get them to answer with a short answer *Yes, there is / No there aren't.* etc. (choose words from the box.) Make sure students don't try to contract the short answer *Yes, there is* to *Yes, there's*.

- Practise the questions in the examples in choral repetition.

- Give students some quick practice in choosing between *Is there . . . ? Are there . . . ?* using word prompts.

   Example:
   T   *boys*
   S1 *Are there any boys?*
   T   *orange juice*
   S2 *Is there any orange juice?*

- Students work in pairs, taking it in turns to ask and answer.

- When they have finished asking and answering, call on students at random to ask and answer a question and check for errors.

3 Spot the differences

- Students work in pairs or in groups to find the differences.

- Find out which pair or group has spotted the greatest number of differences.

- Check their answers.

4 How good is your memory?

d You may need to give the teams help in preparing their questions.

- Set a time limit for preparing questions but make sure they have prepared enough before the two students come back in.

- Keep a record of the scores.

- The game can be repeated with different questions.

5 What happens next?

a Give students a time limit to write their dialogue. Help with vocabulary and correct where necessary.

b Give students time to rehearse their dialogues.

c Choose some pairs to act out their dialogues in front of the class from memory.

Extra activity: Your home town

This is only possible if students are from different towns/cities.

In pairs students write down questions about their partner's home town using *Is there . . . ?*, *Are there . . . ?*

Example:
How many inhabitants are there?
Are there any interesting old buildings?
Are there any churches?
Is there a river?

They also ask about cinemas, theatres, discos, parks, factories, etc.

They tell the rest of the class a little about their partner's home town.

This could be followed up with some written work: a few sentences about either their own home town or their partner's home town.

- inviting people to do things
- accepting invitations and offers
- apologizing and making excuses

I Invitations/offers

- Practise the question and the answer in the example with choral and individual repetition.

- In pairs students work out suitable invitations and responses.

- Check their answers.

- Still in pairs, students practise the questions and responses.

- Students go through the exercise again, this time extending the dialogues with one or two extra questions and responses.

- Some students act out their extended dialogues.

2 Making excuses

- Before looking at the exercise, introduce the idea as follows:

  Get students to invite you to do something.

  Example:
  José, ask me if I'd like to dance.
  Maria, ask me if I'd like to go for a swim.
  Jorge, ask me if I'd like to go to a rock concert.

  Pull a face and make one of the excuses in the list.

- Go through the picture prompts and make sure students can form a correct question for each of them.

- Go through picture prompts a–g and make sure students can form a correct question for each of them.

- Suggest more phrases to introduce excuses in addition to *No thanks.*

  Example:
  Oh, I'm sorry . . . ,
  Sorry, not tonight, I'm afraid.
  I can't, I'm afraid.

- Students work in pairs inviting and making excuses. They move round the class, changing partners during this activity.

3 More excuses

- Give students time to prepare their invitations and excuses.

- Make clear that A must be very insistent, for example, by saying *But what about Monday / Tuesday?*

4 🎧 Sorry, I can't

- Play the conversation through once without stopping. Students do not write anything.

- Play it again and give students enough time to write their answers.

- Play the conversation through a third time so that students can check their answers.

- Students exchange books and correct each other's answers.

- Students act out the dialogue from memory with the help of some word prompts on the board.

- Invite one or two pairs to act out their dialogue for the rest of the class.

5 Role play

- Divide the class into pairs (A and B).

- Tell the Bs to read their instructions on page 80, and the As to read their instructions on page 51.

- Make sure that students only look at their own instructions.

- Ask one pair to demonstrate the activity to the rest of the class.

- When students have finished situation A, they go straight on to situation B.

- Afterwards, ask two or three pairs to act out their conversations in front of the class.

Extra activity: Famous invitations

Students work in groups or two teams.

They must think of invitations and responses spoken by famous people (real or fictional, alive or dead).

They write them down and act them out for the other groups or team who must guess who the characters are.

Example:
A *Would you like to try this apple?*
B *Well . . . all right. It looks delicious.*
(Answer: The snake and Eve)
A *Would you like to try on this shoe?*
B *Yes, please, Your Royal Highness.*
(Answer: the Prince and Cinderella)

Give help with vocabulary if necessary.

---

2 Making excuses

Work in pairs. Student A invites student B to do the things in the pictures. Student B makes excuses.

Example:
A Would you like to go to a concert?
B No thanks, | I've got a headache.

I'm busy / tired.
I'm not feeling well.
I must do my homework.
I must write a letter.
I must wash my hair.

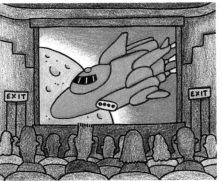

3 More excuses

Now practise inviting and making excuses in pairs, using your own ideas.

4 Sorry, I can't

🖭 Listen to the telephone conversation. Write T (true) or F (false) next to these sentences:

1 Sharon phones David.   . . . . .
2 Sharon remembers David.   . . . . .
3 There's a party at Sharon's. . . . . .
4 Sharon can go to the party. . . . . .
5 Sharon must wash her hair
   before she goes to the club. . . . . .
6 David wants to see a film
   called *Yours For Ever*.   . . . . .
7 David wants to take Sharon
   to the cinema on Friday.   . . . . .

5 Role play

Work in pairs. Student A reads the information below. Student B looks at the information on page 80.

Situation 1
You want to go to the cinema with Student B. It's a horror film.
It starts at 8 o'clock. Phone student B and invite him / her. Try to persuade him / her to come!

Situation 2
Student B phones you and invites you to play tennis. You want to play but you're not free until 6 o'clock.
Another problem is that you haven't got a tennis racket.

Summary of English in situations

- inviting and making offers
- accepting / refusing invitations and offers
- apologizing and making excuses

1 Sound right

a 🖭 Listen to these words. Underline the syllables which you say most strongly or heavily.

student   problem
later   another
over   cinema
horror   persuade
tired   different
mustard   tomorrow
letter   badminton
afraid   hamburger

b Now listen again and circle the syllables which you say very quickly or lightly.

Example:

stu(dent)

What sound is in all of these syllables?

c Now listen and repeat the words. Say the 'heavy' syllables as heavily as possible, and the 'light' syllables as lightly as possible.

2 Work on words

Write words which are opposites of those on the left. Put one letter in each box.

Example:
big   [s][m][a][l][l]

 1 easy   ☐☐☐☐☐☐☐☐
 2 same   ☐☐☐☐☐☐☐☐
 3 above ☐☐☐☐☐
 4 cheap ☐☐☐☐☐☐☐☐☐
 5 late   ☐☐☐☐☐
 6 full   ☐☐☐☐☐
 7 dirty ☐☐☐☐☐
 8 noisy ☐☐☐☐☐
 9 never ☐☐☐☐☐☐☐
10 thin   ☐☐☐☐
11 stupid ☐☐☐☐☐☐☐
12 fast   ☐☐☐☐
13 last   ☐☐☐☐☐
14 tall   ☐☐☐☐☐
15 dry   ☐☐☐

3 Play games in English

The crossword game

a Form two teams. The teacher draws two empty crosswords on the board, like this:

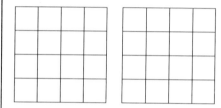

b One student from each of the teams writes a word in his/her team's crossword, across or down. You get 4 points for a 4-letter word, 3 points for a 3-letter word, etc.

c The first two students give the pen or chalk to two other students in their teams who then write another word in their crosswords.

d The game is over when all the squares in the crosswords have been filled, or when the teams can't think of more words to write.
The teacher then adds up the total points. The board can look like this:

H	A	N	D
A	N	D	O
R	O	A	O
D	R	Y	R

hand = 4 points
and   = 3 points
dry   = 3 points
hard = 4 points
an   = 2 points
nor   = 3 points
or   = 2 points
day   = 3 points
do   = 2 points
door = 4 points

TOTAL: 30 points

4 Listen to this

a 🖭 Listen to a girl speaking on the telephone to a boy.

b Now read these questions.

		Yes	No
1	Does Peter answer the phone?	☐	☐
2	Is Peter listening to the radio?	☐	☐
3	Is Peter watching *Eastenders*?	☐	☐
4	Does *Eastenders* finish at seven o'clock?	☐	☐
5	Does Peter want to go out with Becky?	☐	☐
6	Is Peter ready to go out?	☐	☐
7	Does Peter want Becky to come to his house?	☐	☐
8	Does Peter want to bring a friend with him?	☐	☐
9	Does Becky like Nick?	☐	☐

c Listen to the conversation on the phone again and answer the questions. Tick (√) the right answer.

d Now listen to the conversation again. This time you can hear what Peter says. Check your answers.

FUN WITH ENGLISH

1 Sound right

- The aim of the exercise is to give practice in identifying and stressing the correct syllables and to make students aware of the [ə] sound which occurs in many unstressed syllables.

Note: The [ə] sound is one of the most common sounds in English. It presents problems because it is often not easily recognizable from the spelling of the word, for example sof<u>a</u>, pap<u>er</u>, welc<u>ome</u>, Lond<u>on</u>.

a Students work individually.

b Give students some examples of the [ə] sound, for example t<u>o</u>night, writ<u>er</u>, doct<u>or</u>. Tell students that it is the sound which usually occurs in the words *a, an* and *the*.

2 Work on words

- Students work in pairs or groups.
- Students check each other's answers.
- Practise pronouncing the words.
- Remind students of the question *What's the opposite of...?*
- Students work in pairs. Student A tests student B (whose book is closed). Change roles.

3 Play games in English

- Draw the example crossword on the board and explain carefully how the scoring works.
- Once a team has written up a word they cannot change it.
- Play the game two or three times.

4 Listen to this

a The first time they listen, students do not hear the boy's lines.

- Play the exercise once through without stopping. Students do not write anything.

b Give students time to read the questions.

c Play the exercise again, stopping at each pause in the conversation. Give students enough time to mark their answers.

d Play the conversation through a third time. Students check their answers.

- Students exchange books and correct each other's answers.

5 Read and think

- Students work in pairs. Give them enough time to order the story.

- Afterwards, ask students to try to retell the story using the two pictures but with the text covered. Prompt them with mime and words.

6 Now you're here

a Give students a few minutes in pairs or groups to try to decide the meaning of the abbreviations.

b Tell them to ask a British person about the ones they do not know.

- Make sure students can pronounce the abbreviations correctly.

- They compare their answers in class next day.

Extra activity: What's in the square?

Draw a square on the blackboard and divide it into nine smaller squares. Number the squares.

Draw nine small, easily–drawn objects, one in each square.

Example:
a cigarette, a cross, a house, a cup, a knife, a hand

The idea is to remember where all the objects are. Go to the back of the class and ask the students to look at you so that they have their backs to the board.

Ask them what there is in each square.

Example:
What is there in number 4?
There's a tree.

To practise *there are* put two or three objects in each square.

The game can also be played in pairs. Each student draws nine objects on a piece of paper. They exchange papers and ask each other questions about the drawings.

---

5 Read and think

This is a story in ten parts, but the parts are in the wrong order.
Read the ten parts and then put them in the right order. The two pictures are there to help you.

☐ a) The two men walk on down the road until they come to a bridge.

☐ b) Fred and Bert ask him where he got the fish. He tells them, 'I got it from a river near here.'

1 c) Two men, Fred and Bert, are walking along a road.

☐ d) Fred says to Bert, 'When you catch a fish, shout and I can pull you up.'

☐ e) They meet another man. He's coming in the opposite direction. He's carrying an enormous fish.

☐ f) An hour later Bert suddenly shouts, 'Quick, quick. Pull me up! QUICK!'

☐ g) 'It's fantastic!! The fish there are jumping so high you can catch them in your hands – from the bridge!'

☐ h) 'Have you got a fish?' Fred asks. 'How big is it? Enormous?'

☐ i) Then Fred holds Bert's feet while he hangs over the bridge.

☐ j) 'No, I haven't got a fish,' Bert answers. 'There's a train coming!!'

6 Now you're here

a Find out what these letters stand for.

Example:
GB = *Great Britain*

1	a.m.	12	VAT
2	ITV	13	RAC
3	DIY	14	p.m.
4	UFO	15	p.t.o.
5	B & B	16	mph
6	BBC	17	LP
7	DJ	18	H & C
8	e.g.	19	AA
9	WC	20	UK
10	MP	21	BR
11	i.e.	22	M & S

b Now make a list of other common abbreviations like these.
Write down what they mean. Ask a British person to help you.

c Compare your lists in class.

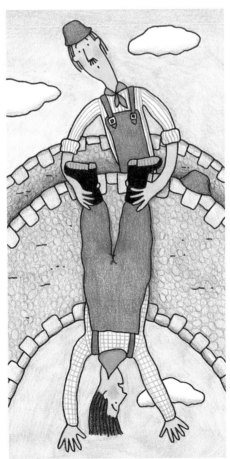

53

UNIT NINE · LESSON ONE

Where were you?

Dominique wanted to play tennis. Rob and Debbie wanted to play too. So they decided to meet at the tennis courts at three o'clock.

Debbie arrived at three o'clock but Rob and Dominique didn't. She waited for twenty minutes but they still didn't arrive. She was very angry. She phoned home but nobody answered. She then walked home, opened the front door and . . .

Did you have a good game?

No, I didn't—I didn't play.

Because Dominique and Rob didn't arrive. I waited twenty minutes for them. Then I phoned you but you didn't answer. Where were you?

Where were you?

Why didn't you play?

Sorry, we were in the garden.

What do you mean 'Where was I'? Where were *you*?

Oh no, how stupid! We were at the tennis courts in White Rock Gardens.

We were at the tennis courts at three o'clock, but you weren't.

Yes, I was.

Which tennis courts?

The tennis courts in Alexandra Park, of course.

GRAMMAR IN ACTION

Grammar summary

- Past simple: regular verbs
  (*I played tennis. Did you play tennis? I didn't play tennis.*)
- Past simple: verb *to be* (*was/were*)

📼 Where were you?

Notes and possible problems

- Past simple (regular verbs): all the verbs in the introductory paragraph and the first paragraph are regular past tense verbs, i.e. they all end in *-ed*.

  Example:
  want – wanted
  arrive – arrived
  study – studied (Note the change in spelling.)

  Make sure that students understand that in negative sentences and in questions, the main verb is in the infinitive, i.e. does not end in *-ed*.

- Rules for the pronunciation of regular (*-ed*) verbs:

  [t] if *ed* follows an unvoiced sound, for example, *watched, worked, finished.*

  [d] if *ed* follows a voiced sound, for example, *phoned, played, arrived.*

  [id] if *ed* follows the sounds 't' or 'd', for example, *decided, waited, needed.*

Note: The difference between the [t] and [d] sounds is not very important at this stage. It is very difficult to hear when other words follow the verb. The [id] ending, however, is important. Students often put the extra [id] syllable in verbs other than those which finish in 't' or 'd'.

- *Where were you?* (photograph 4) The past simple of the verb *to be* is practised in this second dialogue. Students often have problems with the 2nd person singular (*you were*), since they expect it to be *you was*. A typical error is *Where was you last night?*

  Tell students to look at the table on page 84 if they are uncertain.

- *How stupid!* A typical error is *What stupid!*

Presentation of the dialogue

- Set the scene for the dialogue. Rob, Debbie and Dominique decided to play tennis. They agreed to meet at a certain time but things went wrong.

- Write these questions up on the board:

Did Rob and Dominique decide to meet Debbie at two o'clock?	YES/NO
Did Debbie arrive at the tennis courts before Rob and Dominique?	YES/NO
Did she wait for half an hour?	YES/NO
Did she phone home?	YES/NO

- Students listen to the first part of the 'text', as far as line 11, ('the front door and . . .'), twice if necessary.

- Students write their answers like this:
  1 No   2 Yes   3 No   4 Yes

- Students check their answers.

- Write these questions on the board:

Did Debbie play tennis?	YES/NO
Did Rob and Dominique meet Debbie at the tennis courts?	YES/NO
Did Debbie's parents answer the telephone?	YES/NO
Were they in the garden?	YES/NO

- Students listen to the first dialogue, as far as photograph 3, ('. . . in the garden'), twice if necessary.

- Students write and check their answers as before.
  Answers: 1 No   2 No   3 No   4 Yes

- Write up these questions on the board:

  Where was Debbie at 3 o'clock?
  Where were Rob and Dominique at 3 o'clock?

- Students listen to the second dialogue, answer the questions and check their answers.

- Play the whole 'text' again. Students repeat sentence by sentence after the cassette (or after the teacher).

- Students practice reading the dialogues in threes (Mr and Mrs Bond and Debbie/Debbie, Rob and Dominique). Different students read one sentence each of the introductory 'text'.

- Choose groups of three students to act out the dialogues in front of the class, from memory (with help from you and the class, if necessary). Don't insist that the lines are exactly the same as those in the book. Students should be encouraged to improvise.

Exercises

1 Make true sentences

- Ask students to make some true sentences orally from the table.
- Give students time to write some true sentences.
- Ask students to read out some of their sentences.

2 Ask and answer

- Ask the class all the questions yourself. Concentrate particularly on students' pronunciation of past forms.
- Students practise asking the questions. Choral repetition. Make sure they don't put a heavy stress on *did*.
- Students work in pairs. Student A asks all the questions and B answers them. Change roles.

Extra activity: True or false?

Students work individually.

Using the past simple, they write down six sentences about the dialogue, some true, some false.

In pairs or small groups they then read out their sentences. The other students must agree *Yes, that's right. Yes, she did.* etc. or correct the sentences if they are false.

---

3 Interview Debbie

a Students work individually or in pairs to complete the questions.

- Students check their answers.

b Students work individually or in pairs writing Debbie's answers, and then check their answers.

- Students practise the dialogue in pairs.
- Let one or two pairs act out the dialogue for the rest of the class.

4 What did you do?

- Practise pronouncing the short answers *Yes, I did / No, I didn't.*
- Students work in pairs. Student A asks the questions and Student B answers. Change roles.
- Students think of their own questions of the same type. Be prepared to help them with the necessary irregular verbs.

5 Where were you?

- Make sure students understand what they have to do.

  To demonstrate, the teacher writes on a piece of paper *I was in the garden,* for example, and holds it to his / her chest.

- Tell the class the time you were there.

b Encourage the class to ask you questions until they guess where you were. Correct their questions where necessary. Answer their questions with short answers.

c The student who guesses where you were takes your place and the game continues.

- Make sure the student being questioned writes where he / she was on a piece of paper before answering the questions.

Extra activity

Substitution drill practising *was* and *were.*

Students practise a basic sentence pattern changing one item each time and the verb if necessary. You provide prompts.

Student A *The weather was good last week.*
Teacher *yesterday*
Student B *The weather was good yesterday.*
Teacher *excursion*
Student C *The excursion was good yesterday.*

Teacher: *awful party fun last night film my friends angry last week my mother my parents yesterday my brother happy I tired we*

---

1 Make true sentences

Make true sentences from the table.

Example:
Dominique and Rob were at the tennis courts in White Rock Gardens.

Dominique and Rob Debbie Mr and Mrs Bond	was wasn't were weren't	with Rob and Dominique. at the tennis courts at 3 o'clock. at the tennis courts in Alexandra Park. at the tennis courts in White Rock Gardens. at home at 3 o'clock. in the house at 3 o'clock. in the garden at 3 o'clock.

2 Ask and answer

Ask and answer these questions in pairs.

Example:
A *Did Dominique want to play football?*
B *No, he wanted to play tennis.*

1 Did Rob and Debbie want to go swimming?
2 Did they decide to meet at 2 o'clock?
3 Did Debbie arrive late?
4 Did she wait for half an hour?
5 Did she phone the police?
6 Did her parents answer the phone?
7 Did she walk to the beach?
8 Did Rob and Dominique arrive home before her?

3 Interview Debbie

a Complete the questions with *did, was* or *were.*

b Write Debbie's answers to the questions.

You *What . . . . you want to play?*
Debbie *I . . . .*
You *Who . . . . you want to play with?*
Debbie *. . . .*
You *Where . . . . . you decide to meet?*
Debbie *. . . .*
You *What time . . . . you arrive?*
Debbie *. . . . .*

You *. . . . Dominique and Rob there?*
Debbie *. . . .*
You *How long . . . you wait?*
Debbie *. . . .*
You *What . . . you do then?*
Debbie *. . . .*
You *. . . your mother answer the phone?*
Debbie *. . . . .*
You *. . . . . you angry?*
Debbie *. . . .*
You *. . . . Dominique and Rob at home when you arrived?*
Debbie *. . . . .*
You *Where . . . . . they at 3 o'clock?*
Debbie *. . . . .*

4 What did you do?

Work in pairs. Ask and answer these questions about what you did yesterday.

Example:
play tennis?
A *Did you play tennis yesterday?*
B *Yes I did. / No I didn't.*

1 play football?
2 arrive at school on time?
3 listen to pop music?
4 phone a friend?
5 wait for a bus?
6 walk to school?
7 watch television?
8 answer the phone?

5 Where were you?

Work in groups.

a Student A thinks of where he / she was at a certain time yesterday or last weekend, etc.

b Student A tells the rest of the group the time. They try to guess where he / she was at that time.

Example:
A *Yesterday, at 10 o'clock in the evening.*
B *Were you in bed?*
A *No, I wasn't.*
C *Were you at the cinema?*
A *No, I wasn't.*
D *Were you in the bath?*
A *Yes, you're right. I was.*

C A different student takes over from student A.

Grammar summary: page 84

55

Making suggestions

Greg *What shall we do this afternoon?*
Sally *Shall we play tennis?*
Greg *No, it's too hot.*
Sally *Why don't we go for a swim?*
Greg *No, the water's too cold.*
Sally *Well, let's sit on the beach then.*
Greg *Yes OK, good idea.*

1 Act it out

Read the dialogue in pairs. Change roles.

2 What are they suggesting?

One student at a time mimes a suggestion. The rest of the class must guess what he/she is suggesting.

Example:
Let's buy an ice-cream.

3 What shall we do?

Work in pairs.

Student A looks at the pictures and makes suggestions.
Student B answers 'Yes OK, good idea.'

Example:

A *Shall we play mini-golf?*
         or
   Why don't we play mini-golf?
         or
   Let's play mini-golf.

B *Yes OK, good idea.*

1

2

3

4

5

6

ENGLISH IN SITUATIONS

Students practise

- making suggestions
- making arrangements
- making excuses

Example:
A *I'm really thirsty.*
B *Let's have a drink then.*
C *Yes, good idea.*

They must use each of the three ways of making suggestions taught so far.

📼 Making suggestions

- Listen and repeat the dialogue.

- Draw students' attention to the three common ways of making suggestions:

  Shall we . . . ?
  Why don't we . . . ?
  Let's . . . ?

1 Act it out

- The students read the dialogue aloud in pairs. They change roles.

2 What are they suggesting?

- Explain the game and mime an activity yourself, for example mime dancing to elicit *Let's go to a disco.*

- Insist on a full sentence using any one of the three ways of making a suggestion.

Note: You could give out pieces of paper with the ideas written on them which the students have to mime, for example *have a pizza / play tennis / go to the park*, etc.

3 What shall we do?

- Focus attention on the picture and the three ways of making a suggestion and the answer.

- Practise pronouncing the questions and the answer.

- Go through pictures 1–6 and ask students to think of a question for each picture.

- Call out the number of a picture and indicate a pair of students to ask and answer.

- Students work simultaneously in pairs alternately asking and answering.

- Still working in pairs, students think up three mini dialogues.

4 Making excuses

- Look at the picture and ask *Why can't they play badminton?* to elicit the answer *It's too windy.*

- Go through the list of excuses and make sure students understand them. Practise saying them.

- Students work in pairs using the same pictures as before to make suggestions but this time student B makes an excuse (choosing a logical answer from the list).

- Elicit other excuses from the students and put them on the board.

  Example:
  I've got a headache.
  I'm too tired.
  I must wash my hair.

  In pairs they think of appropriate suggestions to match these responses.

  Students read out some of their suggestions to the class.

5 Role play

- As this activity depends on student A not knowing that student B can only agree to the suggestion *watch television* it is better not to get one pair to demonstrate. Otherwise this will take away the element of surprise from the activity.

- Tell B students to read their instructions on page 80.

- Choose one or more pairs to act out their conversation in front of the class.

6 📟 Making arrangements

a Listen and repeat the dialogue line by line.

b PG = Parental Guidance (children under 15 must be accompanied by an adult)

Sep progs = Separate programmes

U = Universal

15 = You must be 15 or over to see the film.

18 = You must be 18 or over to see the film.

Students can find out from British people what these abbreviations mean.

C Students practise the dialogue in pairs, substituting the name of the film they want to see (chosen from the entertainments page) and the name of the cinema where it's on.

- Choose one or two pairs to act out the conversation from memory in front of the class.

7 📟 What's missing?

a Play the conversations once through without stopping. Students do not write anything.

b Play them again, stopping after each conversation. Give students enough time to write their answers.

- Play the conversations through a third time if necessary so that students can check their answers.

- Students correct each other's answers.

- Act out the dialogues from memory.

Extra activity: Noughts and crosses

Form two teams (X and O).

The teacher draws nine squares on the board with short words in them, for example:

too	*why?*	*shall?*
let's	*did?*	*play*
was	*does?*	*were*

Team X choose one of the nine words. They think of a sentence with the word in it.

Example:
Why don't we go for a walk? or
Why are you crying?

If the sentence is correct, the teacher rubs out *why?* and draws a cross (X) in that square.

If the sentence is not correct, the teacher leaves the word in the square.

Team O then choose a word and think of a sentence with the word in it. (It can be *why?* if team X could not include it in a correct sentence.) If their sentence is correct, the teacher rubs out the word and draws a nought (O) in it.

The first team to have a line of three Xs or Os is the winner. The line can be horizontal, vertical or diagonal.

Play the game once more. Change the words in the boxes if you want to revise structures from earlier units.

---

4 Making excuses

Now student A makes the same suggestions as in exercise 3, but student B makes an excuse. Choose from:

No, it's too	hot.
	expensive.
	cold.
	late.
	windy.
	wet.

Example:
A *Why don't we play badminton?*
B *No, it's too windy.*

5 Role play

Work in pairs. Student A reads the instructions below. Student B reads the instructions on page 80.

Student A

You want to do something with Student B. Make suggestions.

Example:
Why don't we go for a walk?

You must *continue* making suggestions until Student B agrees with you.

6 Making arrangements

a 📺 Work in pairs. Practise the dialogue.

David *Let's go to the cinema.*
Paula *Yes OK, good idea.*
David *Which film shall we see?*
Paula *I want to see The Monster from Outer Space.*
David *OK, where shall we meet?*
Paula *Outside the Odeon cinema.*
David *What time shall we meet?*
Paula *At 8 o'clock. The film starts at a quarter past.*

b Look at this film guide from a newspaper. Find out what the following mean:

PG   Sep. progs   U   15   18

WHAT'S ON

FILMS

CANNON CINEMAS 1, 2 & 3: Whiteladies Road, Bristol 733640
1 — Steven Spielberg presents INNER SPACE (PG), in Dolby stereo. Sep. progs. 2.00, 5.00 & 8.00 (Sun. 2.15, 5.00, & 8.00). 2 – Steve Martin ROXANNE (PG). Sep. progs. 2.30, 5.20, & 8.10 (inc. Sun.). 3 – MAURICE (15). Sep. progs. 4.15 & 7.15 (incl. Sun., not Thurs.). Special presentation for one day only Thursday December 3, Sean Connery THE NAME OF THE ROSE (18), 1.30, 4.30 & 7.30. Saturday Late Show at 11 p.m. JAGGED EDGE (15).

CONCORDE CINEMAS, Stapleton Rd, Eastville. 510377
Concorde 1, OUTRAGEOUS FORTUNES (15) 8.00. From Sun. ALAN LADD as SHANE (U). Sun. 5.00 & 7.30. Wk. 8.00, Concorde 2: BLACK WIDOW (15) 8.00 from Sun. BEVERLY HILLS COP II (15) Sun. 5.00 & 7.30 Wk 8.00

GAIETY CINEMA, Wells Road 776224 MADONNA in WHO'S

c Choose a film you want to see. Practise the dialogue again. Use your own ideas instead of the underlined words. Take it in turns to be A and B.

7 What's missing?

📺 Listen to these three conversations.

a Match the conversations with the pictures.

b Fill in the missing information under the pictures.

1 Meeting place: . . . . .
  Time: . . . . .

2 Meeting place: . . . . .
  Time: . . . . .

3 Meeting place: . . . . .
  Time: . . . . .

Summary of English in situations

- making arrangements
- making suggestions
- making excuses

1 Sound right

a 🖭 Listen to these phrases and sentences.

Wait for me.
It's an egg.
What's the time?
Fish and chips.
At eight o'clock.
It's slow but cheap.
Speak to me.
He's from France.
A cup of tea.

b Listen again. Circle the words or syllables which are said lightly or quickly.

Example:

Wait (for) *me.*

c Listen and repeat the phrases and sentences.
Notice that these words are usually said very lightly or quickly:

a   an   the
for   at   to   from   of
and   but

2 Listen to this

🖭 Listen to the six voices and write down their jobs.
Choose from the jobs in the box.

teacher	waiter
doctor	photographer
taxi driver	bank clerk
soldier	telephone operator
dentist	farmer
pilot	mechanic
shop assistant	disc jockey
chemist	secretary

1 ....
2 ....
3 ....
4 ....
5 ....
6 ....

3 Work on words

1 📼 Sound right

- The aim of the exercise is to help make students aware of unstressed syllables in English (i.e. words which are not given a strong emphasis and are consequently difficult for foreign learners to hear).

Note: Words in English which are given a strong emphasis are invariably words carrying information (especially verbs, nouns, adverbs and adjectives).

The words which are not usually emphasized and which are said as quickly as possible are generally short words (articles, prepositions, *and, but,* etc.). It is the combination of stressed and unstressed words which gives English its characteristic rhythm.

Foreign speakers often tend to stress all the words in the sentence equally which makes their English sound stilted and 'foreign'. They also have difficulty hearing unstressed syllables.

C Students practise repeating the phrases after the cassette or after the teacher and in pairs. Get them to clap or to beat time on the table to get the rhythm and stress correct.

- Ask individual students to read sentences and correct their pronunciation if necessary.

- Focus attention on the kinds of words which are not usually emphasized, for example *for, an, the.*

- Write up these sentences and ask students which words are not emphasized and how the sentences are said:

  Look at the book.
  A bottle of wine.
  I'm from Italy.

2 📼 Listen to this

- There is no example so make sure students are clear about what they have to do.

- Make sure students know what all the jobs are.

- Play the exercise through once without stopping. Students do not write anything.

- Play it again, stopping after each 'job'. Give students enough time to write their answers.

- Play the exercise through a third time so that students can check their answers.

- Students exchange books and correct each other's answers.

- Explain, if necessary, the useful vocabulary in the tapescript.

Extra activity: Jobs
Working in pairs, students choose another job. (Write a number of different jobs on slips of paper and hand them out if you want to be sure of variety.)
Students write a few sentences similar to those they have just heard in Exercise 2.
They read them out and the rest of the class must guess which job it is.

3 Work on words

- Students work on their own or in pairs.

- Write the crossword on the board and ask one student at a time to fill in a word.

4 Play games in English

Think of a word

a Each team should have one piece of paper and appoint a secretary to write down the words.

b Write the chosen letter on the board.

● When a team think they have finished, ask the secretary to come to the board and write up the words. If they have made a mistake, give the other team the chance to write up their words.

● Award points and keep a record of the score.

● Play several rounds of the game.

5 Read and think

a Give students time to read the story.

● Explain any unknown words. Encourage students to ask you *What does X mean?*

b Students answer the questions individually or in pairs.

● Students check each other's answers.

● Many students watch soap operas. Have a quick chat about them:

Which ones are popular in their countries?
Who are the main characters?
Who are the goodies?
Who are the baddies?
What is happening in the story at the moment?
Have they seen any British soap operas? What do they think of them?

6 Now you're here

a Give students a few minutes in pairs or groups to try to decide the meaning of the abbreviations.

b Tell them to ask a British person about the ones which they do not know.

● Make sure students can pronounce the abbreviations correctly.

c Compare their answers in class the next day.

4 Play games in English

Think of a word

a Form two teams. On a piece of paper, each team writes these categories:

a country	
a sport	
something you eat	
something you drink	
something you wear	

b The teacher says a letter, for example B. The two teams try to think of words in the five categories which begin with that letter.

a country	Belgium
a sport	Basketball
something you eat	Banana
something you drink	Beer
something you wear	Boots

The first team to finish is the winner. The teacher then says another letter.

5 Read and think

a Read this story from a newspaper.

Unhappy ending

Mrs Joyce Harris from Birmingham telephoned the fire brigade when she noticed her house was on fire. Ten minutes later a fire engine arrived. Mrs Harris was outside her house. She was very worried

'My husband and son!' she shouted. 'They're still inside!'

Four firemen rushed into the house. They discovered Mr Harris and his teenage son Wayne in the sitting room. They were in front of the television. The room was full of smoke.

The firemen picked them up and carried them outside. But Mr Harris and his son were not pleased. In fact they were angry.

'Why did you stay in the house when it was on fire?' a fireman asked Mr Harris.

Mr Harris answered, 'We didn't want to leave because we wanted to watch the end of *Dallas*!'

b Are these sentences true or false?

	True	False
1 Mr Harris telephoned the fire brigade.	☐	☐
2 Mrs Harris waited for the fire brigade outside her house.	☐	☐
3 Her husband and son were still inside the house.	☐	☐
4 Mrs Harris discovered her husband and son in the sitting room.	☐	☐
5 The television was on fire.	☐	☐
6 The firemen carried the television outside.	☐	☐
7 Mrs Harris was very angry with the firemen.	☐	☐
8 Mr Harris stayed in the house to watch television.	☐	☐
9 Mr Harris and his son liked *Dallas*.	☐	☐

6 Now you're here

a The following are all common abbreviations. Find out what they mean.

Example:
Sat. = *Saturday*

1 Mon.	9 plc
2 info.	10 hr
3 prog.	11 min.
4 Feb.	12 dept.
5 tel.	13 incl.
6 Bros.	14 in.
7 etc.	15 ft.
8 no.	16 lb.

b Make a list of other abbreviations you see and try to find out what they mean.
Ask a British person if he/she can think of any more.

c Compare your list with other students' lists.

Dominique's day out

One Saturday morning Dominique went to London. He went by coach with the other students on his course.

They left at 9 o'clock in the morning, and they got to London at 11 o'clock.

First they did some sightseeing and then they had lunch. After that they had the afternoon free.

Dominique had a good time. He took a lot of photos and bought a lot of souvenirs. But at the end of the day . . .

What's the matter, Sue?

I'm worried about Dominique. Miss Fox rang an hour ago . . .

What did she say?

Dominique didn't come back with them. He missed the coach.

Where is he now?

I don't know. I'm very worried.

The telephone rings

Hello . . . 712660.

Is that Mrs Bond?

How did you miss the coach?

Oh, I met some French students and I forgot the time. Then I got lost . . .

Dominique! Where are you?

I'm at the station. I came back by train.

Don't worry, Dominique! I'm coming to get you now. Stay there!

Just a moment, Mrs Bond. There's another problem.

What is it?

I caught the wrong train. I'm not at Hastings station. I'm at Brighton . . .

Grammar summary

- Past simple: (irregular verbs)
  (go – went   leave – left   get – got)

🎦 Dominique's day out

Notes and possible problems

- Past simple (irregular verbs): all the verbs in the introduction and dialogue (except *to miss*) are irregular (see Grammar summary, page 85).

- *Dominique had a good time* (line 9). means Dominique enjoyed himself. Some students may think this means *Dominique had good weather.*

- *First . . . then . . . after that . . .* (line 6) These are useful words / expressions for connecting a narrative. Make sure students do not omit *that* in *after that.*

- *He missed the coach* (photograph 3). A typical mistake *He lost the coach.*

- *I caught the wrong train.* This use of the verb *to catch* will surprise many students.

Presentation of the dialogue

- If you have any pictures / postcards of London, bring them into class. Pass them around, stick them up on the board or around the classroom and talk about them for a few minutes.

- Set the scene for the dialogue: Dominique and the other students on his course went to London one day . . .

- Write these sentences up on the board:

Dominique went to London by train.	TRUE / FALSE
The students left Hastings in the morning.	TRUE / FALSE
They did some sight-seeing in the morning.	TRUE / FALSE
Dominique enjoyed himself in London.	TRUE / FALSE

- Students listen to the first part of the text, as far as line 11 (the end of the day . . .), twice if necessary.

- Students write their answers like this:
  1 False   2 True   3 True   4 True

- Check students' answers.

- Write these sentences on the board:

Mrs Bond was worried.	TRUE / FALSE
Mrs Bond rang Miss Fox.	TRUE / FALSE
Dominique missed the coach.	TRUE / FALSE

- Students listen to the first part of the dialogue.

- Students write their answers as above, and then check them.
  1 True   2 False   3 True

- Write the following questions on the board:

  Did Dominique phone Mrs Bond?
  How did he come back from London?
  Who did he meet in London?
  Where was he when he telephoned?

- Students listen to the second part of the dialogue.

- Students write their answers as above, and then check them.
  1 Yes   2 By train.   3 Some French students.
  4 At Brighton station.

- Play the tape again. Students listen with books open, and then repeat the dialogue, line by line.

Exercises

1 Questions and answers

a Students work individually or in pairs and check each other's answers.

b Make sure that the student who is answering has the answers covered or the book closed.

2 What happened when?

a Students work individually or in pairs and then check each other's answers.

b Give students 2–3 minutes to memorize the whole story (looking again at exercise 1 and 2).

● Tell students to shut their books or cover the page.

● Students retell the story in pairs. Then choose students at random, getting each one to say one sentence. Prompt with single words or a mime.

Extra activity: Correct the sentences

This is useful if students need further practice with the past simple.

Read out the sentences below. Students spot the deliberate mistake and correct it.

Example:
T *Dominique went to Cambridge.*
S1 *No, he didn't. He went to London.*

1 The students went by train.
2 They left at 6 o'clock.
3 They had breakfast in London.
4 Dominique took a few photos.
5 He bought a lot of clothes.
6 He missed the train home.
7 He met some old friends.
8 He got drunk.
9 He caught the train to Hastings.
10 He rang Miss Fox to ask for help.

---

3 What did you do?

a Students should note down their partner's answers.

b Encourage students to invent further questions to ask each other. Give them time to think of three or four more.

c Students should note down their partner's answers.

4 Quick questions

● Ask students what the questions will be. Make sure they can form the questions correctly.

● Show how the exercise works by moving around the class yourself, asking different students *Did you go to the cinema last week?* If you get a positive answer, mime writing their names down in your book.

● Tell students to move around the class. Expect a lot of noise and movement. That's good. Real communication should be taking place.

5 Start of the day

● Look at the picture of Patrick. Point out that the information about what time he did the activities is missing.

● Ask students what questions they must ask to find out the missing information, and quickly practise them.

a Students A reads the information below the exercise and student B turns to page 81 for his/her information.

b and c Student A questions student B about Patrick and fills in the missing information. Then student B questions student A about Suzanna and fills in the missing information about her.

● Make sure students write in the missing information but don't 'cheat' by looking at their partner's information.

● Check their answers.

1 Questions and answers

a Match the questions on the left with the answers on the right.

Example: 1 – i

1 When did they go to London?
2 How did they go?
3 What time did they leave?
4 What time did they get to London?
5 What did they do in London?
6 Did Dominique have a good time?
7 Who did Dominique meet?
8 Why did Dominique miss the coach?
9 How did Dominique come home?
10 Where did the train go to?

a) Yes, he did.
b) Some French students.
c) To Brighton.
d) By coach.
e) At eleven o'clock.
f) By train.
g) They went sightseeing.
h) At nine o'clock.
i) On Saturday.
j) Because he forgot the time.

b Work in pairs. Student A asks the same questions, student B answers them without looking at the answers above. Change roles.

2 What happened when?

a In what order did these things happen in the story?

☐ Dominique got lost.
☐ Miss Fox rang Mrs Bond.
☐ The coach went to London.
☐ Dominique got to Brighton.
☐ Dominique caught the wrong train.
☐ The coach left Hastings.
☐ Dominique forgot the time.
☐ Dominique missed the coach.
☐ Dominique did some sightseeing.

b Retell the whole story.

3 What did you do?

a Work in pairs. Find out what your partner did yesterday evening. Ask him/her questions using the verbs in the box.

| go out | listen | meet | ring |
| read | go to bed | eat | have |

Ask questions like these:
Did you go out?
What did you have for dinner?

b Think of your own questions using other verbs.

c Now find out what he/she did last summer, using these verbs:

| go | stay | spend | buy | do | have |

Ask questions like these:
Did you go abroad?
Where did you stay?
Did you have a good time?

d Tell the rest of the class what your partner did yesterday evening/last summer.

4 Quick questions

Go round the class, asking and answering quick questions like this:
Did you go to the cinema last week?

Find as many students as you can who:

went to the cinema last week
bought some clothes yesterday
had a bath last night
took some photos last weekend
came to school late yesterday
wrote a letter at the weekend.

The 'winner' is the student with the most names after five minutes.

5 Start of the day

a Work in pairs. Student A reads the information about Suzanna below. Student B reads the information about Patrick on page 81.

b Student A asks student B questions about Patrick, and fills in the missing information about him.

Example:
A *What time did he get up this morning?*
B *He got up at half past seven.*

c Student B asks student A the same questions about Suzanna and fills in the missing information about her.

Suzanna

Got up at: *7.30*
Had breakfast at: *8.00*
Had for breakfast: *toast and coffee*
Had a shower: *Yes*
Left home at: *8.40*
Got to school at: *8.55*
Came to school by: *bus*

Patrick

Got up at: . . . . .
Had breakfast at: . . . . .
Had for breakfast: . . . . .
Had a shower: . . . . .
Left home at: . . . . .
Got to school at: . . . . .
Came to school by: . . . . .

Grammar summary: page 85

1 What are they?

Write down the correct names of the clothes.

Shopping

Shop assistant *Can I help you?*
First customer *No, I'm just looking, thanks.*

(pause)

Shop assistant *Can I help you?*
Second customer *Yes, I'm looking for a pair of jeans.*
Shop assistant *What size are you?*
Second customer *I'm size 30, I think.*
Shop assistant *These are all 30 waist.*

(one minute later)

Second customer *Can I try these on, please?*
Shop assistant *Yes, the changing room's over there.*

(a little later)

Second customer *They're too big. Have you got size 28?*
Shop assistant *Yes, here you are.*

(one minute later)

Second customer *Yes, they're OK. How much are they?*
Shop assistant *They're £24.99.*
Second customer *Right, I'll have them, please.*

ENGLISH IN SITUATIONS

Students practise
● buying clothes
● describing how someone is dressed
● talking about colours / sizes

I What are they?

● Teach some more clothes vocabulary, if necessary, by using the clothes worn by students in the class. Give practise in pronouncing the new vocabulary.

📼 Shopping

● Introduce the dialogue. Explain that it takes place in a shop.

● Put these questions on the board:

What kind of shop is it?
What's the first customer doing?
What does the second customer buy?
What size is she?
How much does she pay?

● Students listen to the dialogue with books closed and try to answer the questions.

● Students check their answers.

● Students listen again.

● Students listen once more with books open and repeat line by line.

2 Act it out

a Students practise the dialogue in threes substituting their own sizes, and changing roles.

b Ask students to improvise the conversations if possible.

● Choose two pairs of students to act out the conversation in front of the class. Alternatively write some word prompts on the board.

Example:
help you?
looking for / pair of shoes
size?

Measurements

- Explain that *large* = *big*. Some students often confuse *large* with *wide*.

Extra activity: All change

Whether you do this activity or not will depend very much on your class. Some students might not like it; others will think it's fun. It's up to you to judge.

Get students to take off as many of their clothes as they decently can, for example shoes, sweaters, jackets, belts. Put them all at the front of the class. Students put on clothes which are not theirs.

Elicit statements about the clothes they have on.

Example:
These shoes are too small.
This jacket is just right.

---

3 🔊 What's missing?

- Explain that students are going to hear a conversation between a girl and a shop assistant.

- Play the exercise through once. Students listen only.

- Play it again, pausing to give students time to write their answers.

- Play the conversation through a third time so that students can check their answers.

- Students exchange books and correct each other's answers.

- Act out the dialogue with the help of word prompts.

Extra activity: Memory game

Students work in pairs. They look at each other's clothes for 30 seconds, then sit back to back, so they can't see each other.

A asks B about the things he/she is wearing.

Examples:
A *What colour's my jumper?*
B *It's red.*
A *Right. And what colour are my trainers?*
B *They're grey.*
A *No, they're not. They're blue.*

Students then change roles.

Get one pair to demonstrate the activity to the class first (then put the two students with a different partner).

Make sure students are sitting back to back so that they can't 'cheat'.

---

4 Bring me a . . .

- A game to revise clothes vocabulary.

b Keep a record of the score.

- Think of more examples of things to bring, for example *a watch, a comb, a tissue.*

5 What's wrong?

- Remind students that *this* is used for singular nouns and *these* is used for plural nouns.

- In pairs, students complete the speech bubbles.

- Check their answers.

- Call out the number of one picture at a time and indicate two students to ask and answer like this:

  Teacher *Picture 3*
  Student A *What's wrong? Can I help you?*
  Student B *Yes, this T-shirt is too small.*

- Continue in this way until you have called out all the numbers *twice.*

Measurements

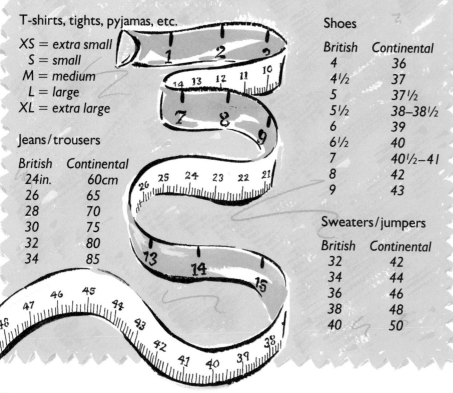

British shops are slowly changing over to the metric system (instead of inches/feet/yards). Many department stores use both systems whereas most small clothes shops still usually use the British measurements.

T-shirts, tights, pyjamas, etc.

XS = extra small
 S = small
 M = medium
 L = large
XL = extra large

Jeans/trousers

British	Continental
24in.	60cm
26	65
28	70
30	75
32	80
34	85

Shoes

British	Continental
4	36
4½	37
5	37½
5½	38–38½
6	39
6½	40
7	40½–41
8	42
9	43

Sweaters/jumpers

British	Continental
32	42
34	44
36	46
38	48
40	50

2 Act it out

a Practise the dialogue opposite in groups of three. Use your own sizes.

b Work in pairs. Imagine you want to buy other clothes. Act out the dialogue.

3 What's missing?

Listen to the dialogue, and then fill in the missing information in the table below.

	Clothes	Colour	Price	Size
1	...	...	...	...
2	...	...	...	...
3	...	...	...	...

4 Bring me a ...

a Form two teams. One student from each team stands at the front of the class.

b The teacher then asks these two students to bring certain things from the other people in their teams.

Examples:
a white sock
a black shoe
a red sweater
a brown jacket
a green handbag

The first team to give each object to the teacher gets a point.

5 What's wrong?

What's wrong with these clothes?

These trainers are too big

Choose from the words in the box.

big	small	long	short

1...   2...

3...   4...

Summary of English in situations

- buying clothes
- talking about sizes and colours

1 Sound right

a 📼 Listen and underline the words or syllables which are said heavily.

Example:
They got to London at eleven o'clock.

1 Dominique went to London.
2 He went by coach.
3 He took some photographs.
4 How did you miss the coach?
5 I met some French students, and I forgot the time.
6 I'm coming to get you now.
7 I caught the wrong train.
8 I'm not at Hastings station.

b Now practise saying the sentences. Try to say the 'heavy' words and syllables as heavily as possible, and the others as quickly or lightly as possible.

2 Work on words

At the station

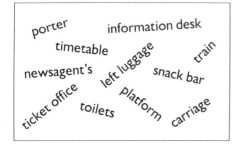

porter
information desk
timetable
newsagent's   left luggage   train
                        snack bar
ticket office   platform
        toilets   carriage

What are the things you can see in the picture? Fill them in below.

1 ....
2 ....
3 ....
4 ....
5 ....
6 ....
7 ....
8 ....
9 ....
10 ....
11 ....

FUN WITH ENGLISH

1 🔊 Sound right

- The aim of the exercise is to make students aware of word stress (i.e. how the important words which carry information are said more strongly than words which do not carry information, such as *a, an, and.*)

a Remind students of 'Sound right' in Unit 9 and how 'unimportant' words are said as quickly and lightly as possible.

- Explain that this time they have to listen and mark the emphasized, stressed words. Remind them that these are usually the longer ones which carry information.

- Ask students to anticipate the stressed words before they hear the cassette.

- Play the cassette twice.

- Students work individually, then check their answers with their partner.

b Students repeat the sentences after the cassette or after the teacher.

2 Work on words

- Practise pronouncing the words in the box.

- Students work in pairs to label the picture.

- Students check their answers.

- Students think of other *station* vocabulary and say how stations and rail travel are different in their own countries.

3 Read and think

- Students work in pairs to identify the speakers in the picture.
- Check their answers.
- Practise using the expressions in short, improvised dialogues.

4 🎦 Listen to this

- There is no example so make sure students understand what they have to do.
- Play the tape through once without stopping. Students do not write anything.
- Play the tape again, stopping at each pause. Give students enough time to write their answers.
- Play the tape through a third time so that students can check their answers.
- Students exchange books and correct each other's answers.

5 Play games in English

Alibi

- This is a role play activity designed to give students practice in asking and answering questions in the past tense. The more drama you can inject into this activity the better it will go. Allow at least 25 minutes for it.
- Set the scene as dramatically as you can.

a Choose two 'good' students to be George and Susan.

- Give the two students who go outside time to read their instructions.
- Focus the rest of the class's attention on George and Susan's alibi and go through instructions b), c), d) and e) with them so they know exactly what they have to do.
- Put the 'detectives' into two or three groups and get them to start writing their questions.
- Go out and check that George and Susan understand their instructions and have begun preparing the details of their alibi.

- Divide your time between the suspects and detectives. It's important that the suspects' story is difficult to break down so you may want to 'tip off' Susan and George about the kinds of questions the detectives are preparing.

  On the other hand help the detectives to ask the kinds of questions that may break the alibi, for example *How much was the meal? What time did you leave the restaurant?* Don't begin the interrogation until you are satisfied that George and Susan have prepared a strong alibi.

- The interrogation can be carried out in two possible ways:

  Either arrange the detectives in a semicircle with a chair in the middle and get two students to bring in Susan and proceed as in instructions c), d) and e).

  Or arrange the detectives in two groups with a chair in the middle of either group.

- George and Susan come in together. Susan is interviewed by Group A and George by Group B. Then they change places. This avoids one student having to wait outside the class and means smaller groups of detectives but it is very important that George and Susan cannot overhear each other's answers.

- Encourage the detectives to improvise questions and not just to ask the ones they have prepared.

- When the interrogation is over the detectives confer to see if there are any differences in the couple's stories.

- The detectives explain the differences (if any) to you (the judge) and you give the verdict.

6 Now you're here

- Students ask you the questions. Answer yes each time so they have to ask the extra questions in brackets.
- Students ask each other the questions in pairs.
- Tell students to ask a British person the same questions after class and make notes of their answers.
- Students tell the rest of the class about their most interesting answers the next day.

3 Read and think

Who says what?

Read the following and decide which of the people in the picture on page 64 says each of them.

1 . . .
> Single or return?

2 . . .
> Bye! Have a good journey.

3 . . .
> I want to go to Manchester tomorrow. Can you tell me the times of trains?

4 . . .
> With or without milk?

5 . . .
> Is this the right platform for the London train?

6 . . .
> Can I have a ticket to London, please?

7 . . .
> See you soon. Don't forget to write!

8 . . .
> What time of day do you want to travel?

9 . . .
> Can I have a cup of tea, please?

10 . . .
> Yes, it is. It'll be in in about five minutes.

4 Listen to this

This morning Susan, the maid, took a cup of tea to Lady Bartley . . .

Now listen to what happened after that and mark the sentences with a tick (√) or a cross (×).

The Bartleys had dinner at 8.15. ☐
They had steak for dinner. ☐
After dinner they saw a film. ☐
They didn't go out during the evening. ☐
Lady Bartley went to bed half an hour before Lord Bartley. ☐
They slept in the same bedroom. ☐

5 Play games in English

Alibi

The police think Lady Bartley was murdered at about 11 o'clock. They want to interview George (the gardener) and Susan (the maid).

a Two students, George and Susan, go out of the room. They read their instructions on page 81.

b The other students in the class are detectives. They must think of at least twenty questions to ask George and Susan.

George and Susan say:

they left the house at 7 o'clock
they went to London
they had dinner in a restaurant
they went to the cinema
they went to a disco.

Examples of questions the detectives can ask:
What time did you go out last night?
Where did you have dinner?
What was the name of the disco?

c The detectives ask Susan the questions and write down her answers. They then do the same with George.

MURDER AT
BARTLEY TOWERS
A. D. YOUNGER

d If there are three or more differences in their answers, they are guilty – they killed Lady Bartley.

6 Now you're here

Ask a British person these questions. If the answer is 'yes', ask a second question, using the word in brackets. Write down the answers you get.

Example:
A *Did you buy anything yesterday? (What?)*
B *Yes, I did.*
A *What did you buy?*
B *A newspaper and a new pair of shoes.*

- Did you drink any coffee yesterday? (How much?)
- Did you spend any money? (How much?)
- Did you ring anyone? (Who?)
- Did you lose anything? (What?)
- Did you read a newspaper? (Which?)
- Did you get any letters? (Who from?)
- Did you watch television? (What?)
- Did you go to bed late? (What time?)

Tell the rest of the class your most interesting answers.

UNIT ELEVEN · LESSON ONE

Trivial Pursuit

Sammy It's your turn now, Dominique. Throw the dice.

Dominique Three. 1–2–3. Green.

Debbie OK, boys. Which is longer, a metre or a yard?

Rob That's easy – a yard.

Debbie Wrong!

Sammy Give me the dice. It's our turn . . . Five. 1–2–3–4–5. Blue.

Rob Which is hotter, 100 degrees Celsius or 100 degrees Fahrenheit?

Sammy 100 degrees Celsius is hotter than 100 degrees Fahrenheit.

Rob Brilliant!

Debbie Let me throw now . . . One. Orange.

Dominique Which is more intelligent – a dolphin or a whale?

Debbie Eh . . . that's more difficult . . . er . . . a dolph . . . – no, a whale!

Dominique Wrong!

Rob It's my turn then . . . Four. Yellow.

Sammy Which planet is the nearest to Earth?

Dominique I think it's . . . it's Venus.

Rob Good, Dominique! You're cleverer than I thought!

Debbie But that was much easier than our last question!

Rob Rubbish!

Dominique It's my turn . . . Two. Red.

Debbie What's the most common word in the English language?

Dominique Please!

Rob No! It's–

Sammy Too late. The answer's 'the'.

Rob But I knew it! This is a silly game!

Debbie It's just because you're losing!

1 Who's who?

Who does the following? Tick (✓) the right answer.

Choose from Debbie (A)   Sammy (B)   Rob (C)   Dominique (D)

		A	B	C	D
1	Who plays with Dominique?	□	□	□	□
2	Who plays with Debbie?	□	□	□	□
3	Who thinks a yard is longer than a metre?	□	□	□	□
4	Who knows 100 °Centigrade is hotter than 100 °Fahrenheit?	□	□	□	□
5	Who thinks a whale is more intelligent than a dolphin?	□	□	□	□
6	Who knows Venus is the nearest planet to Earth?	□	□	□	□
7	Who thinks 'please' is the most common word in English?	□	□	□	□
8	Who thinks Trivial Pursuit is a silly game?	□	□	□	□

2 Make comparisons

a Write sentences using the words and information in the pictures.

Example: kilometre (short) mile

A kilometre is shorter than a mile.

1 30°C (hot) 30°F

<table>
<tr><td colspan="2">

Grammar summary
</td></tr>
</table>

- Comparative and superlative of adjectives
  (*big – bigger – the biggest   bad – worse – the worst*)

🖭 Trivial Pursuit

Notes and possible problems

- *Trivial Pursuit* is a well-known board game, consisting of general knowledge questions.

- *a dice* Technically the singular word is *a die* and *dice* is the plural word but most people nowadays use dice for both the singular and plural (i.e. one dice, two dice, etc.).

- *metre/yard* (line 5) 1 yard = 0.91 metres.

- 0° Celsius = 32° Fahrenheit
  20°Celsius = 68° Fahrenheit

- *Brilliant!* (line 15) Here it means *very clever*.

- *Rubbish!* (line 33) Students may know the literal meaning. Here it is used as an expression of disagreement like *Nonsense!* or *That's ridiculous!*

Presentation of the dialogue

- Ask students to think of all the games they play. Write *Board games* and *Card games* on the board. Put the names of the games the students mention in the appropriate column. Talk briefly about them.

- Set the scene for the dialogue. Dominique and Rob are playing Trivial Pursuit against Sammy and Debbie.

- Write these questions on the board:

  Which is longer, a metre or a yard?
  Which is hotter, 100° Celsius or 100° Fahrenheit?
  Which is more intelligent, a dolphin or a whale?
  Which planet is the nearest to Earth?
  What's the most common word in English?

  Encourage students to answer the questions if they can, before listening to the cassette.

- Students listen to the dialogue with books closed, twice if necessary.

- Students write their answers to the questions above and then check each other's answers.

- Students listen and repeat the dialogue, line by line.

Exercises

1 Who's who?

- Students work individually or in pairs to tick the appropriate name in each case.
- Check their answers.

2 Make comparisons

a Students write sentences individually.
- Check their answers.

b Students write sentences individually or in pairs.
- Check their answers.

3 Compare them

a Focus attention on the table of information.

● Ask the class a variety of questions as in the example, using the adjectives given.

● Ask students how to form a comparative with the adjectives given.

Note: *heavy* changes to *heavier*.

b This activity could be more fun if student B is given one minute to memorize the information and then answers A's questions from memory.

● Get one pair of students to demonstrate the activity to the class first.

● Make sure students change roles at some stage so that both have a chance to ask and answer questions.

C Ask students a variety of questions, this time using superlative forms.

● Ask students how to form superlatives with the adjectives given. Make sure they don't forget the *the*, as in *the biggest*.

● Students 'test' each other in the same way as they did in b).

Extra activity

If you feel students still need extra practice, ask three or four students to write similar details (real or fictitious) on the board. The class use this information to ask and answer questions like those in Exercise 3.

---

4 School subjects

a Elicit a list of subjects and write it on the board. Students copy the list.

b Go through the list of adjectives and make sure students understand them and can pronounce them correctly.

● Get students to compare the subjects *orally* using the adjectives given.

C Students can work in pairs or small groups. Remind them of the irregular comparative/superlative forms:

good – better – the best   and   *bad – worse – the worst*

● Ask students to write six sentences (three with *better* and three with *worse*).

d Tell students that long adjectives form their superlative with *the most*, for example *the most expensive*. Tell them to look at the table on page 85 if necessary.

● Ask students to write three sentences as in the example.

e Students compare their sentences either in pairs, groups or by the teacher calling on individual students to read out their sentences.

5 Class survey

● Before forming groups ask students what questions they must ask to find who is the oldest, etc.

Example:
How tall are you? What size are your shoes?

a Students form groups and ask each other the questions.

b It is probably quickest to choose likely candidates and vote with a show of hands or have a vote in which students write on a ballot sheet.

Example:
Maria is the best at English.
Pascal is the most hard-working.

Extra activity: Quiz

Students work in two teams and make up their own quiz using comparatives and superlatives.

Example:
Which is longer, a kilometre or a mile?
Which is the biggest ocean in the world?

Each team should prepare the same number of questions, 6–10, depending on the time available.

They ask a particular student in the opposing team a question.

The team gets two points if he/she knows the answer, one point if he/she needs help from the rest of the team.

2 Jupiter (big) Mars

3 kilo (heavy) pound

4 100 mph (fast) 100 kph

b Now write sentences comparing the things in the pictures using the words in the box.

light   slow   cold   small   long

Example:
A mile is longer than a kilometre.

3 Compare them

a Look at the information in the table.

	Sammy	Rob	Dominique	Debbie
Age	16 yrs, 3 mths	15 yrs, 4 mths	16 yrs, 1 mth	16 yrs, 8 mths
Height	1.65 metres	1.72 metres	1.76 metres	1.62 metres
Weight	52 kilos	65 kilos	63 kilos	50 kilos
Shoe size	36	41	43	37

b Work in pairs. Ask and answer questions like this:

A *Who's older, Sammy or Rob?*
B *Sammy's older than Rob.*
A *Who's got bigger feet, Sammy or Debbie?*
B *Debbie's got bigger feet than Sammy.*

Use adjectives like the ones in the box.

old / young   heavy / light
tall / short   big / small

c Now ask and answer questions like this:

A *Who's the oldest?*
B *Debbie is.*
A *Who's got the biggest feet?*
B *Dominique has.*

4 School subjects

a Make a list of the subjects you do at school. They probably include some of the following.

English	chemistry
history	gymnastics
maths	biology
physics	art
geography	religious knowledge

b Compare the subjects on your list, using adjectives like the ones in the box.

easy / difficult	boring
useful	enjoyable
important	interesting

Example:
English is more important than gymnastics.

c Now write sentences like these:

I'm better at English than maths.
I'm worse at chemistry than biology.

d Now write sentences like these:

I think English is the most important school subject.
My best subject is maths.
My worst subject is history.

5 Class survey

a Form groups. Ask each other questions to find out who is:

- the | oldest | in the group
  | youngest |
  | tallest |
  | shortest |

- the student with the biggest / smallest feet
- the student from the biggest family.

b Now vote on which student in the class is:

- the best at English
- the most hard-working
- the laziest
- the noisiest.

Grammar summary: page 85

67

Asking permission

Tomas Is it all right if I come home late this evening?
Mrs Hall Yes, all right. Where are you going?
Tomas To a party.
Mrs Hall What time does it finish?
Tomas Oh, about midnight.
Mrs Hall All right, but you must be home by half past twelve.
Tomas Don't worry, I will.
Can I have a front door key, please?
Mrs Hall Yes, of course.
Tomas And is it OK if I use your bike?
Mrs Hall No, I'm sorry. It hasn't got any lights.

1 Act it out

a Practise the dialogue above in pairs.

b Now write dialogues for the following situations.
Use these phrases:

Can I . . . ?
Is it all right if I . . . ?
Yes, of course / Yes, all right.

Example:

A *Is it all right if I close the window?*
B *Yes, of course.*

1

2

3

4

5

6

c Act out your dialogues in pairs. Change roles.

d Now think of reasons for not giving permission in each of the situations.

Example:
A *Is it all right if I open the window?*
B *No, I'm sorry, I'm cold.*

e In pairs, practise refusing permission.

f Think of other situations where you must ask permission.
In pairs, practise asking permission.

Example:
A *Can I borrow your tennis racket?*
B *Yes, of course.*
        or
  No, I'm sorry, I'm using it.

Students practise

- asking permission to do things
- giving / refusing permission
- talking about dates / seasons

Asking permission

- Ask students to listen to the dialogue (books closed) and tell you who is talking.

- Write these questions on the board:

  Where does the student want to go?
  What time must he / she be home?
  What two things does the student want?

- Play the dialogue again. Students answer. Check their answers.

- Students listen to the dialogue with books open and repeat line by line.

Act it out

b Students write the dialogues in pairs. Check their answers.

c Pick pairs at random to demonstrate the dialogues. Insist on appropriate intonation.

d Students only have to write the excuse. It is not necessary to write out all the questions again.

e Call out the number of a picture and nominate two students to ask and answer. Continue in the same way until you have called out all the numbers twice.

f Elicit some of the students' own examples of asking permission and write them up on the board.

2 Dates

a Students practise pronouncing the list of ordinal numbers on page 86.

● Choral and individual repetition. Don't let the activity drag. Keep a good pace and rhythm going in order to maintain interest.

● Practise around the class 1st to 31st, jumping from student to student.

● Call out cardinal numbers for example *3*. The class call back the ordinal number *the third*.

● Practise pronouncing the months and seasons.

● Practise the months quickly around the class.

b Focus attention on the difference between the way the date is written and the way it is said.

Write five or six examples up on the board:

11/6/53   *13th June 1987*
1st September 1960   *4/2/66*

● Ask students how these dates are said, making sure they do not forget *the* and *of*.

● Point out that in dates such as 1801 and 1907, the *0* is pronounced as in the letter *O* (the same as in telephone numbers).

● Write these questions on the board:

When were you born?
When did you come to England?
When will you go home?

Ask one or two students the questions. Then let them ask and answer in pairs. They form new pairs and ask and answer again.

d Ask students questions like:

What's the first/fifth/second month of the year?
When's Christmas? When's your birthday? When's Easter?

● Form teams. Students ask each other similar questions. Set a time limit for answering. Insist on good pronunciation. Keep a record of the score.

3 A survey

● Practise the question *When's your birthday?*

a and **b** Each student should try to ask everybody, unless the class is very large.

Extra activity: Whose birthday?

Students write out the dates of their birthday on two pieces of paper.

Example:
20th July   *20th July*

Students give the pieces of paper to the teacher who puts them all in a bag/box. The teacher gives two pieces of paper with different dates on to each student (but not their own). Students go round the class asking *When's your birthday?*

The 'winner' is the first student to find the two people whose pieces he/she has got.

---

4 A quiz

a Keep a record of the score.

b Give students time to prepare some questions.

5 The four seasons

● Ask some students to read out their sentences.

6 What's the preposition?

● Students have their books closed.

● Write the time expressions from the box on page 69 on the board in random order without prepositions.

● Ask students to tell you the missing prepositions or draw three columns headed *on*   *in*   *at*. Students must put the phrases in the correct columns.

● Students open their books. Focus their attention on the phrases with *on, in* and *at*.

2 Dates

a Learn the ordinal numbers (first, second, etc.) and months on page 86.

b Note that you write 21 (st) August, 1988, or 21/8/88, but you say 'the twenty-first of August, nineteen eighty-eight'.

c Write the date of your birthday and the birthdays of other people in your family.

d Form two teams. Ask each other questions like:
What's the third month of the year?
What's the eleventh month of the year?

3 A survey

a Each student writes down on a piece of paper the twelve months of the year.

b Students then go round the class asking: 'When's your birthday?'
They tick (√) the month of the year for each answer and add the date.

Example:
A *When's your birthday?*
B *The third of March.*

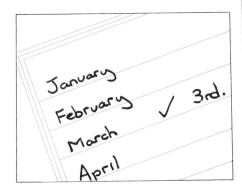

c The teacher then asks:
'Which month is the most 'popular' for birthdays?'
'Which month is the least 'popular' for birthdays?'
'Are there any students in the class with the same birthday?'

4 A quiz

a Form two teams. Students have their books closed. The teacher asks one team at a time:

1 Which is the shortest month of the year?
2 Which month has the longest day?
3 Which month has the shortest day?
4 In which month is the third letter P?
5 Which month comes after June?
6 Which month comes before September?
7 Which month comes between January and March?
8 In which month is the last letter L?
9 Which month has the shortest name?
10 Which month has the longest name?
11 Which month doesn't always have the same number of days?
12 Which three months begin with the same letter?

b Now ask each other similar questions. You have 3 minutes to prepare your questions.

5 The four seasons

a Write two sentences about each season in your country.

Examples:
I go skiing in the winter.
It's hot in the summer.

b Compare your sentences in groups.

6 What's the preposition?

a Look at the phrases below.

on	Monday Tuesday morning 3rd June my birthday
in	the morning the summer July 1989
at	night 10 o'clock Christmas the weekend

b Now complete the following sentences, without looking back at the box.
Choose between *in, on* and *at*.

1 My birthday is . . . 5th August.
2 I go to church . . . Sunday.
3 I get up . . . the morning.
4 I was born . . . 1975.
5 I sleep . . . night.
6 It's usually hot . . . the summer.
7 It often snows . . . January.
8 We sometimes go skiing . . . Christmas.

Summary of English in situations

- asking permission
- giving/refusing permission
- talking about dates

1 Sound right

a Find pairs of words (one from each box) which rhyme.
Example: *what – hot*

WHAT	hate
know	blue
one	tea
caught	HOT
two	good
me	light
great	said
would	laugh
bed	short
write	so
word	sun
half	bird

b Form two teams. Students from each team take it in turns to add to the list of rhyming words on the blackboard.

The team with the longest list is the winner.

c Now practise pronouncing the groups of rhyming words on the blackboard.

2 Listen to this

Listen to the descriptions of six people and fill in the missing information.

The tallest man: . . . . metres.
The tallest woman: . . . . metres.
The heaviest man: . . . . kilos.
The lightest baby: . . . . grams.
The oldest person: . . . . years,
                     . . . . days.
The oldest mother: . . . . years,
                     . . . . days.

3 Work on words

What's the missing word?

Example:
England / English
France / *French*

1 short / long
   near / . . .
2 ½ / half
   ¼ / . . .
3 a telephone / a phone
   a bicycle / . . .
4 weight / kilos
   temperature / . . .
5 he / him
   I / . . .
6 hot / hotter
   easy / . . .
7 to know / knew
   to think / . . .
8 6th / sixth
   2nd / . . .
9 to go / to come
   to stand up / . . .
10 July / summer
    October / . . .
11 60 seconds / a minute
    60 minutes / . . .
12 August / a month
    winter / . . .
13 a man / men
    a person / . . .
14 Monday / on
    December / . . .
15 a wife / a husband
    a daughter / . . .
16 to take / took
    to go / . . .
17 a plane / an airport
    a train / . . .
18 a taxi / a driver
    a plane / . . .
19 to listen / to
    to wait / . . .
20 7 / a week
    365 / . . .

FUN WITH ENGLISH

I Sound right

- The aim of the exercise is to show that words with different spellings often have the same pronunciation.

a Students work in pairs.

- Copy the two sets of words on to the board and elicit the correct answer.

C Practise pronouncing the words.

2 ▣ Listen to this

- Explain that students are going to hear information about world records—*the tallest man, the oldest person*, etc. Focus attention on the information grid.

- Play the exercise through once without stopping. Students do not write anything.

- Play it again, stopping after each description. Give students enough time to write their answers.

- Play the exercise through a third time, so that students can check their answers.

- Students exchange books and correct each other's answers.

- There are several dates of birth and death, etc. on the cassette. On a fourth listening you could ask four or five more questions, for example *When was Robin Wadlow born? When did Zeng Jinlian die?*

3 Work on words

- The missing word is not always immediately obvious. If students seem puzzled as they start the exercise, do a few more examples with them.

hard / soft	*fat / . . . . .*
paint / painter	*act / . . . . .*
hear / ears	*see / . . . . .*
horse / legs	*car / . . . . .*

- Students work in pairs or in groups.

4 Play games in English

Flump

a Focus attention on the explanation and the examples.

- Explain that *flump* is an invented verb which does not exist.

- Write a verb *to sing* on a piece of paper and hold it against your chest, hidden from the class.

- Encourage students to ask you questions to guess the verb.

- Help them with question forms and insist on correct questions.

b When they have guessed your verb, choose a student to think of a different verb. He or she writes it on a piece of paper, comes out to the front, and follows your example.

- Impose a limit of 15 questions of which no more than 3 can be straight guesses.

- With a weaker class, write up auxiliary verbs and question words on the board to help them.

    Example:
    Do . . . ?
    Did . . . ?
    Can . . . ?
    Is it . . . ?
    Where . . . ?
    When . . . ?
    What . . . ?
    How often . . . ?

- Check that the verb the student has chosen is known to the class and guessable.

5 Read and think

- Students work in pairs.

- Put a time limit and tell pairs who find the right answers quickly to keep it a secret until everyone has had a chance to finish.

6 Now you're here

- Give students practice in asking the questions and let them guess the answers but don't give them the correct answers.

a One British person might not know all the answers. Students might have to question several. Suggest other ways of finding out the answers — encyclopaedias, the *Guinness Book of Records*, etc.

b Students can compare their answers in class the next day.

4 Play games in English

Flump

a One student (Student A) thinks of a verb. The other students in the class try to guess the verb by asking questions like this:

Student B *Can you **flump**?*	Student A *Yes I can.*
Student C *Can everybody **flump**?*	Student A *No, not everybody.*
Student D *Are you good at **flumping**?*	Student A *Yes, quite good.*
Student E *Do you often **flump**?*	Student A *Yes, quite often.*
Student F *When do you **flump**?*	Student A *In the summer.*
Student G *Is it easy to **flump**?*	Student A *Yes, quite easy.*
Student H *Are you **flumping** now?*	Student A *No, I'm not.*
Student I *Did you **flump** yesterday?*	Student A *Yes, I did.*
Student J *Where did you **flump**?*	Student A *In the sea.*
Student K *Is the answer 'swim'?*	Student A *Yes, it is.*

b Student K then thinks of a different verb.

5 Read and think

a Read the following information carefully.

Kim   Tom   Ben

Nick

Meg

Tom is older than Ben.
Kim is younger than Meg.
Meg is older than Nick.
Nick is younger than Tom.
Ben isn't younger than Kim.
Tom isn't older than Meg.
Nick is younger than Kim.

b Now answer these questions.

1 Who is the oldest?
2 Who is the youngest?
3 Who is the oldest boy?

6 Now you're here

a Ask a British person these questions. Make notes of their answers.

1 Which is the second biggest city in Britain?
2 Which is the oldest university in Britain?
3 Which is the biggest county in Britain?
4 Which is the most common girls' name in Britain?
5 Which is the most popular television programme?
6 Which is the most popular radio programme, Radio 1, 2, 3 or 4?
7 Who is the richest person in Britain?
8 What is the youngest age at which you can marry?
9 What is the most expensive car you can buy in Britain?
10 Which is usually the driest month of the year?
11 Which is usually the wettest month of the year?
12 Which is the most popular newspaper?
13 How wide is the English Channel, at its narrowest point?
14 What is the most common name for a pub?
15 Who is the youngest member of the royal family?

b Tell other students in the class your most interesting answers.

UNIT TWELVE · LESSON ONE

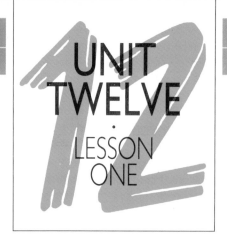

I'm going to miss you!

I'm starving. Why don't we go in and have a pizza?

I haven't got any money left.

It's all right—it's your last evening in England. We can pay for you.

Two minutes later.

What are you going to have, Dominique?

Um . . . I think I'm going to have a Pizza Napolitana.

Are you going to write to us, Dominique?

Yes, of course. Don't worry. I'm not going to forget you.

Are you really going to miss us?

Yes, of course I am.

Five minutes later.

What's the first thing you're going to do back in France?

I'm going to eat some French food!

Careful, Dominique—I think Sammy's going to cry!

No, I'm not—don't be silly!

What are you going to miss most about England?

Um . . . I'm not sure, but I know what I'm *not* going to miss.

What's that?

English sausages!

Grammar summary
• future tense with *going to* (*I'm going to miss you.   Are you going to miss us?* *I'm not going to forget you.*)

⛶ I'm going to miss you!

Notes and possible problems

• Future tense with *going to*: This tense is used when you talk about what you plan to do in the future (*I'm going to get up early tomorrow.*). It can also be used when you think or understand that something is going to happen in the future, often because you can see it (*It's going to rain.*).

It is formed with the verb *to be* + *going to* + the infinitive of the main verb.

• *I'm starving.* A colloquial expression meaning *I'm very hungry.*

• *back in France* Short for *when you are back in France.*

• *Careful, Dominique* This is short for *Be careful Dominique.*

Presentation of the dialogue

• Talk briefly to the students about going home. When are they going home? How are they going to travel? Are they happy/sad about leaving? Have they bought any presents/souvenirs? Are they going to come back to Britain? Keep it brief.

• Tell students what the dialogue is about. It's Dominique's last evening in England so he's going out with Rob, Sammy and Debbie.

• Write these statements on the board:

Dominique's going to pay for the pizzas.	TRUE/FALSE
Dominique's going to have Pizza Napolitana.	TRUE/FALSE
Dominique's going to write to them.	TRUE/FALSE
He's not going to miss them.	TRUE/FALSE
Dominique's going to miss English sausages.	TRUE/FALSE

• Students listen to the dialogue with books closed. Play the cassette twice if necessary.

• Students answer true or false. Check their answers.

1 False   2 True   3 True   4 False   5 False

• Students listen with books open, repeating the dialogue line by line.

• Students form groups of four and act out the dialogue from memory.

Exercises

1 Questions and answers

a Students work in pairs or individually.

b Student A asks the questions and B answers them. They then change roles. Make sure that the student who is answering has the answers covered or the book closed.

● Check their answers.

● Make sure students don't use short forms in their answers, for example *Yes, she's.*

2 What's going to happen?

● Students work in pairs to make a sentence for each picture.

● Check their answers. Sometimes more than one answer will be possible.

● Make sure students use contracted forms wherever possible.

Extra activity: Mime

In pairs or small groups students prepare a short mime. They act it out for the class but stop before it is finished.

Example:
Young man and woman sitting side by side. He goes down on one knee and proposes to her.

They freeze the action there.

The rest of the class has to suggest what's going to happen next.

Example:
She's going to say yes.
She's going to say no.
She's going to laugh at him.
She's going to kiss him.
They're going to get married.

When a number of suggestions have been offered, the mime is concluded. Another pair perform their mime, and so on.

---

3 Hastings and Rouen

● This exercise contrasts the present and future tenses.

a First ask students to make sentences about Dominique from the two lists orally.

● Give students time to write some sentences.

● Students compare their sentences in pairs.

● Ask some students to read out their sentences.

b Give students time to think of some personal examples of differences between what they do in Britain and what they're going to do when they go home. Students compare their answers in pairs or groups. They also read out some of their sentences in class.

4 Find out

● Check that students understand all the questions.

● Students work in pairs taking it in turns to ask and answer. Get them to note down their partner's answers briefly.

● Ask some students to report to the class about their partner (one or two of the most interesting answers only).

Extra activity: When I get home, I'm going to . . .

One student completes the sentence.

Example:
When I get home, I'm going to have a cup of coffee.

The next student adds an idea of his/her own.

Example:
When I get home, I'm going to have a cup of coffee and a shower.

The next student adds yet another idea and so on.

---

1 Questions and answers

a Match the questions on the left with the answers on the right.

Example: 1 – d

1 Are they going to eat hamburgers?
2 Is Dominique going to pay?
3 Are his friends going to pay?
4 Is Dominique going to miss his friends?
5 Is Sammy going to cry?
6 Is Sammy going to miss Dominique?

a) Yes, he is.
b) Yes, they are.
c) No, she isn't.
d) No, they aren't.
e) Yes, she is.
f) No, he isn't.

b Work in pairs. Student A asks the same questions. Student B answers without looking in the book. Change roles.

2 What's going to happen?

Describe what's going to happen in each of these pictures.

She's going to answer the phone.

1

2

3

4

5

3 Hastings and Rouen

a Compare Dominique's life in Hastings with his life at home, in Rouen, next week. Use the information in the table below.

In Hastings	In Rouen
with the Bonds	with his parents
instant coffee	real coffee
a bicycle	a moped
on the left	on the right
English	French
tennis	rugby
The Daily Mail	*Le Monde*
ketchup	mayonnaise

Write sentences like this:

In Hastings he lives with the Bonds. Next week, in Rouen, he's going to live with his parents again.

b Now make a list of other differences between life in Britain and in your country. Compare them in the same way.

4 Find out

Ask the person next to you the following questions.

- When are you going to go back to your country?
- Are you going to miss anything about Britain? (What?)
- Are you going to miss anybody? (Who?)
- Are you going to write to anybody in Britain? (Who?)
- Are you going to cry when you leave?
- What's the first thing you're going to do when you get home?
- What's the first thing you're going to eat?
- Are you going to come back to Britain? (When?)

Grammar summary: page 85

73

📺 Saying goodbye

Mrs Hall *Have you got everything?*
Tomas *Just a minute—passport, ticket, money . . . Yes, I've got everything.*
Mrs Hall *I hope you enjoyed yourself.*
Tomas *Yes, I really did. Thank you very much for everything.*
Mrs Hall *Don't forget to write to us.*
Tomas *Don't worry, I won't.*
Mrs Hall *Have a good journey.*
Tomas *Thanks . . . And thank you again for looking after me so well. Goodbye!*
Mrs Hall *Bye!*

1 Act it out

Practise the dialogue above in pairs. Change roles.

2 Questions and answers

a Match the questions on the left with the responses on the right.

Example: 5 – b

1 Can I try them on, please?
2 Can I speak to Mario, please?
3 Would you like a drink?
4 Is it OK if I have a bath?
5 How much is it?
6 Who's speaking?
7 What's the matter?
8 When's your birthday?
9 Is that everything?
10 Bye! See you tomorrow.
11 Can you pass the salt, please?
12 I can't come to the party, I'm afraid.

a) Yes, that's all, thanks.
b) It's £2.99.
c) Nothing.
d) Cheerio.
e) Yes, there's a changing room over there.
f) Yes, here you are.
g) No, I'm sorry, there's no hot water.
h) That's a pity.
i) No, I'm sorry, he's not in.
j) On 11th August.
k) This is Laura.
l) Yes, please.

b Work in pairs. Student A says the sentences on the left. Student B responds without looking at the answers on the right.

3 A quiz

a What do you say if:

1 somebody asks you if you want an ice cream?
2 you want to dance with somebody?
3 you want to know what something costs?
4 somebody needs help?
5 you want to try on a pair of jeans?
6 you want to know the date?
7 you want to know the time?
8 you want to use the telephone?
9 somebody asks if he/she can smoke in your room?
10 you want to buy a cup of coffee?
11 you want to speak to Chris on the phone?
12 you answer the phone and somebody asks for you?

b Look at the pictures and fill in the speech bubbles.

1

2

Students practise

- saying goodbye and thank you and revise the situational English from Units 1–11

📼 Saying goodbye

- Students listen to the conversation on the cassette, with books closed.

- Ask a few questions.

  Example:
  Who's speaking?
  What's the student going to do?
  Did he/she have a good time in Britain?

- Students listen again and repeat, sentence by sentence.

1 Act it out

- Students can practise the dialogue in pairs, from memory if possible.

2 Questions and answers

- This exercise revises many of the important and useful phrases from all the previous English in Situations lessons.

a Students work in pairs to match the phrases.

- Check their answers.

- Students can suggest alternative answers to those on the right.

3 A quiz

- A revision quiz.

a Give students time to write their answers in pairs.

- Students check their answers.

b Give students time to fill in the speech bubbles in pairs.

- Students check their answers.

- There are many possible answers. Get students to suggest different alternatives.

4 What do they say?

a Students write the dialogue in pairs.

● Students check their answers.

b Students practise the dialogue in pairs, then change roles.

● In this dialogue, there are many possible answers. Encourage students to improvise and use words and phrases they have heard, as much as possible.

5 ▱ Where are they?

● Play the conversations through once without stopping. Students do not write anything.

● Play them again, stopping after each conversation. Give students enough time to write their answers.

● Play the conversations through a third time, so that students can check their answers.

● Students exchange books and correct each other's answers.

● Go through the useful vocabulary in the tapescript.

● Students can act out the dialogues for each picture from memory.

┌───┐
│ **Extra activity: Where are we?**   │
├───┤
│ In pairs students decide on a place, for example, *post office, shoe shop, station, bus, pub.*

They write a short dialogue, similar to those in Exercise 5, which could be heard in that place.

They then act out the dialogue in front of the class who must guess the location. │
└───┘

3

4

4 What do they say?

In this dialogue, A is Mrs Baker, B is a foreign student staying with her. They are having supper.

A *hungry?*
B *yes*
A *salt?*
B *yes*
A *here like it?*
B *yes*
A *more?*
B *no*
A *sure?*
B *yes full*
A *coffee?*
B *yes*
A *black?*
B *white*

a The conversation is written in the shortest possible way. Write it out in full.

b Practise the *polite* version of the dialogue in pairs.

5 Where are they?

Listen to these short conversations.
Write the number of the conversation in the box under the correct picture.

1 London picture quiz

a Divide the class into two or more teams.

b Each team should match the name of each building/place with the correct photograph. Choose names from the box below.

10 Downing Street
Madame Tussaud's
Trafalgar Square
Tower Bridge
The Tower of London
Marble Arch
The Houses of Parliament
St Paul's Cathedral
Wembley stadium
Piccadilly Circus
Buckingham Palace
Westminster Abbey

c They should then match the photographs with the correct descriptions below.

d A correct name gets one point. A correct sentence gets another point.

A This is where the Prime Minister lives.
B Here you can see wax models of famous people.
C This is the Queen's residence in London.
D MPs debate and argue here, and there is a clock tower with a famous bell in it.

E This building was rebuilt by Christopher Wren after the Great Fire of London, 1666. It has a famous 'whispering gallery'.
F English kings and queens are usually married here. Many of them are also buried here, as well as many famous writers.

G This place has a memorial to Admiral Nelson, and is also famous for its many pigeons.
H This round place is often called the centre of London. There is a statue of Eros in the middle of it.
I It is quite near the City of London. It opens to let ships through.

As this is the final section of the book the normal format has
been changed to two quizzes about Britain.

I London picture quiz

- Set a time limit. Teams must agree on one possible
  answer in each case.

- Either trust the teams to work correctly or appoint
  checkers who sit with another group as you go through
  the answers and count up that group's points.

- Finally go through the quiz and give the correct answers.

2 UK quiz

- This exercise is intended to increase students' knowledge of the UK in an enjoyable way.

- Set a time limit.

- The teams must agree on one answer. You can only accept the first answer they give.

- Read each question aloud.

- One point for each correct answer. Keep a record of the score.

- Finally go through the quiz and give the correct answers.

- An alternative and rather more active and noisy way of conducting this quiz is to divide the class into several teams (four or five is ideal). Students have their books closed. Read out the questions (perhaps putting up items on the board if necessary).

  If a team knows the answer, they must put up their hands —not call out the answer. The first team to put up a hand gets a chance to answer the question. If they answer correctly, they get 1 point. If the answer is wrong, the next team to put up a hand gets a chance to answer.

  If you insist on getting answers only from teams with hands up, students will soon realise that calling out the answers only helps other teams and not themselves.

  It's useful to have a couple of helpers here: one to keep the score, the other to help spot which hands go up first.

Progress test 3: see page 00

2 UK quiz

a Divide the class into two teams, A and B.

b Team A answers question 1, team B question 2, etc. If one team can't answer a question, the other team tries to answer it.

Questions

1 What does 'lb' mean?

2 68° Fahrenheit is
   a) 15°
   b) 20°
   c) 25° Celsius.

3 Is a mile about
   a) 1,000
   b) 1,600
   c) 2,000 metres?

4 What does 'mph' mean?

5 Is the capital of Eire
   a) Belfast
   b) Edinburgh
   c) Dublin?

6 What is Wembley famous for?

7 What are these?
   a) *The Guardian*
   b) *The News of the World*
   c) *The Independent*

8 What are these?
   a) Harrods
   b) Selfridges
   c) Marks & Spencer

9 Which of these cities is in Wales?
   a) Cardiff
   b) Bristol
   c) York

10 What does 'L' on a car or motorbike mean?

11 What number do you dial if you want the police?

12 Channels 1 and 2 on British television are BBC. What is Channel 3?

13 You must go to school in Britain
    a) from the age of 5 until you are 16
    b) from the age of 6 until you are 17
    c) from the age of 7 until you are 18.

14 What is the population of Britain?
    a) 35 million
    b) 45 million
    c) 55 million

15 When can you vote in Britain?
    a) When you are 18.
    b) When you are 20.
    c) When you are 21.

16 What is the name of the largest political party in Britain?

17 How old must you be to buy an alcoholic drink in a pub?
    a) 16
    b) 18
    c) 20

18 Is the Princess of Wales married to
    a) Prince Andrew
    b) Prince Philip
    c) Prince Charles?

19 Which of these cities is in Scotland?
    a) Manchester
    b) Glasgow
    c) Southampton

20 What are these?
    a) Vauxhall
    b) Rover
    c) Jaguar

21 'Ulster' is another name for
    a) Scotland
    b) Northern Ireland
    c) the Republic of Ireland.

22 What are these?
    a) Arsenal
    b) Tottenham Hotspur
    c) Queens Park Rangers

23 What are these?
    a) Gatwick
    b) Heathrow
    c) Stanstead

24 What are these?
    a) Kent
    b) Surrey
    c) Hampshire

25 Where is the Loch Ness Monster supposed to live?
    a) England
    b) Scotland
    c) Wales

26 What sort of programmes can you hear on BBC1 Radio 1?
    a) classical music
    b) news and talks
    c) pop music

PAIRWORK: STUDENT B

This material is for use by student B in the information gap exercises earlier in the book.

Unit 2 Lesson 2 Exercise 2 (page 14)

Picture B

Work in pairs. Student A looks at picture A on page 14. Student B looks at picture B above. Try to find the six differences between the two pictures. Ask questions like: *Where are the clothes?*

Unit 2 Lesson 2 Exercise 5 (page 15)

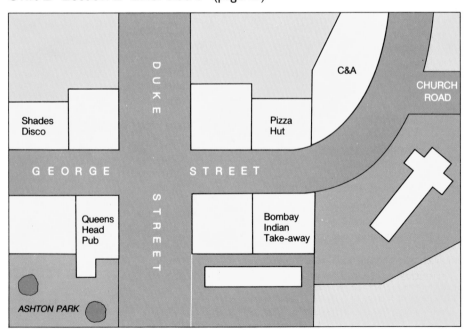

Look at the map.

You want to know where these places are:

1 the post office
2 Barclays Bank
3 the Cannon cinema
4 Boots the Chemist
5 the bus station
6 St Peter's Church

Fill in the information that student A gives you.

Ask each other questions like:

B *Excuse me. Where's the post office, please?*
A *It's on the corner of George Street and Duke Street, opposite the Cannon Cinema.*

Unit 4 Lesson 1 Exercise 4 (Page 25)

a Work in pairs. Student A looks at the information about Paul on page 25. Student B looks at the information about Carmen below.

b Student A asks questions about Carmen like this:

A *Does she like English pop music?*
B *Yes, she does.*

c Student B asks questions about what Paul likes or doesn't like.

Paul

English pop music: . . .
English food: . . .
Spanish food: . . .
English weather: . . .

Carmen

English pop music:	YES
English food:	NO
Spanish food:	YES
English weather:	NO

Unit 4 Lesson 2 Exercise 4
(Page 26)

Work in pairs. Student A looks at the list of programmes on Radio 1 on page 26.

Student B looks at the list of programmes below.

Ask each other questions, and fill in the missing information on your page.

Example:
What time does Simon Mayo start?

Unit 5 Lesson 2 Exercise 8 (Page 33)

Examples:
B *How much do the shoes cost?*
A *They cost £35.99.*
  How much does the jacket cost?
B *It costs £49.50.*

TUESDAY

1 MW 1053 +
1089 kHz
285 + 275 m
VHF/FM
88·90·2

**VHF/FM Stereo between
10.0pm and 12 midnight**
News on the half hour from
6.30am until 8.30pm,
then 10.0 and 12 midnight

5.30am Adrian John

☐ **Simon Mayo**
with the **Breakfast Show**.
Just before 8.0, an exclusive
preview of the new Top 40.

9.30 Simon Bates

11.0 ☐

with **Mike Read** at Portobello
Beach, Edinburgh

12.30pm Newsbeat
with Frank Partridge

☐ **Gary Davies**
with this week's Top 40

3.0 Bruno Brookes

5.30 ☐
with **Frank Partridge**

5.45 Peter Powell
At 6.30 Peter reviews the new
Top 40 singles.

☐ **Robbie Vincent**
with special guests

10.0-12.0 John Peel

79

Unit 7 Lesson 2 Exercise 3 (Page 44)

```
881000
210633    Bond J.R, 1 Su...
362786    Bond Kay, 18 Robertson Ho,Hastings ...     Tun Wells 36743    Bone C
712718    Bond K, 42 Priory Rd ...                    Tun Wells 22485    Bone C.
354564    Bond K.L, 19 Cavendish Dv ...               Tun Wells 28750    Bone C
ge  673   Bond L.A, South Riding,Upper Cumberland Wlk ...              Bone (
s 217591  Bond L.R, Leighton,Dower Ho Cres,Southborough  Hastings 435597  Bone (
lls 42819 Bond L.T,                                       Brede 882703    Bone (
field 3626           20 Gresham Wy,Filsham Pk,St. Leonards-o-s ..Hastings 437315  Bone
-s 212151 Bond M, Sunnyside,Cackle St ...                                 Bone
tford 2789 Bond M, 2 Quarry Cres ...                     Tun Wells 33214   Bone
rden 2592  Bond M.A, 7 Holly Clo,Hailsham Rd ...         Burwash 883236    Bone
bury 2260  Bond N.C, 4 Earls Rd ...                       Tun Wells 43297   Bone
           Bond Norman F.G, Linden,Swiffe La,Broad Oak ...  Forest Rw 3308   Bon
           Bond N.H, 13 Kendal Pk ...                      South Godstone 893168  Bon
ngs 422744 Bond N.J, Belnor,Chapel La ...                  Smallfield 2443   Bon
ngs 754384 Bond P.D, 2 The Grange ...                        Otford 4616     Bo
e Gn 830338 Bond P.E.T, 8 Grange Wy ...
tings 441497 Bond P.F, 21a East Hill Fm,Kemsing ...        Burwash 882294    Bo
tings 429843 Bond R.A, Unit 14 Waldron Ct Mutton Hall Hill ...  Hastings 429077  Bo
ersham  380  Bond R.A, Roseneath,Shrub Rd ...             Copthorne 714586   B
gh Gn 884491 Bond R.C, 166 Sedlescombe Rd Nth,St. Leonards-o-S  Fairseat 822889   B
mans Pk  403 Bond R.G, 8 Woodland Clo,Crawley Dwn ...      Hastings 422952    B
n Wells 34592 Bond R.H.C, Five Acres,Oakfarm La ...        Sevenoaks 452818   B
astings 712533 Bond R.M, 73 Edmund Rd ...
Hastings 52668 Bond Robert W, Ashgrove Cott,Gracious La ...  Westerham 62567
 Oxted 716714  Bond S, 20 Rodney Av ...                    Edenbridge 862780
n Wells 510196 Bond S.A, 57 Quebec Av ...                   Hastings 712660
lastings 753684 Bond S.E, 16 Sunnyside ...                  Fairseat 823642
tchingham  451  Bond S.G, 7/39 Cornwallis Gdns ...          W Malling 848105
 Crowboro 4996  Bond S.W, 45 Timberbank,Meopham,Gravesend ... Hastings 751267
tchingham  430  Bond T, 11 Auden Rd,Larkfield ...           Tun Wells 41129
 Oxted 712201   Bond T, 15 The Dene ...
Hastings 813587 Bond T, 6 Vale Rd,Southborough ...           Hastings 754080
 Oxted 717562   Bond T.C, 2 Warren Cotts,Stonelands,W Hoathly ...  E Grinstead 28632
 Hawkhurst 2564 Bond T.J, 8 Geary Pl,Westfield ...
aplehurst 892438 Bond T.P, 51 Forest View Rd ...             Bexhill-o-s 224220
evenoaks 458060 Bond V.C, 7 Reedswood Rd,St.Leonards-o-s.    Tenterden 2658
 Uckfield 2569  Bond V.F, 1 New Brassey Ct,6,Brassey Rd ...   Uckfield 3219
 Buxted 3492    Bond W, 17 Heather Dv,St. Michaels ...
 Crowboro 64110 Bond W.F, 16 Keld Dv ...                      Bexhill-o-s 218410
E Grinstead 28890 Bond W.G, Pound Ho,Willsley Pound ...        Rotherfield 244
E Grinstead 314599 Bond William.J, 180 Ninfield Rd ...
 Tonbridge 356862 Bond W.W, Loft Cott 4 New Rd ...             Paddock Wd 346
 Rye 225222    Bondelivery Service Ltd –
 Crowboro 2815  29 Eldon Wy ...                                Horam Rd 22
 Sandhurst  518 Bonding Systems Ltd,Adhesives Mfrs,  Vines Cross Rd,Horam  Paddock Wd 34
 Cooden 4453                                                   Tonbridge 3567
 Biddenden 291813 Bond's Delivery Service, 29 Eldon Wy ...     Tonbridge 3627
 Hastings 751739 Bonds E, 14 Lodge Rd ...                      Tonbridge 351
                Bonds G, 29 College Av ...                       Oxted 717
                Bonds R.J, 81 Higham La ...                    Sevenoaks 463
 Borough Gn 882470 Bone A.N.G, 103 Home Pk,Hurst Gn ...        Groombdge
 Smallfield 2907  Bone B.J, 14 Hurst Fm Road,Weald ...          Newick
                  Bone C.A, Hamsell Manor Barn,Eridge ...      Frittenden
E Grinstead 25091 Bone C.A, Fir Tree Cott,Station Rd ...        Hadlow 85
              ...M Parsonage Fm ...                           Tonbridge 39
```

Work in pairs. Student A looks at the page from the Hastings telephone directory on page 44. He/She then asks student B for the missing information.

Student B looks at the page from the Hastings telephone directory above and asks student A for the missing information.

Example:
B *What's V.C. Bond's telephone number?*
A *Hastings 712242.*

Unit 7 Lesson 2 Exercise 8
(Page 45)

Student A is going to ask you some questions. Use the information below in your answers. Use complete sentences when you answer.

Tiffany's
8.30
number 91
bus station
next to the Town Hall / opposite the Odeon cinema

Unit 8 Lesson 2 Exercise 5
(Page 51)

Situation 1
Student A phones you to invite you to go out. You don't want to go out with him/her. Make excuses, but be friendly.

Situation 2
You phone student A and invite him/her to play tennis with you. You say where (the place) and when (the time). You've got two tennis rackets, but you haven't got any balls.

Unit 9 Lesson 2 Exercise 5
(Page 57)

The *only* thing you want to do tonight is watch television. *Don't* tell student A this, but make excuses when he/she suggests doing something.

Examples:
No, I'm too tired.
I've got a headache.

Unit 10 Lesson 1 Exercise 5
(Page 61)

a Work in pairs. Student A reads the information about Suzanna on page 61. Student B reads the information about Patrick below.

b Student A asks student B questions about Patrick, and fills in the missing information about him.

Example:
A *What time did he get up this morning?*
B *He got up at half past seven.*

c Student B asks student A the same questions about Suzanna and fills in the missing information about her.

Patrick

Got up at: 7.30
Had breakfast at: *8.20*
Had for breakfast: *cornflakes and tea*
Had a shower: *No*
Left home at: *8.45*
Got to school at: *9.00*
Came to school by: *car*

Suzanna

Got up at: . . . . .
Had breakfast at: . . . . .
Had for breakfast: . . . . .
Had a shower: . . . . .
Left home at: . . . . .
Got to school at: . . . . .
Came to school by: . . . . .

Unit 10 Lesson 3 Exercise 5
(Page 65)

Instructions for Susan and George

The police think that you two murdered Lady Bartley last night at about 11.00.

You say that both of you:

- went to London at 7 o'clock, by taxi.
- came back at 12 o'clock, by taxi.
- had dinner in a restaurant.
- saw a film.
- went to a disco.

Prepare your story of what you did last night. The police will ask you questions, one at a time. You must try to tell *exactly* the same story.

Example questions:
What time did you go out?
How did you go to London?
What time did you have dinner?
Where did you have dinner?
Which film did you see?

If there are three or more differences in the stories you tell the police, then *you* killed Lady Bartley!

GRAMMAR SUMMARY

Unit 1

to be (present tense)

Affirmative	
I am	(I'm)
you are	(you're)
he is	(he's)
she is	(she's)
it is	(it's)
we are	(we're)
you are	(you're)
they are	(they're)

Negative	
I am not	I'm not
you are not	{ you aren't { you're not
he is not	{ he isn't { he's not
she is not	{ she isn't { she's not
it is not	{ it isn't { it's not
we are not	{ we aren't { we're not
you are not	{ you aren't { you're not
they are not	{ they aren't { they're not

Questions
Am I . . . ?
Are you . . . ?
Is he . . . ?
Is she . . . ?
Is it . . . ?
Are we . . . ?
Are you . . . ?
Are they . . . ?

Possessive adjectives

Personal pronoun	Possessive adjective
I	my
you	your
he	his
she	her
it	its
we	our
you	your
they	their

Apostrophe 's' genitive

When you talk about something which a person has or owns, put 's (an apostrophe + s) after the noun.

Example:
Dominique's bags.
A girl's name.

Unit 2

Demonstratives

This (singular)
These (plural) } Here/near you

That (singular)
Those (plural) } There/not near you

Plurals of nouns

Nouns usually add — s in the plural

Examples:
a bedroom – two bedrooms
a bag – three bags

The definite article

The definite article in English is always *the*.
It is the same with all nouns, singular or plural, masculine or feminine.

Examples:
the boy – the boys
the girl – the girls
the room – the rooms

Unit 3

to have got (present tense)

Affirmative			
I	have (I've)	got . . .
you	have (you've)	got . . .
he	has (he's)	got . . .
she	has (she's)	got . . .
it	has (it's)	got . . .
we	have (we've)	got . . .
you	have (you've)	got . . .
they	have (they've)	got . . .

Negative
I haven't got . . .
you haven't got . . .
he hasn't got . . .
she hasn't got . . .
it hasn't got . . .
we haven't got . . .
you haven't got . . .
they haven't got . . .

Questions
Have I got . . . ?
Have you got . . . ?
Has he got . . . ?
Has she got . . . ?
Has it got . . . ?
Have we got . . . ?
Have you got . . . ?
Have they got . . . ?

Short answers
Yes, I have. / No, I haven't.
Yes, you have. / No, you haven't.
Yes, he has. / No, he hasn't.
Yes, she has. / No, she hasn't.
Yes, it has. / No, it hasn't.
Yes, we have. / No, we haven't.
Yes, you have. / No, you haven't.
Yes, they have. / No, they haven't.

Indefinite articles

a   before words starting with a consonant (b, c, d, etc), or a consonant sound.

Examples:
a bike
a university

an   before words starting with a vowel sound (a, e, i, o, u)

Examples:
an Amstrad
an old bike

Adjective + noun

Adjectives usually go before the noun.

Example:
a French girl
a terrible temper

Adjectives do not change. They are the same with masculine and feminine nouns, both in the singular and plural.

Example:
an English girl – two English boys

Unit 4

The present simple tense

Affirmative		
I	like	
You	like	
He	likes	coffee.
She	likes	
It	likes	
We	like	
You	like	
They	like	

Negative		
I	do not (don't)	
You	do not (don't)	
He	does not (doesn't)	like coffee.
She	does not (doesn't)	
It	does not (doesn't)	
We	do not (don't)	
You	do not (don't)	
They	do not (don't)	

Questions	
Do I	
Do you	
Does he	
Does she	like coffee?
Does it	
Do we	
Do you	
Do they	

Short answers
Yes, I do. / No, I don't.
Yes, you do. / No, you don't.
Yes, he does. / No, he doesn't.
Yes, she does. / No, she doesn't.
Yes, it does. / No, it doesn't.
Yes, we do. / No, we don't.
Yes, you do. / No, you don't.
Yes, they do. / No, they don't.

Unit 5

Adverbs of frequency

- Adverbs of frequency tell you how often a person does something or how often something happens.

- The most common adverbs of frequency are:

always   usually   often   sometimes   hardly ever   never.

- Adverbs of frequency usually go before the main verb.

Example:
She always asks too many questions.

- Adverbs of frequency usually go after the verb *to be* (am, are, is, etc.) and auxiliary verbs (can, will, must, etc.)

Example:
He is always right.

Unit 6

can (present tense)

Affirmative	
I can	
You can	
He can	
She can	speak English.
It can	
We can	
You can	
They can	

Negative	
I can't	
You can't	
He can't	
She can't	speak English.
It can't	
We can't	
You can't	
They can't	

Questions	
Can I	
Can you	
Can he	
Can she	speak English?
Can it	
Can we	
Can you	
Can they	

Short answers

Yes, I can./No, I can't.
Yes, you can./No, you can't.
Yes, he can./No, he can't.
Yes, she can./No, she can't.
Yes, it can./No, it can't.
Yes, we can./No, we can't.
Yes, you can./No, you can't.
Yes, they can./No, they can't.

Unit 7

Present continuous (progressive) tense

Use the present continuous when you talk about what is happening now, at this moment.

Example:
I'm peeling the potatoes.

Affirmative

| I'm
You're
He's
She's
It's
We're
You're
They're | working. |

Negative

I'm	not		
You	aren't/	You're not	
He	isn't/	He's not	
She	isn't/	She's not	working.
It	isn't/	It's not	
We	aren't/	We're not	
You	aren't/	You're not	
They	aren't/	They're not	

Questions

| Am I
Are you
Is he
Is she
Is it
Are we
Are you
Are they | working? |

Short answers

Yes, I am./No, I'm not.
Yes, you are./No, you aren't.
Yes, he is./No, he isn't.
Yes, she is./No, she isn't.
Yes, it is./No, it isn't.
Yes, we are./No, we aren't.
Yes, you are./No, you aren't.
Yes, they are./No, they aren't.

Unit 8

some/any

- Positive sentences: *some*

  Example:
  I want some Coca-Cola.

- Negative sentences: *any*

  Example:
  We haven't got any Coca-Cola.

- Questions: *any*

  Example:
  Have you got any Pepsi Cola?

Singular	Plural
There is/isn't Is there . . . ?	There are/aren't Are there . . . ?

Unit 9

Past simple tense: regular verb

Affirmative

| I
You
He
She
It
We
You
They | arrived yesterday. |

Negative

| I
You
He
She
It
We
You
They | didn't arrive yesterday. |

Questions

| Did | I
you
he
she
it
we
you
they | arrive yesterday? |

Short answers

Yes, I did./No, I didn't.
Yes, you did./No, you didn't.
Yes, he did./No, he didn't.
Yes, she did./No, she didn't.
Yes, it did./No, it didn't.
Yes, we did./No, we didn't.
Yes, you did./No, you didn't.
Yes, they did./No, they didn't.

Past simple tense: to be

Affirmative

I	was
You	were
He	was
She	was
It	was
We	were
You	were
They	were

Negative

I	was not	(wasn't)
You	were not	(weren't)
He	was not	(wasn't)
She	was not	(wasn't)
It	was not	(wasn't)
We	were not	(weren't)
You	were not	(weren't)
They	were not	(weren't)

Questions

Was I ...?
Were you ...?
Was he ...?
Was she ...?
Was it ...?
Were we ...?
Were you ...?
Were they ...?

Unit 10

Past simple: irregular verbs

Affirmative
He went to London.

Negative
He didn't go to London.

Questions
Did he go to London?

Present / Infinitive	Past
go	went
leave	left
get	got
do	did
have	had
take	took
buy	bought
ring	rang
say	said
come	came
meet	met
forget	forgot
catch	caught

Unit 11

Comparatives of adjectives

- Add the ending –er to short adjectives.

  Example:
  A metre is longer than a yard.

- Put the word *more* before long adjectives.

  Example:
  A dolphin is more intelligent than a whale.

Superlatives of adjectives

- Add the ending –est to short adjectives.

  Example:
  Venus is the nearest planet to Earth.

- Put the word *most* before long adjectives.

  Example:
  What is the most common word in English?

  NB Put *the* before the superlatives.

Irregular comparatives/superlatives

	comparative	superlative
good	better	the best
bad	worse	the worst

Unit 12

Future tense: going to

Affirmative

I'm / You're / He's / She's / It's / We're / You're / They're going to leave.

Negative

I'm not / You aren't/You're not / He isn't/He's not / She isn't/She's not / It isn't/It's not / We aren't/We're not / You aren't/You're not / They aren't/They're not going to leave.

Questions

Am I / Are you / Is he / Is she / Is it / Are we / Are you / Are they going to leave?

Short answers	
Yes, I am.	No, I'm not.
Yes, you are.	No, you aren't.
	You're not.
Yes, he is.	No, he isn't.
	No, he's not.
Yes, she is.	No, she isn't.
	No, she's not.
Yes, it is.	No, it isn't.
	No, it's not.
Yes, we are.	No, we aren't.
	No, we're not.
Yes, you are.	No, you aren't.
	No, you're not.
Yes, they are.	No, they aren't.
	No, they're not.

Days of the week

Sunday
Monday
Tuesday
Wednesday
Thursday
Friday
Saturday

Months of the year

January
February
March
April
May
June
July
August
September
October
November
December

Seasons

Spring
Summer
Autumn
Winter

Numbers

Cardinal		Ordinal	
1	one	1st	first
2	two	2nd	second
3	three	3rd	third
4	four	4th	fourth
5	five	5th	fifth
6	six	6th	sixth
7	seven	7th	seventh
8	eight	8th	eighth
9	nine	9th	ninth
10	ten	10th	tenth
11	eleven	11th	eleventh
12	twelve	12th	twelfth
13	thirteen	13th	thirteenth
14	fourteen	14th	fourteenth
15	fifteen	15th	fifteenth
16	sixteen	16th	sixteenth
17	seventeen	17th	seventeenth
18	eighteen	18th	eighteenth
19	nineteen	19th	nineteenth
20	twenty	20th	twentieth
21	twenty-one	21st	twenty-first
22	twenty-two	22nd	twenty-second
23	twenty-three	23rd	twenty-third
24	twenty-four	24th	twenty-fourth
25	twenty-five	25th	twenty-fifth
26	twenty-six	26th	twenty-sixth
27	twenty-seven	27th	twenty-seventh
28	twenty-eight	28th	twenty-eighth
29	twenty-nine	29th	twenty-ninth
30	thirty	30th	thirtieth
31	thirty-one	31st	thirty-first
40	forty	40th	fortieth
50	fifty	50th	fiftieth
60	sixty	60th	sixtieth
70	seventy	70th	seventieth
80	eighty	80th	eightieth
90	ninety	90th	ninetieth
100	one | hundred a |	100th	one | hundredth a |
101	one | hundred and one a |	101st	one | hundred and first a |

Unit 1
Lesson 1

first
meeting
French
language course
husband
rude
bag
over there
heavy

Unit 2
Lesson 1

bathroom
loo
bedroom
suite
wardrobe
drawer
clothes
shower
doll

Unit 2
Lesson 2

-ness
floor
excuse me
post office
opposite
cinema
between
chemist's
you're welcome

Unit 3
Lesson 1

hi
news
how about . . . ?
at the moment
what's . . . like?
terrible
lucky
computer
a few
game
moped
cc
bike

Unit 3
Lesson 2

spell
full
address
sorry?
postcode

Unit 4
Lesson 1

record
mean (v.)
anything
kind (n.)
singer
word
of course
want (v.)
hear

Unit 4
Lesson 2

turn on
what's the matter?
listen to
pardon?
week
charts (n.)
I'm sorry
understand
hopeless
explain
quick

Unit 5
Lesson 1

parents
ask
many
question (n.)
know
everything
about
live
work
holiday
and so on
embarrassing
habit
sing
bath (n.)

This list contains the new, active vocabulary introduced in each unit. The words are listed in the order in which they appear in the text.

voice
remember
really
sometimes
wear
jeans
tight
forget
nearly
come round
talk about
instead
dance (v.)

Unit 5
Lesson 2

cash (v.)
traveller's cheque
passport
here you are
sign (v.)
fill in
date (n.)
money

Unit 6
Lesson 1

accent
guess (v.)
Spain
Italy
wrong
again
what a pity
speak
a bit of
worry (v.)
come on
let's
swim (v., n.)

Unit 6
Lesson 2

rule (n.)
late

meal
smoke (v.)
use (v.)
without
permission
play (v.)
loud

Unit 7
Lesson 1

lay the table
peel (v.)
potato
upstairs
probably
as usual
shower (n.)
help (v.)
busy
write
letter
kind (a.)
starve

Unit 7
Lesson 2

double
zero
message
ring (v.)

Unit 8
Lesson 1

beach
barbecue
evening
hamburger
only
sausage
left (a.)
I'm afraid
mustard
ketchup
different

Unit 8
Lesson 2

would you like
to . . . ?

Unit 9
Lesson 1

too
decide
meet
court
arrive
wait for
still
angry
phone (v.)
nobody
answer (v.)
then
walk (v.)
open (v.)
front door
garden
stupid

Unit 9
Lesson 2

afternoon
hot
cold
water
sit
idea

Unit 10
Lesson 1

morning
go (went)
by coach
with
leave (left)

get to (got to)
sightseeing
lunch
free
take (took)
photo
buy (bought)
end
ring (rang)
hour
ago
say
miss (v.)
train
station
meet (met)
forget (forgot)
get lost
stay (v)
another
catch (caught)

Unit 10
Lesson 2

look for
a pair of
size
think
waist
later
try on
changing room

Unit 11
Lesson 1

Trivial Pursuit
turn (n.)
throw
dice
green
long
yard
easy
give
blue
degree
Celsius
Fahrenheit
brilliant
orange
intelligent
dolphin
whale
difficult
yellow

planet
earth
clever
think (thought)
last (a.)
rubbish
red
common
know (knew)
silly
because
lose

Unit 11
Lesson 2

party
finish (v.)
key
light (n.)

Unit 12
Lesson 1

miss (v.)
pay (v.)
food
write
careful
cry (v.)
sure

Unit 12
Lesson 2

ticket
enjoy
journey
look after
well

THE BRITISH ISLES

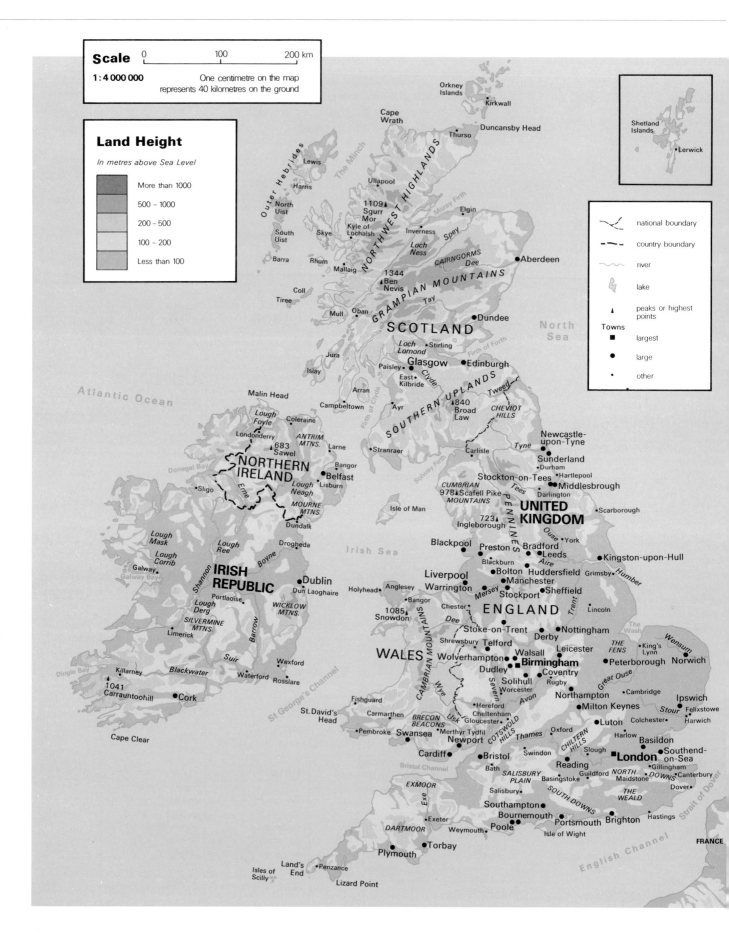

Scale

0   100   200 km

1 : 4 000 000

One centimetre on the map represents 40 kilometres on the ground

Land Height

In metres above Sea Level

More than 1000

500 – 1000

200 – 500

100 – 200

Less than 100

national boundary

country boundary

river

lake

peaks or highest points

Towns

largest

large

other

Orkney Islands

Kirkwall

Shetland Islands

Lerwick

Cape Wrath

Thurso

Duncansby Head

NORTH WEST HIGHLANDS

Lewis

The Minch

Ullapool

Harris

Outer Hebrides

North Uist

1109 Sgurr Mor

Morey Firth

Elgin

Inverness

Kyle of Lochalsh

Skye

Spey

CAIRNGORMS

Dee

Aberdeen

South Uist

Loch Ness

Barra

Rhum

Mallaig

1344 Ben Nevis

GRAMPIAN MOUNTAINS

Coll

Tay

Tiree

Mull

Oban

Dundee

SCOTLAND

North Sea

Jura

Loch Lomond

Stirling

Islay

Glasgow

Edinburgh

Firth of Forth

Paisley

Clyde

East Kilbride

Arran

Ayr

SOUTHERN UPLANDS

Tweed

840 Broad Law

CHEVIOT HILLS

Atlantic Ocean

Malin Head

Campbeltown

Stranraer

Carlisle

Tyne

Newcastle-upon-Tyne

Lough Foyle

Coleraine

Londonderry

ANTRIM MTNS.

Larne

Sunderland

Durham

Hartlepool

683 Sawel

Bangor

Belfast

Stockton-on-Tees

Tees

Middlesbrough

NORTHERN IRELAND

Lisburn

Solway Firth

CUMBRIAN

Darlington

Donegal Bay

Erne

Lough Neagh

978 Scafell Pike MOUNTAINS

PENNINES

UNITED KINGDOM

Scarborough

Sligo

MOURNE MTNS.

Isle of Man

723 Ingleborough

Ouse

York

Dundalk

Kingston-upon-Hull

Lough Mask

Lough Ree

Drogheda

Blackpool

Preston

Bradford

Lough Corrib

Boyne

Irish Sea

Blackburn

Leeds

Aire

Galway

Shannon

IRISH REPUBLIC

Dublin

Liverpool

Bolton

Huddersfield

Grimsby

Humber

Galway Bay

Dun Laoghaire

Holyhead

Anglesey

Warrington

Manchester

Sheffield

Portlaoise

Bangor

Mersey

Stockport

Lincoln

Lough Derg

WICKLOW MTNS.

Chester

ENGLAND

Trent

SILVERMINE MTNS.

1085 Snowdon

Dee

Stoke-on-Trent

Nottingham

The Wash

Limerick

Barrow

CAMBRIAN MOUNTAINS

Shrewsbury

Telford

Derby

Wensum

Suir

Blackwater

Wexford

Wolverhampton

Walsall

Leicester

THE FENS

King's Lynn

Norwich

1041 Carrauntoohill

Killarney

Dudley

Birmingham

Peterborough

Cork

Rosslare

Dudley

Solihull

Coventry

Rugby

Dingle Bay

Waterford

Worcester

Great Ouse

WALES

Wye

Severn

Avon

Northampton

Cambridge

Ipswich

Fishguard

Hereford

Milton Keynes

Stour

Felixstowe

Cape Clear

St. David's Head

Carmarthen

BRECON BEACONS

Cheltenham

Gloucester

Usk

COTSWOLD HILLS

Oxford

Luton

Harlow

Colchester

Harwich

Pembroke

Swansea

Merthyr Tydfil

Newport

Thames

CHILTERN HILLS

Slough

Basildon

Cardiff

Bristol

Swindon

Reading

London

Southend-on-Sea

Bristol Channel

Bath

SALISBURY PLAIN

Basingstoke

Guildford

NORTH DOWNS

Gillingham

Maidstone

Canterbury

EXMOOR

Salisbury

SOUTH DOWNS

THE WEALD

Dover

Southampton

Bournemouth

Portsmouth

Brighton

Hastings

Exeter

DARTMOOR

Weymouth

Poole

Isle of Wight

Strait of Dover

Plymouth

Torbay

FRANCE

Land's End

Penzance

English Channel

Isles of Scilly

Lizard Point

88

Unit 1 Lesson 1 Exercise 1

1	f	5	b
2	e	6	h/g
3	g/h	7	a
4	c	8	d

Unit 1 Lesson 1 Exercise 5

I	my
we	our
it	its
he	his
they	theirs
she	her
you	yours

Unit 1 Lesson 2 Exercise 5

Ria	14	Holland	Dutch
Hans	16	Switzerland	Swiss
Estelle	17	France	French
Manuel	15	Spain	Spanish
Maki	17	Japan	Japanese
Miguel	16	Brazil	Brazilian

Unit 1 Lesson 3 Exercise 2

a)	1	d)	5
b)	6	e)	3
c)	2	f)	4

Unit 1 Lesson 3 Exercise 3

boy	girl
yes	no
first	last
good	bad
Mr	Mrs
here	there
nice	horrible
husband	wife
rude	polite
hello	goodbye
heavy	light
short	tall
early	late
man	woman
morning	evening

Unit 2 Lesson 1 Exercise 1

1	✓	6	X
2	X	7	X
3	X	8	✓
4	✓	9	✓
5	X		

Unit 2 Lesson 1 Exercise 3

1 These are our bedrooms.
2 These drawers are full.
3 These rooms are bedrooms.
4 Those bedrooms are big.
5 Those are Dominique's bags.
6 Those are her books.

Unit 2 Lesson 2 Exercise 1

1	in	6	on
2	on	7	next to/on the left of
3	next to	8	next to/on the right of
4	above	9	in
5	below	10	on

Unit 2 Lesson 2 Exercise 2

In picture A the records are on the stereo, but in picture B they are on the floor/in front of the wardrobe.

In picture A the cassettes are in the drawer, but in picture B they are on the desk.

In picture A the table is next to the bed, but in picture B it is in front of the stereo/on the left of the desk.

In picture A the lamp is in the corner, but in picture B it is on the Amstrad.

In picture A the Walkman is next to the Armstrad, but in picture B it is next to the cassettes.

Unit 2 Lesson 2 Exercise 3

(possible answers)

1 The ABC Cinema is between the Chinese take-away and the record shop.
2 The Midland Bank is next to the post office.
3 McDonald's is on the corner of Queens Road and Station Road.
4 The amusement arcade is in Station Road.
5 The Oxford School of English is on the right of the church.
6 Boots the Chemist is on the left of the church.
7 The Red Lion Pub is opposite the sports centre.

STUDENT'S BOOK KEY

8 The record shop is between the ABC Cinema and McDonald's.
9 The Chinese take-away is next to the ABC Cinema.
10 The park is on the corner of Queens Road and Station Road.

Unit 2 Lesson 3 Exercise 1

1	this	5	hour
2	here	6	our
3	near	7	him
4	quiet	8	shall

Unit 2 Lesson 3 Exercise 2

1	Mrs	6	all right	11	a wardrobe	16	a town
2	our	7	below	12	surname	17	Spanish
3	hers	8	a month	13	bye	18	tomorrow
4	there	9	a square	14	south	19	£1
5	forty	10	a cross	15	hungry	20	buses

Unit 2 Lesson 3 Exercise 3

1 Football statium
2 English Language Centre
3 Linton Hotel

Unit 2 Lesson 3 Exercise 4

A	Kim	E	Di
B	Beth	F	Tim
C	Liz	G	Mark
D	Nick	H	Sue

Unit 2 Lesson 3 Exercise 6

a chemist's:	aspirins toothpaste a film sun cream make-up
a newsagent's:	a newspaper sweets a magazine postcards
a post office:	stamps
a greengrocer's:	bananas apples oranges

Unit 3 Lesson 1 Exercise 1

1 d 2 a 3 e 4 f 5 b 6 g 7 c

Unit 3 Lesson 2 Exercise 2

1	girl	6	news
2	bad	7	half
3	name	8	moped
4	lucky	9	brother
5	friend	10	computer

Unit 3 Lesson 2 Exercise 5

1 Have your money ready (10p, 5p, £1).
2 Pick up the receiver and listen for the dialling tone.
3 Put in your money.
4 Dial the number you want.
5 Speak when somebody answers.
6 Don't forget to take your unused coins back.

Unit 3 Lesson 3 Exercise 2

A 4 B 3 C 4 D 3

Unit 3 Lesson 3 Exercise 3

a 1 b 3 c 6 d 2 e 4 f 5

Unit 3 Lesson 3 Exercise 4

A 3 B 1 C 4 D 2

Unit 4 Lesson 1 Exercise 1

1	Does...	Yes, she does.
2	Does...	No, it doesn't.
3	Do...	Yes, they do.
4	Does...	No, he doesn't.
5	Does...	Yes, he does.
6	Do...	No, they don't.
7	Does	No, she doesn't.

Unit 4 Lesson 2 Exercise 1

1	3.00	6	8.35
2	8.10	7	10.45
3	1.30	8	11.55
4	4.05	9	1.50
5	7.15	10	12.58

Unit 4 Lesson 2 Exercise 2

a) twenty-five past eight
b) nine o'clock
c) five to five
d) a quarter to three
e) ten past four
f) six minutes to four
g) half past seven

Unit 4 Lesson 3 Exercise 2

	Pop music	Football	Modern fashion
Gary Carter	√	√	O
Sandra Brent	O	X	√
Charles Wentworth-Smythe	X	O	√

Unit 4 Lesson 3 Exercise 4

I	Italy	7	football
2	sister	8	park
3	hi	9	computer
4	ugly	10	milk
5	car	II	terrible
6	student	12	crisps

Unit 5 Lesson I Exercise I

Rob's father	forgets people's names. wears tight jeans.
Dominique's father	sings in the bath. has a terrible voice.
Debbie's mother	likes the Rolling Stones. embarrasses her.
Dominique's mother	asks too many questions. dances to his records. wants to know about his friends.

Unit 5 Lesson 2 Exercise I

I 23p 2 56p 3 £1.42 4 £2.15 5 £1.87

Unit 5 Lesson 2 Exercise 2

1 3 coins – 10p 5p 1p
2 3 coins – 20p 2p 1p
3 I coin – 20p
4 7 coins – £1 £1 £1 50p 20p 20p 5p
5 6 coins – £1 20p 20p 5p 2p 2p
6 7 coins – £1 50p 20p 10p 2p 1p

Unit 5 Lesson 2 Exercise 5

1 27p
2 29p
3 49p
4 35p

Total £1.40

Unit 5 Lesson 3 Exercise I

problem	habit
question	remember
everything	forget
holiday	fourteen
embarrassing	forty
terrible	music

Unit 5 Lesson 3 Exercise 3

I	8.00	4	7.30
2	8.35	5	8.45
3	8.20	6	7.45

1 She has a shower at eight o'clock.
2 She leaves home at twenty-five to nine.
3 She gets dressed at twenty past eight.
4 She gets up at half past seven.
5 She catches a bus at a quarter to nine.
6 She has breakfast at a quarter to eight.

Unit 5 Lesson 3 Exercise 4

I	yes	5	yes
2	no	6	yes
3	yes	7	no
4	yes	8	no

Unit 5 Lesson 3 Exercise 5

I	You ask a question.	7	You play games.
2	You eat a hamburger.	8	You ride a bike.
3	You speak English.	9	You read a magazine.
4	You wear jeans.	10	You drink coffee.
5	You catch a bus.	II	You open a door.
6	You listen to the radio.	12	You cash a cheque.

Unit 6 Lesson I Exercise I

I h 2 d 3 g 4 a 5 f 6 e 7 b 8 c

Unit 6 Lesson 2 Exercise 2

	come home late	smoke in his/her room	have a bath everyday	have friends in his/her room
Marco	✓	X		✓
Pia	X	X	X	✓
Martine	X	✓	X	X
Takao	✓	✓	X	✓

Unit 6 Lesson 2 Exercise 6

(possible answers)

No entry:
You mustn't drive/cycle up this street.

Wet paint:
You mustn't touch.

STUDENT'S BOOK KEY

Silence:
You mustn't talk.
You must be silent.

Please keep off the grass:
You mustn't walk on the grass.
You must keep off the grass.

Pay as you enter:
You must have the exact fare.
You must pay as you get on the bus.

No smoking:
You mustn't smoke.

No parking:
You mustn't park your bicycle / car here.

Unit 6 Lesson 3 Exercise 3

a) head   e) ear   h) foot   k) hair
b) hand   f) stomach   i) leg   l) eye
c) arm   g) toe   j) finger   m) nose
d) mouth

Unit 6 Lesson 3 Exercise 4

1 d   4 g
2 f e   5 c
3 b   6 a h

Unit 7 Lesson 1 Exercise 1

(possible answers)

Is Mrs Bond laying the table? No, she isn't.
Are Mr and Mrs Bond writing a letter? No, they aren't.
Is Debbie having a shower? Yes, she is.
Is Dominique listening to music? No, he isn't.
Is Rob working? No, he isn't.
Are Debbie and Rob peeling the potatoes? No, they aren't.

Unit 7 Lesson 1 Exercise 2

(possible answer)

I'm lying on the beach. It's hot. Some people are swimming in the sea. A girl is windsurfing and two men are fishing from the pier. See you soon. Love Dominique.

Unit 7 Lesson 1 Exercise 3

1 writes
2 he is (he's) writing
3 washes
4 it is (it's) raining   rains
5 I'm having
6 speaks   doesn't speak
7 are you watching
8 are you cooking   I'm starving

Unit 7 Lesson 2 Exercise 1

1 3023126   4 341 4913
2 400368   5 0862 67598
3 403710

Unit 7 Lesson 2 Exercise 6

a) Ring Fina before 8.
    Her number: 351 8818

b) Anna rang.
    She has 2 tickets for concert tonight – starts 8.30. Meet her outside bus station at 8.

Unit 7 Lesson 3 Exercise 1

C 1 thin   4 thank
   2 sink   5 thought
   3 sick   6 some

Unit 7 Lesson 3 Exercise 2

1 √   6 X
2 √   7 √
3 X   8 X
4 X   9 √
5 √   10 √

Unit 7 Lesson 3 Exercise 4

to ring	to phone
all right	OK
starving	hungry
right	correct
hi	hello
to speak	to talk
to start	to begin
to shut	to close
quick	fast
pardon?	sorry?
to arrive	to get to
toilet	loo
terrible	horrible
dad	father
bike	bicycle
at the moment	now
too	also
you're welcome	not at all
a bit	a little
great	fantastic
famous	well-known
big	large
to finish	to end
till	until

Unit 8 Lesson 1 Exercise 1

At the barbecue there	are some English people.
	's some Coca-Cola.
	are some sausages.
	's some ketchup.
	's some music.
	aren't any hamburgers.
	isn't any mustard.
	are some French students.

Unit 8 Lesson 1 Exercise 3

In picture A there are some	hamburgers
	sausages
	cassettes
	bottles of orange juice.

In picture B there aren't any.

Unit 8 Lesson 2 Exercise 4

1 F 2 T 3 F 4 F 5 F 6 T 7 F

Unit 8 Lesson 3 Exercise 1

student	problem
later	another
over	cinema
horror	persuade
tired	different
mustard	tomorrow
letter	badminton
afraid	hamburger

Unit 8 Lesson 3 Exercise 2

1 difficult	6 empty	11 clever
2 different	7 clean	12 slow
3 below	8 quiet	13 first
4 expensive	9 always	14 short
5 early	10 fat	15 wet

Unit 8 Lesson 3 Exercise 4

1 yes	4 no	7 no
2 no	5 yes	8 yes
3 yes	6 no	9 no

Unit 8 Lesson 3 Exercise 5

1 c	6 i
2 e	7 d
3 b	8 f
4 g	9 h
5 a	10 j

Unit 8 Lesson 3 Exercise 6

1 ante meridian	12 value added tax
2 Independent Television	13 Royal Automobile club
3 do-it-yourself	14 post meridian
4 unidentified flying object	15 please turn over
5 bed and breakfast	16 miles per hour
6 British Broadcasting Corporation	17 long playing (record)
7 disc jockey	18 hot and cold
8 for example	19 Automobile Association
9 water closet	20 United Kingdom
10 member of parliament	21 British Rail
11 that is	22 Marks and Spencer

Unit 9 Lesson 1 Exercise 1

Dominique and Rob	weren't at the tennis courts in Alexander Park.
	were at the tennis courts at 3 o'clock.

Debbie	wasn't with Rob and Dominique.
	was at the tennis courts at 3 o'clock.
	was at the tennis courts in Alexandra Park.
	wasn't at the tennis courts in White Rock Gardens.

Mr and Mrs Bond	weren't with Rob and Dominique.
	weren't at the tennis courts at 3 o'clock.
	weren't at the tennis courts in Alexandra Park.
	weren't at the tennis courts in White Rock Gardens.
	were at home at 3 o'clock.
	weren't in the house at 3 o'clock.
	were in the garden at 3 o'clock.

Unit 9 Lesson 1 Exercise 3

What did you want to play?
I wanted to play tennis.

Who did you want to play with?
I wanted to play with Rob and Dominique.

Where did you decide to meet?
We decided to meet at the tennis courts.

What time did you arrive?
I arrived at 3 o'clock.

Were Dominique and Rob there?
No they weren't.

STUDENT'S BOOK KEY

How long did you wait?
I waited for twenty minutes.

What did you do then?
I phoned home.

Did your mother answer the phone?
No, she didn't.

Were you angry?
Yes, I was.

Were Dominique and Rob at home when you arrived?
No they weren't.

Where were they at 3 o'clock?
They were at the tennis courts in White Rock Gardens.

Unit 9 Lesson 2 Exercise 6

b PG   parental guidance
Sep. progs   separate programmes
U   universal
15   you must be over 15
18   you must be over 18

Unit 9 Lesson 2 Exercise 7

1 C Bus station   8.00
2 A Leisure centre   7.45
3 B outside school   2.25

Unit 9 Lesson 3 Exercise 1

Wait for me.
It's an egg.
What's the time?
Fish and chips.
At eight o'clock.
It's slow but cheap.
Speak to me.
He's from France.
A cup of tea.

Unit 9 Lesson 3 Exercise 2

1 soldier   4 disc jockey
2 pilot   5 taxi
3 photographer   6 mechanic

Unit 9 Lesson 3 Exercise 3

Across	Down
1 Sausages	1 Shower
2 Potatoes	3 Shoes
4 Socks	5 Garden
5 Grass	7 Knife
6 Skirt	
8 Fork	
9 Tights	
10 Beach	
11 Plate	

Unit 9 Lesson 3 Exercise 5

1 False   6 False
2 True   7 False
3 True   8 True
4 False   9 True
5 True

Unit 9 Lesson 3 Exercise 6

1 Monday   9 public limited company
2 information   10 hour
3 programme   11 minute
4 February   12 department
5 telephone   13 inclusive/including
6 brothers   14 inch (es)
7 etcetera   15 foot (feet)
8 number   16 pound (s) (weight)

Unit 10 Lesson 1 Exercise 1

1 i   6 a
2 d   7 b
3 h   8 j
4 e   9 f
5 g   10 c

Unit 10 Lesson 1 Exercise 2

The coach left Hastings.
The coach went to London.
Dominique did some sightseeing.
Dominique forgot the time.
Dominique got lost.
Dominique missed the coach.
Dominique caught the wrong train.
Miss Fox rang Mrs Bond.
Dominique got to Brighton.

Unit 10 Lesson 2 Exercise 1

1	a pair of gloves	15	a pair of trainers
2	a dress	16	a pair of jeans
3	a jumper	17	a pair of underpants
4	a necklace	18	a pair of sunglasses
5	a sweatshirt	19	a pair of boots
6	a blouse	20	a pair of tights
7	a shirt	21	a pair of knickers
8	a bra	22	a pair of shorts
9	a vest / T-shirt	23	a bracelet
10	a jacket	24	a hat
11	a skirt	25	a coat
12	a pair of shoes	26	a scarf
13	a tie	27	a belt
14	a pair of trousers	28	a pair of socks

Unit 10 Lesson 2 Exercise 3

1	T-shirt	yellow	£6.99	small
2	denim skirt	blue	£16.25	10
3	tights	black	£1.20	

Unit 10 Lesson 2 Exercise 5

1 These trousers are too long / big.
2 This skirt's too long / big.
3 This T-shirt's too small / short.
4 These jeans are too tight / short.

Unit 10 Lesson 3 Exercise 1

1 Dominique went to London.
2 He went by coach.
3 He took some photographs.
4 How did you miss the coach?
5 I met some French students, and I forgot the time.
6 I'm coming to get you now.
7 I caught the wrong train.
8 I'm not at Hastings Station.

Unit 10 Lesson 3 Exercise 2

1	information desk	7	platform
2	ticket office	8	carriage
3	timetable	9	porter
4	snack bar	10	toilets
5	left luggage	11	newsagents
6	train		

Unit 10 Lesson 3 Exercise 3

1 F 2 I 3 B 4 H 5 C 6 E 7 J 8 A 9 G 10 D

Unit 10 Lesson 3 Exercise 4

X
X
✓
✓
✓
X

Unit 11 Lesson 1 Exercise 1

1	Rob	5	Debbie
2	Sammy	6	Dominique
3	Rob	7	Dominique
4	Sammy	8	Rob

Unit 11 Lesson 1 Exercise 2

a 1 30°C is hotter that 30°F.
   2 Jupiter is bigger than Mars.
   3 A kilo is heavier than a pound.
   4 100 mph is faster than 100 kph.

b   A mile is longer than a kilometre.
     30°F is colder than 30°C.
     Mars is smaller than Jupiter.
     A pound is lighter than a kilo.
     100 kph is slower than 100 mph.

Unit 11 Lesson 2 Exercise 6

1	on	5	at
2	on	6	in
3	in	7	in
4	in	8	at

Unit 11 Lesson 3 Exercise 1

what	hot
know	so
one	sun
caught	short
two	blue
me	tea
great	hate
would	good
bed	said
write	light
word	bird
half	laugh

Unit 11 Lesson 3 Exercise 2

The tallest man:	2.72 m
The tallest woman:	2.47 m
The heaviest man:	4.42 k
The lightest baby:	283 gm
The oldest person:	120 years 237 days
The oldest mother:	57 years 129 days

Unit 11 Lesson 3 Exercise 3

1	far	11	an hour
2	a quarter	12	a season
3	a bike	13	people
4	degrees	14	in
5	me	15	a son
6	easier	16	went
7	thought	17	a station
8	second	18	a pilot
9	to sit down	19	for
10	autumn	20	a year

Unit 11 Lesson 3 Exercise 5

1 Neg   2 Nick   3 Tom

Unit 12 Lesson 1 Exercise 1

1 d	4 a
2 f	5 c
3 b	6 e

Unit 12 Lesson 1 Exercise 2

1 She's going to fall in the pool.
2 They're going to eat some sandwiches.
3 It's going to rain.
4 He's going to miss the bus.
5 They're going to buy some ice-creams.

Unit 12 Lesson 1 Exercise 3

In Hastings	*In Rouen*
He drinks instant coffee.	He's going to drink real coffee again.
He rides a bicycle.	He's going to ride a moped again.
He drives on the left.	He's going to drive on the right again.
He speaks English.	He's going to speak French again.
He plays tennis.	He's going to play rugby again.
He reads *The Daily Mail*.	He's going to read *Le Monde* again.
He eats ketchup.	He's going to eat mayonnaise again.

Unit 12 Lesson 2 Exercise 2

1 e	7 c
2 i	8 j
3 l	9 a
4 g	10 d
5 b	11 f
6 k	12 h

Unit 12 Lesson 2 Exercise 3

a 1 Yes, please./No, thank you.
   2 Would you like to dance?
   3 How much is this, please?
   4 Can I help you?
   5 Can I try these on, please?
   6 What's the date today, please?
   7 What time is it, please?
   8 Can I make a phone call, please?
   9 Yes, of course.
     No, I'm sorry you can't.
  10 Could I have a coffee, please?
  11 Can I speak to Chris, please?
  12 This is X speaking.

b 1 How do you do?
   2 That's all right.
   3 You're welcome./Not at all.
   4 Yes, please./No, thank you.

Unit 12 Lesson 2 Exercise 4

(suggested answer)

A Are you hungry?
B Yes, I am.
A Would you like some salt?
B Yes, please.
A Here you are. Do you like it?
B Yes, it's lovely.
A Would you like some more?
B No thank you.
A Are you sure?
B Yes, thank you I'm full.
A Would you like some coffee?
B Yes, please.
A Do you want it black?
B No, white please.

Unit 12 Lesson 2 Exercise 5

2	1
4	6
3	5

Unit 12 Lesson 3 Exercise 1

1 The Houses of Parliament   D
2 Westminster Abbey   F
3 Buckingham Palace   C
4 Tower Bridge   I
5 Madame Tussaud's   B
6 10 Downing Street   A
7 Piccadilly Circus   H
8 St Paul's Cathedral   E
9 Trafalgar Square   G

Unit 12 Lesson 3 Exercise 2

1 pound(s)
2 20° Celsius
3 1,600 metres
4 miles per hour
5 Dublin
6 football
7 newspaper
8 shops
9 Cardiff
10 learner driver
11 99
12 ITV
13 from the age of 5 until you are 16
14 55 million
15 When you are 18.
16 Conservative party
17 18
18 Prince Charles
19 Glasgow
20 cars
21 Northern Ireland
22 football teams
23 airports
24 counties
25 Scotland
26 pop music

TAPESCRIPTS

Unit 1 Lesson 2 Exercise 5

Hello. My name's Manuel Santos, but my family and friends always call me Manolo. I'm from Granada in the south of Spain. I'm fifteen but my sixteenth birthday is next month.

Hello. My name's Estelle Verrier, and I'm French as you can probably hear. My home town is Vichy in the centre of France. It's a very beautiful old city. I'm not as old as Vichy. I'm only seventeen!

Hi. I'm Maki Tadeshi. I'm a Japanese student from Sapparo, in the north of Japan. I'm eighteen soon – my birthday's next week, in fact.

Hi. I'm Hans Beck. I come from a small town in Switzerland called Biel. I speak German and French, and a little English. I look older than I am. People think I'm eighteen, but in fact I'm only sixteen.

I'm from Sao Paulo in the south of Brazil. Brazilian people speak Portuguese, not Spanish. I'm sixteen years old. Oh, I almost forgot. My name's Salazar—Miguel Salazar.

Hello. My name's Ria Muhren. I'm Dutch. I live in a town in south-east Holland called Arnhem. It has about 100,000 people. I'm fourteen. I've got two brothers. They're ten and twelve.

Unit 1 Lesson 3 Exercise 2

Where do these conversations take place? Listen carefully.

Number one

A Can I cash these traveller's cheques, please?
B Yes, can I see your passport, please . . . Thank you. Can you sign your name here, please . . . How would you like the money?
A In fives, please.

The conversation takes place in a bank. So you write number 1 under the picture of a student in a bank.

Now listen to these conversations and write the correct number under each picture.

Number 2

A Any more fares?
B Victoria Station, please.
A 65p, please . . . Thank you.
B Can you tell me when to get off, please?
A Right you are love . . . Any more fares, please?

Number 3

A Yes, what's the problem?
B It's my back. I've got a terrible pain just here.
A I see. Can you just take your shirt off and lie down over there . . .

Number 4

A Have you got the latest Dire Straits album, please?
B Yes, it's over there.
A But have you got it on cassette?
B Yes, of course.
A How much is it?
B It's £6.95.
A All right, I'll have it, please.

Number 5

'Right. Sit down and shut up. Now take out your books, please, and open them at page 39. Stop talking at the back there! Ah don't tell me Wayne—you've forgotten your book again.

Number 6

A What do you want?
B Ooh, I'm hungry. I think I'm going to have a Super Mac with chips.
A I'll just have a cheeseburger, I think.

Unit 2 Lesson 3 Exercise 3

Conversation number 1

A Excuse me, where's (the football ground), please?
B Erm, go down this road, and then turn right into Queen's Road. Then erm take the first left turn—that's Castle Street. Er, there's a post office on the corner. Then go along Castle Street until you get to a crossroads. Um, turn left at the crossroads, and it's on your right. You can't miss it—you won't be the only one there. Not quite, anyway!

Conversation number 2

A Excuse me, can you tell me the way to (the English Language Centre), please?
B Yes of course. Go to the end of this road. Turn left into Queen's Road. Go along Queen's Road until you come to a roundabout. Turn left at the roundabout, and it's on your right opposite the museum.

Conversation number 3

A Excuse me, I'd like to know where (the Linton Hotel) is.
B Do you know this town at all?
A No, I'm a stranger here.
B Ah, well, go to the end of this street, turn left and you're in Queen's Road. Erm, go along Queen's Road, and then take the third turning on the right. There's a pub on the corner, called the Queen's Head. Go down the High Street. Erm, pass the Technical College on your right. Turn left opposite the tennis courts, and then you'll see it on your right next to the cinema.

Unit 3 Lesson 2 Exercise 2

1 G-I-R-L
2 B-A-D
3 N-A-M-E
4 L-U-C-K-Y
5 F-R-I-E-N-D
6 N-E-W-S
7 H-A-L-F
8 M-O-P-E-D
9 B-R-O-T-H-E-R
10 C-O-M-P-U-T-E-R

Unit 3 Lesson 3 Exercise 3

Listen to this example first:

Number 1

A Psst!
B What is it?
A Have you got a pen I can borrow?
B No, I haven't got a pen. Is a pencil all right?
A Yes, fine thanks.

The conversation takes place in a classroom. So you write number 1 under the picture of students in a classroom.

Now listen to these conversations and write the correct number under each picture.

Number 2

A I'm thirsty. Have you got any money?
B What does it take?
A 10ps. But I've only got 50p. Have you got any change?
B Yes, I think so . . .

Number 3

A Have you got the time, please?
B Sorry?
A Can you tell me what time it is?
B No, I'm sorry, I haven't got a watch.

Number 4

A Have you got a stamp? I want to send this letter to my boyfriend.
B No, I'm sorry I haven't. Why don't you go to the post office?
A It's closed . . .

Number 5

A Can I help you?
B Yes, have you got these trainers in my size?
A What size are you?
B 41, I think . . .

Number 6

A Excuse me, have you got a light, please?
B Sorry?
A Have you got a light?
B No, I'm sorry, I don't smoke.

Unit 4 Lesson 3 Exercise 2

Listen to this interview with Gary Carter first.

I Excuse me. Can I just ask you a few questions?
GC Who? Me?
I Yes, it won't take a moment.
GC Yeah, all right then. What do you want to know?
I Can you tell me what you think of modern pop music?
GC Well, it's great, isn't it?
I So you like it?
GC Yeah, of course I do.
I How about football? Do you like football?
GC Yeah, Arsenal are magic! I never miss a match.
I So Arsenal's your favourite team?
GC Yeah, you can say that again!
I How about Tottenham?
GC No, they're rubbish!
I What about modern clothes—you know, fashion?
GC What do you mean?
I Well, do you like it?
GC Yes, it's all right I suppose. I just wear what's comfortable. I don't think about clothes very much.
I Well, that's all. Thank you very much.
GC Is that all? Don't you want to ask me anything else?

Now listen to this interview with Sandra Brent.

I Excuse me, have you got a moment. I'd just like to ask you a few questions?
SB Yes, all right, but I haven't got long. I've got a meeting in ten minutes.
I Can you just tell me what you think of modern fashion?
SB Oh, I love it! I think it's ever so exciting. I mean it's so colourful.
I And do you like modern music as well as modern clothes?
SB Well, I used to like it, and I used to listen to pop music on Radio 1. But I don't really know very much about it nowadays. Some of it sounds all right . . .
I And do you like football?
SB No, I can't stand it. It's so BORING! I can't understand how anyone can like it—22 grown men running around after a silly ball!

Now listen to the last interview, with Charles Wentworth-Smythe.

I Excuse me, sir!
WS Yes, what is it?
I Can I just ask you a few questions?
WS Yes, by all means. Go ahead.
I I'd just like to know what you think of modern pop music?
WS I don't like it at all. Far too noisy. Singers with long hair, some of them even wear ear rings. No, no, can't stand it.
I How about modern fashion?
WS Clothes, you mean? Yes, well, I rather like them. Very attractive, very pretty . . .ummm . . .
I And what do you think of football?
WS Football? Not a bad game. Of course, I prefer cricket myself, and golf. But I never watch it on television or go to a match.

TAPESCRIPTS

I Thank you very much, sir.
WS Not at all. Don't mention it!

Unit 5 Lesson 2 Exercise 5

Woman Morning. Can I help you?
Girl Yes, can I have two bananas, please?
Woman Yes, that's 29p. Anything else?
Girl Yes, can I have a can of lemonade, please?
Woman Right, that's 35p.
Girl Oh yes, and a packet of peanuts. How much are they?
Woman Small, medium or large?
Girl Medium, please.
Woman They're 27p.
Girl Yes, that's fine.
Woman Is that all?
Girl No, can I have a bar or milk chocolate, please?
Woman Is this all right?
Girl How much is it?
Woman It's 49p.
Girl Yes, OK.
Woman Anything else?
Girl No, that's all, thanks.

Unit 5 Lesson 3 Exercise 3

Hi. My name's Nicola. I'm a friend of Rob's. We go to the same school. Just in case you're interested, I'm going to tell you what I do every morning. My alarm clock rings at a quarter past seven. I'm never awake at that time. I lie in bed for the next 15 minutes, half-asleep. Then at exactly half past seven, I get up.

It takes me about five minutes to open my eyes, find my dressing gown and go downstairs. My sister's always in the bathroom at that time, and she spends hours in there, so I have my breakfast while I'm waiting. I make my own breakfast. It's always the same —two pieces of toast, with marmalade, and two cups of tea with two spoonfuls of sugar in. I sit down to eat it at a quarter to eight.

At eight o'clock my mother and father come down for their breakfast, and I know it's time for me to go upstairs for my shower. By the time I've had my shower, I'm wide awake for the first time. Then I brush my teeth, and put on my make-up.

Then I look at my watch, and it's always twenty past, so I'm late as usual. I run into my bedroom and get dressed. This never takes long because I wear the same every day—my school uniform.

Quarter of an hour later, at twenty-five to nine, I'm dressed and ready to leave home. I shout goodbye to my father—my mum's left for work already, and run to the bus stop.

At a quarter to nine, the bus comes round the corner and I get on it. Just as the bus starts moving, I always remember the homework I forgot to do or the books I left behind at home.

Unit 6 Lesson 2 Exercise 2

This is Marco.

Marco My family are very nice. They let me do what I want. For example, I can come home late at night, I can have friends in my room and I can have a bath whenever I want one. Oh, but there's one thing I mustn't do and that's smoke in my room. Nobody in the family smokes and they say they hate the smell of cigarettes.

And here is Pia.

Pia My family are very nice too, but they don't give me as much freedom as Marco's family. So, for example, I can't come home when I like. I must be home before 11, otherwise they worry about me. I'm not allowed to smoke in the house, but that's not a problem for me because I don't smoke anyway. One problem is hot water. There's never enough so I can't have a bath or shower when I want one. But, on the other hand, my landlady likes my friends so she doesn't mind if I bring them home with me and they always come up to my room.

Next is Martine.

Martine I'm sorry to have to say it but my family are not so nice. They don't let me do a lot of things. Just because I'm a girl they say I must come home early—before 10 o'clock! And I can't bring my friends home with me—they say we are too noisy! And they have another ridiculous rule—I can only have three baths a week! But I can smoke as much as I like because they all smoke themselves!

Finally, this is Takao

Takao I am very happy with my English family. I can come home late if I want to—but I never do because I am usually up in my room doing my homework. My friends sometimes come round to help me because, as you can hear, I find English very difficult. When I first arrived, my landlady said I could smoke in my room if I wanted to but I never smoke so that's no problem. But there is one problem with my family. At home we keep very clean, but it is difficult here in England because there is not enough hot water, so I can't have a bath every day as I do in Japan.

Unit 6 Lesson 3 Exercise 2

Open your mouth. Close your mouth. Touch your nose. Close your eyes. Pull your hair. Open your eyes. Turn your head to the left. Put one finger in your right ear. Put your hands on your stomach. Shake hands with the student next to you. Put one foot on your chair. Fold your arms. Touch your toes. Stand on one leg. Put your tongue out . . . Stand like that for the rest of the lesson.

Unit 7 Lesson 2 Exercise 6

Message A

Voice 1 Hello! Can I speak to Manolo, please?
Voice 2 I'm afraid you can't. He's out at the moment. Can I take a message?
Voice 1 Yes, please. Can you ask him to ring me before 8 o'clock. This is Fina.
Voice 2 Can you spell that, please?
Voice 1 Yes, F-I-N-A. Fina.
Voice 2 Has Manolo got your number?
Voice 1 Yes, I think he has. But just in case, it's 351 8818.
Voice 2 Just a moment . . . that's 351 8818. OK, I'll ask him to ring you before 8.
Voice 1 Thanks very much. Goodbye!
Voice 2 Bye, Fina.

Message B

Voice 1 Hello! Mary Lawrence speaking.
Voice 2 Oh, hello. Can I speak to Mitsuko, please?
Voice 1 No, I'm sorry, she's out shopping.
Voice 2 Oh, what a pity. Can I leave a message?
Voice 1 Yes, of course.
Voice 2 Can you tell her I've got two tickets for a concert tonight. It starts at 8.30. Can she meet me outside the bus station at 8?
Voice 1 OK, I'll tell her. Who's speaking, please?
Voice 2 This is Anna. Thank you very much, Mrs Lawrence.
Voice 1 You're welcome, Anna. Goodbye.
Voice 2 Bye.

Unit 7 Lesson 3 Exercise 2

Here is an example first.

'In the picture, the weather is terrible. It's raining.'

This is not true, because the sun is shining and the weather is good, so you put a cross.

Now listen to these sentences.

Number 1:   Four people are playing tennis.
Number 2:   A dog's swimming in the lake.
Number 3:   Three people are having a picnic.
Number 4:   Six boys are playing football.
Number 5:   A boy and a girl are walking hand in hand.
Number 6:   A woman's jogging.
Number 7:   Three people are sitting on a park bench.
Number 8:   Two of them are talking, and one's reading a book.
Number 9:   A boy's fishing in the lake.
Number 10: A plane's flying over the park.

Unit 8 Lesson 2 Exercise 4

Sharon Hello!
David Hi Sharon, this is David.
Sharon David . . . ? Oh, David!
David You remember me, don't you?
Sharon Oh yes, I remember you.
David Would you like to come to a party tonight?
Sharon A party? Where is this party?
David It's at my place.
Sharon Oh, I'm afraid I'm busy this evening.
David Oh that's a pity. Then would you like to go out tomorrow night, to a club maybe?
Sharon Tomorrow night . . . um no, I'm sorry, I must wash my hair tomorrow.
David Well, how about Thursday night? There's a good film on at the Odeon—it's called 'Yours for ever'.
Sharon No thanks, David. I don't like love stories.
David Well, what about Friday?
Sharon Friday? No, I'm sorry, I can't . . .

Unit 8 Lesson 3 Exercise 4

Girl Hello, this is Becky. Can I speak to Peter, please?
Boy (This is Peter speaking.)
Girl Oh good, it is you! You sound different on the phone. (pause) What are you doing?
Boy (I'm watching television.)
Girl What programme are you watching?
Boy ('Eastenders', of course.)
Girl Oh, I never watch 'Eastenders'. . . . What time does it finish?
Boy (Eight o'clock.)
Girl Oh, it's nearly eight now. Would you like to come out afterwards?
Boy (Yes, all right.)
Girl Good. What time can you be ready?
Boy (Oh, I don't know . . . at about half past, I suppose.)
Girl In about half an hour then. Shall I come round to your house?
Boy (No, it's better if we meet in town.)
Girl All right, I'll meet you outside the post office at half past eight.
Boy (Nick will probably come with me.)
Girl Oh no, not Mick! Can't you go anywhere without him?
Boy (But he's my best mate!)
Girl Oh, all right then. I'll see both of you outside the post office at half past eight then.

TAPESCRIPTS

Unit 9 Lesson 2 Exercise 7

A
Boy Are you doing anything special this evening?
Girl No, I don't think so.
Boy Shall we go and see a film?
Girl No, I went to the cinema last night.
Boy Why don't we go bowling then?
Girl Is it very expensive?
Boy No, not really.
Girl OK. What time shall we meet?
Boy What's the time now?
Girl It's just after seven.
Boy All right, let's say we'll meet at a quarter to eight.
Girl But where shall we meet?
Boy At the leisure centre.
Girl Inside or outside?
Boy Inside — it's bound to be raining!
Girl OK, fine . . .

B
Girl What are you doing this afternoon?
Boy Nothing special. Why?
Girl Well, why don't we go horse riding? There's a good riding school only three kilometres from here.
Boy Yes, OK — but how do we get there?
Girl Well, there's a bus which goes from outside the school.
Boy OK, so we can meet outside the school then. What time does the bus go?
Girl Every half hour. So we can catch the half past two bus.
Boy All right, I'll meet you at the bus stop at twenty–five past then.
Girl Well, don't be late! . . .

C
Boy I'm starving. Shall we go somewhere to eat?
Girl Yes, I'm hungry too. Why don't we have a pizza?
Boy Yes, good idea. Do you know a good pizza place?
Girl Yes, there's a Pizza Express in the shopping centre. Do you know it?
Boy No, I don't I'm afraid.
Girl Where shall we meet then?
Boy How about the bus station?
Girl Yes, fine. The Pizza Express is only two minutes from there. What time shall we meet?
Boy Half past seven?
Girl No, that's a bit early. Shall we say eight o'clock?
Boy Yes, OK. See you later then . . .

Unit 9 Lesson 3 Exercise 2

1 Attention! By the left, quick march! Left, right, left, right, left–turn.

2 We're now flying at a height of 35,000 feet and our expected arrival time in Palma is 11.15, that is in 25 minutes . . . So just sit back and enjoy yourselves for the rest of the flight.

3 Now could we have the bride and groom together . . . a bit closer . . . that's lovely . . . and now a big smile . . . great . . .

4 . . . That was Jimmy Riddle's latest single, and I'm sure that'll be another big hit for him. And now, at number 14 in the charts this week, we've got the Casuals and 'Count on Me' . . .

5 Where did you say you want to go? Parkside Avenue? Where's that, — I've never heard of it. Hold on, I'll have a look at my map . . .

6 I'm afraid you've got one or two problems. You'll need new tyres on the front, and the brakes aren't working very well, are they? So if you leave it with me, I'll ring you when it's finished.

Unit 10 Lesson 2 Exercise 3

Shop assistant Can I help you?
Girl Yes, have you got this T-shirt in yellow?
Shop assistant What size are you?
Girl Small.
Shop assistant Just a moment . . . Yes, this one's your size.
Girl How much is it?
Shop assistant 6.99.
Girl OK fine, I'll have it. And I'm looking for a blue denim skirt.
Shop assistant What size are you?
Girl 10, I think.
Shop assistant They're over here . . . Let's see . . . Yes, here we are, size 10.
Girl Can I try it on, please?
Shop assistant Yes, of course. The fitting rooms are over there.

Girl No, I'm afraid it's too big. Have you got size 8?
Shop assistant Yes, here you are.

(pause)

Girl Yes, that's just right. How much is it?
Shop assistant £16.25
Girl All right. Oh, I just remembered. Can I have a pair of black tights, please.
Shop assistant Yes, these are £1.20 . . .

Unit 10 Lesson 3 Exercise 4

Maid Good morning, my lady. Your cup of tea.

Lord B What's the matter, Susan? What's happened?
Maid It's . . . It's Lady Bartley . . . Your wife, my lord . . . She's dead . . .
Police Inspector Lord Bartley, I'm Inspector Hindmarch. I'm sorry, but I must ask you a few questions.
Lord B Yes, of course, Inspector. I quite understand.
Inspector Now, first of all, what time did you have dinner last night?
Lord B Oh, I suppose it was about half past eight.

Inspector And did you have dinner with your wife or alone?
Lord B Oh, with my wife of course.
Inspector And what did you have for dinner?
Lord B Is that really important, Inspector?
Inspector Could you please just answer my question, Lord Bartley?
Lord B Oh, let me see . . . we had chicken . . . and vegetables of course. Nothing very special.
Inspector And what did you do after dinner,
Lord B We watched a film. I think it was called . . .
Inspector So you went to the cinema?
Lord B No, no, we watched it here, on the video. We stayed in all evening.
Inspector And what time did you go to bed?
Lord B Well, my wife went to bed at 11 o'clock. She said she was tired. And I went to bed . . . when was it? I can't remember . . .
Inspector What time *did* you go to bed, Lord Bartley?
Lord B Oh, at about 11.30, I suppose. That's right, about half past eleven.
Inspector And did you sleep in the same bedroom as your wife?
Lord B No, I didn't. We sleep . . . we slept in different bedrooms.
Inspector Lord Bartley, I must ask you—did you kill your wife?
Lord B No, of course I didn't kill my wife! Of course I didn't kill her!

Unit 11 Lesson 3 Exercise 2

The tallest man in the world was Robert Wadlow from Alton, Illinois, USA. He was born in 1918 and by the time he was 21 he had grown to the height of 2.72 metres. He died one year later, at the age of 22.

The tallest woman in the world was from Central China. Her name was Zeng Jinlain and she was born in 1964. When she died in 1982 at the age of only 18, she was 2.47 metres.

The heaviest man who ever lived was Jon Minnoch from Washington, USA. He was born in 1941 and reached his heaviest weight in 1976, when he was 442 kilos. He worked as a taxi driver until his death in 1983.

The lightest baby to survive was Marian Chapman. She was born in South Shields, England in 1938. When she was born, six weeks before she was expected, she weighed only 283 grams. By the time she was 21 she weighed a fairly normal 48 kilos.

Lots of people have claimed to be the world's oldest person. A Japanese man, Shigechiyo Izumi, was 120 years and 237 days old when he died on 21 February 1986. When asked about the secret of a long life he said simply 'not to worry'.

The oldest mother in the world was Mrs Ruth Kistler who had a daughter, Susan, in Glendale, California on 18 October, 1956 when she was 57 years, 129 days old.

Unit 12 Lesson 2 Exercise 5

Number 1

A Can I cash a traveller's cheque here?
B Yes, have you got any means of identification?
A Yes, I've got my passport . . .

Number two

A What's the score?
B 40 – 0
A You're not playing very well.
B I know. It's the racket—it's too heavy . . .

Number three

A Yes, can I help you?
B Are there any squash courts free?
A Not at the moment, I'm afraid, but there's one free at 2.30
B OK, can I book that one, please? . . .

Number four

A Are they the right size?
B No, I'm afraid they're too big. Have you got a size 28?
A Yes, I think so. I'll just have a look . . .

Number five

A No, no, no, you don't hold the reins like that! What did I tell you? Sit up straight in the saddle! . . .

Number six

A How much is that?
B What did you have?
A Two milkshakes and two cakes.
B That's £1.80 altogether, please . . .

TESTS

Placement test

The placement test (pages 104–107) consists of 100 multiple choice questions. Students should work through them at their own speed, marking their answers with a cross on the answer sheet on page 107. With the help of the mark sheet on page 108 (which should be photocopied on to an acetate), tests can be corrected quickly and students allotted to classes/groups according to their total score. As far as *OK* is concerned, we suggest the following:

0–40 correct answers = Book 1
40–60 correct answers = Book 2
60–80 correct answers = Book 3
80–100 correct answers = Book 4

If time allows, you may find it helpful to supplement the placement test with a brief interview and a short piece of extended writing.

Progress tests

Progress tests are included for use after every four units. These are of two types:

1 quick multiple choice tests with 25 questions (pages 109–111). These cover the main grammar points of the preceding four units, and also include questions on the second and third lessons ('English in situations' and 'Fun with English'). These tests can be done quickly and marked in class, ideally at the end of every week.

2 more demanding tests which concentrate on the grammar taught in the 'Grammar in action' lessons (pages 112–113). These tests are probably best done for homework, over the weekend.

Individual teachers can decide whether to use the first or second type of test or both.

Note: You may make photocopies of the following pages but please note that copyright law does not normally permit multiple copying of published material.

Choose the best answer.
Mark your answers (a) b) c) or d)) with a cross (×) on the answer sheet.

1 .... your name?
   a) Why's
   b) What's
   c) How's
   d) Who's

2 .... old are you?
   a) Who
   b) What
   c) How
   d) When

3 a) I'm 17 years old.
   b) I've 17 years old.
   c) I are 17 years old.
   d) I've 17 years.

4 This is .... interesting book.
   a) the
   b) a
   c) an
   d) ....

5 a) They're beautiful girls.
   b) They're girls beautiful.
   c) They're beautifuls girls.
   d) They're girls beautifuls.

6 John and I .... English.
   a) we are
   b) are
   c) we
   d) am

7 a) I've cold.
   b) I has cold.
   c) I are cold.
   d) I'm cold.

8 .... Italian?
   a) You are
   b) Is you
   c) You
   d) Are you

9 There .... ten students in the class.
   a) is
   b) are
   c) be
   d) am

10 Is this your pen?
   a) No, not.
   b) No, isn't.
   c) No, it isn't.
   d) No, this isn't.

11 She's a student. .... brother's a teacher.
   a) His
   b) Her
   c) She
   d) She's

12 We're Swedish. .... names are Tomas and Karl.
   a) Our
   b) We
   c) Us
   d) His

13 Give it to ....
   a) he
   b) I
   c) she
   d) her

14 Show .... the photographs.
   a) their
   b) they
   c) them
   d) theirs

15 What's .... name of this book?
   a) a
   b) the
   c) an
   d) ....

16 .... a bicycle?
   a) You have
   b) Has you
   c) Have you got
   d) You've got

17 Peter .... a tennis racket.
   a) hasn't got
   b) haven't
   c) not has
   d) haven't got

18 Has Anna got a boyfriend? ....
   a) No, she hasn't.
   b) No, she hasn't got.
   c) No, she haven't.
   d) No, she not.

19 a) He no can speak Spanish.
   b) He can't speaks Spanish.
   c) He can't to speak Spanish.
   d) He can't speak Spanish.

20 .... on the right in Britain.
   a) You mustn't to drive
   b) You not must drive
   c) You mustn't driving
   d) You mustn't drive

21 Whose desk is this? ....
   a) It's of Robert.
   b) It's Robert.
   c) It's Robert's.
   d) It's to Robert.

22 a) You he likes.
   b) He likes you.
   c) He you likes.
   d) You likes he.

23 I speak French and English. David only .... English.
   a) speak
   b) does speak
   c) do speak
   d) speaks.

24 Does Michelle like John?
   a) No, she not.
   b) No, she doesn't.
   c) No, she don't.
   d) No, she doesn't like.

25 a) He don't smoke.
   b) He not smoke.
   c) He doesn't smokes.
   d) He doesn't smoke.

26 a) What means this word?
   b) What does mean this word?
   c) What does this word mean?
   d) What is this word mean?

27 Walk!
   a) Run not.
   b) Not run.
   c) Don't run.
   d) No run.

28 Listen! I .... to you.
   a) am talking
   b) talk
   c) do talk
   d) am talk

29 We can't go out now. ....
   a) It rains.
   b) It's raining.
   c) It rain.
   d) It raining.

30 a) Come at nine o'clock in Friday.
   b) Come on nine o'clock on Friday.
   c) Come at nine o'clock on Friday.
   d) Come at nine o'clock at Friday.

31 Do you go .... school by bus?
   a) at
   b) in
   c) on
   d) to

32 a) What you are doing?
   b) What's you doing?
   c) What are you doing?
   d) What are you do?

33 She usually .... to bed at about
   11.30.
   a) go
   b) is going
   c) does go
   d) goes

34 .... people over there are German.
   a) These
   b) This
   c) That
   d) Those

35 Come and look at .... photograph.
   a) these
   b) that
   c) this
   d) those

36 How many chairs are there?
   a) There are five.
   b) There is five.
   c) It is five.
   d) They are five.

37 .... five people in my family.
   a) There are
   b) They are
   c) It is
   d) There is

38 I haven't got .... money.
   a) no
   b) some
   c) ....
   d) any

39 There is .... sugar in this coffee.
   a) a lot of
   b) much
   c) many
   d) a lot

40 How much money have you got?
   a) Much.
   b) Not much.
   c) A lot of.
   d) Not many.

41 There are .... people here already.
   a) a few
   b) a little
   c) much
   d) a lot

42 .... late this morning?
   a) Were you
   b) Was you
   c) You were
   d) You was

43 Was she at school yesterday?
   a) No, she weren't.
   b) No, she wasn't.
   c) No, she not.
   d) No, wasn't.

44 Were there many people at the party?
   a) Yes, there were.
   b) Yes, they were.
   c) Yes, it was.
   d) Yes, there was.

45 How long ....?
   a) waited he
   b) did he waited
   c) he waited
   d) did he wait

46 Did Tim and Mark win the match?
   a) No, they not.
   b) No, they did.
   c) No, they didn't.
   d) No, they don't.

47 Sarah .... out last night.
   a) didn't went
   b) didn't goes
   c) didn't go
   d) no went

48 Why .... to your party?
   a) they not come
   b) they didn't come
   c) not they came
   d) didn't they come

49 .... to a disco last night?
   a) Went you
   b) Did you go
   c) Did you went
   d) You go

50 I came to England .... English.
   a) for learning
   b) for to learn
   c) to learn
   d) to learning

51 a) I never go to bed before ten.
   b) I go never to bed before ten.
   c) Never I go to bed before ten.
   d) I go to bed before ten never.

52 She's .... than me.
   a) more old
   b) older
   c) more older
   d) most old

53 He's .... at tennis than football.
   a) more good
   b) better
   c) best
   d) more better

54 England is .... than Spain.
   a) expensiver
   b) more expensiver
   c) more expensive
   d) the more expensive

55 It was .... day of the summer.
   a) the hottest
   b) the most hot
   c) the most hottest
   d) hottest

56 You're not .... me.
   a) as tall than
   b) as taller as
   c) tall as
   d) as tall as

57 I .... television this evening.
   a) am going to watch
   b) watching
   c) watch
   d) go to watch

58 a) What time is the train going to
      leave?
   b) What time the train is going to
      leave?
   c) What time is going to leave the
      train?
   d) What time going to leave is the
      train?

59 I enjoy .... early.
   a) to get up
   b) getting up
   c) to getting up
   d) get up

60 a) You will come with me
      tomorrow?
   b) Do you come with me
      tomorrow?
   c) Come you with me tomorrow?
   d) Will you come with me
      tomorrow?

61 Oh no! .... my key.
   a) I lost
   b) I've lost
   c) I'm lost
   d) I've lose

62 a) Where they have gone?
   b) Where have they gone?
   c) Where have they went?
   d) Where have they go?

63 a) I've never be to America.
   b) I never been to America.
   c) I've never been to America.
   d) I never was to America.

64 a) They didn't arrive yet.
   b) They haven't arrive yet.
   c) They hasn't arrived yet.
   d) They haven't arrived yet.

65 He .... school last June.
   a) left
   b) has left
   c) did leave
   d) has leave

66 I .... in England since 20th May.
   a) was
   b) am
   c) been
   d) have been

67 We .... to the cinema yesterday.
   a) were
   b) went
   c) have gone
   d) have been

68 .... English since I was twelve.
   a) I'm learning
   b) I've learned
   c) I learn
   d) I've learning

69 I spoke to a girl .... was from Barcelona.
   a) which
   b) ....
   c) who
   d) whose

70 We went to a disco .... was open till 4 a.m.
   a) who
   b) where
   c) ....
   d) which

71 I was in England .... two weeks.
   a) during
   b) for
   c) in
   d) on

72 When I looked out of the window, ...
   a) it was raining
   b) it were raining
   c) it rained
   d) it's raining

73 What .... at ten o'clock when I phoned?
   a) did you do
   b) you were doing
   c) were you doing
   d) did you

74 .... a bath when I opened the door.
   a) He had
   b) He has had
   c) He's having
   d) He was having

75 I .... home when the party was over.
   a) was driving
   b) drive
   c) drove
   d) have driven

76 He left without .... goodbye.
   a) to say
   b) say
   c) saying
   d) said

77 I don't mind ....
   a) waiting
   b) I wait
   c) to wait
   d) that I wait

78 Did you .... yesterday afternoon?
   a) go shop
   b) went shopping
   c) go to shop
   d) go shopping

79 He speaks English ....
   a) good but slow.
   b) well but slow.
   c) good but slowly.
   d) well but slowly.

80 a) I come if you pay for me.
   b) I'll come if you pay for me.
   c) I'll come if you paid for me.
   d) I come if you'll pay for me.

91 The match .... on Saturday.
   a) is going to play
   b) is going to be played
   c) is playing
   d) is going to be playing

92 a) If he asked you out, would you go?
   b) If he asks you out, would you go?
   c) If he asked you out, will you go?
   d) If he asked you out, do you go?

93 a) You'd pass the exam, if you will work harder.
   b) You passed the exam, if you worked harder.
   c) You'll pass the exam, if you would work harder.
   d) You'd pass the exam, if you worked harder.

94 Do you think they'll win? Yes, I ....
   a) hope
   b) hope that
   c) hope so
   d) hope it

95 Will she pass the exam?
   a) No, I don't think so.
   b) No, I don't think it.
   c) No, I don't think.
   d) No, I not think so.

96 .... this letter for me.
   a) I want that you post
   b) I want you to post
   c) I want you post
   d) I want you posting

97 They didn't ask .... to their party.
   a) that I come
   b) me come
   c) me for to come
   d) me to come

98 Didn't I tell ....?
   a) you shut the door
   b) you to shut the door
   c) you the door to shut
   d) that you shut the door

99 There's .... wrong with this pen.
   a) anything
   b) somebody
   c) something
   d) anybody

100 I didn't speak to ....
   a) anybody
   b) anything
   c) nobody
   d) somebody

ANSWER SHEET

1	a	b	c	d	51	a	b	c	d
2	a	b	c	d	52	a	b	c	d
3	a	b	c	d	53	a	b	c	d
4	a	b	c	d	54	a	b	c	d
5	a	b	c	d	55	a	b	c	d
6	a	b	c	d	56	a	b	c	d
7	a	b	c	d	57	a	b	c	d
8	a	b	c	d	58	a	b	c	d
9	a	b	c	d	59	a	b	c	d
10	a	b	c	d	60	a	b	c	d
11	a	b	c	d	61	a	b	c	d
12	a	b	c	d	62	a	b	c	d
13	a	b	c	d	63	a	b	c	d
14	a	b	c	d	64	a	b	c	d
15	a	b	c	d	65	a	b	c	d
16	a	b	c	d	66	a	b	c	d
17	a	b	c	d	67	a	b	c	d
18	a	b	c	d	68	a	b	c	d
19	a	b	c	d	69	a	b	c	d
20	a	b	c	d	70	a	b	c	d
21	a	b	c	d	71	a	b	c	d
22	a	b	c	d	72	a	b	c	d
23	a	b	c	d	73	a	b	c	d
24	a	b	c	d	74	a	b	c	d
25	a	b	c	d	75	a	b	c	d
26	a	b	c	d	76	a	b	c	d
27	a	b	c	d	77	a	b	c	d
28	a	b	c	d	78	a	b	c	d
29	a	b	c	d	79	a	b	c	d
30	a	b	c	d	80	a	b	c	d
31	a	b	c	d	81	a	b	c	d
32	a	b	c	d	82	a	b	c	d
33	a	b	c	d	83	a	b	c	d
34	a	b	c	d	84	a	b	c	d
35	a	b	c	d	85	a	b	c	d
36	a	b	c	d	86	a	b	c	d
37	a	b	c	d	87	a	b	c	d
38	a	b	c	d	88	a	b	c	d
39	a	b	c	d	89	a	b	c	d
40	a	b	c	d	90	a	b	c	d
41	a	b	c	d	91	a	b	c	d
42	a	b	c	d	92	a	b	c	d
43	a	b	c	d	93	a	b	c	d
44	a	b	c	d	94	a	b	c	d
45	a	b	c	d	95	a	b	c	d
46	a	b	c	d	96	a	b	c	d
47	a	b	c	d	97	a	b	c	d
48	a	b	c	d	98	a	b	c	d
49	a	b	c	d	99	a	b	c	d
50	a	b	c	d	100	a	b	c	d

MARK SHEET

#	a	b	c	d		#	a	b	c	d
1	a	**(b)**	c	d		51	**(a)**	b	c	d
2	a	b	**(c)**	d		52	a	**(b)**	c	d
3	**(a)**	b	c	d		53	a	**(b)**	c	d
4	a	b	**(c)**	d		54	a	b	**(c)**	d
5	**(a)**	b	c	d		55	**(a)**	b	c	d
6	a	**(b)**	c	d		56	a	b	c	**(d)**
7	a	b	c	**(d)**		57	**(a)**	b	c	d
8	a	b	c	**(d)**		58	**(a)**	b	c	d
9	a	**(b)**	c	d		59	a	**(b)**	c	d
10	a	b	**(c)**	d		60	a	b	c	**(d)**
11	a	**(b)**	c	d		61	a	**(b)**	c	d
12	**(a)**	b	c	d		62	a	**(b)**	c	d
13	a	b	c	**(d)**		63	a	b	**(c)**	d
14	a	b	**(c)**	d		64	a	b	c	**(d)**
15	a	**(b)**	c	d		65	**(a)**	b	c	d
16	a	b	**(c)**	d		66	a	b	c	**(d)**
17	**(a)**	b	c	d		67	a	**(b)**	c	d
18	**(a)**	b	c	d		68	a	**(b)**	c	d
19	a	b	c	**(d)**		69	a	b	**(c)**	d
20	a	b	c	**(d)**		70	a	b	c	**(d)**
21	a	b	**(c)**	d		71	a	**(b)**	c	d
22	a	**(b)**	c	d		72	**(a)**	b	c	d
23	a	b	c	**(d)**		73	a	b	**(c)**	d
24	a	**(b)**	c	d		74	a	b	c	**(d)**
25	a	b	c	**(d)**		75	a	b	**(c)**	d
26	a	b	**(c)**	d		76	a	b	**(c)**	d
27	a	b	**(c)**	d		77	**(a)**	b	c	d
28	**(a)**	b	c	d		78	a	b	c	**(d)**
29	a	**(b)**	c	d		79	a	b	c	**(d)**
30	a	b	**(c)**	d		80	a	**(b)**	c	d
31	a	b	c	**(d)**		81	**(a)**	b	c	d
32	a	b	**(c)**	d		82	a	b	**(c)**	d
33	a	b	c	**(d)**		83	**(a)**	b	c	d
34	a	b	c	**(d)**		84	a	b	c	**(d)**
35	a	b	**(c)**	d		85	a	b	c	**(d)**
36	**(a)**	b	c	d		86	**(a)**	b	c	d
37	**(a)**	b	c	d		87	a	**(b)**	c	d
38	a	b	c	**(d)**		88	a	b	**(c)**	d
39	**(a)**	b	c	d		89	a	b	**(c)**	d
40	a	**(b)**	c	d		90	a	b	c	**(d)**
41	**(a)**	b	c	d		91	a	**(b)**	c	d
42	**(a)**	b	c	d		92	**(a)**	b	c	d
43	a	**(b)**	c	d		93	a	b	c	**(d)**
44	**(a)**	b	c	d		94	a	b	**(c)**	d
45	a	b	c	**(d)**		95	**(a)**	b	c	d
46	a	b	**(c)**	d		96	a	**(b)**	c	d
47	a	b	**(c)**	d		97	a	b	c	**(d)**
48	a	b	c	**(d)**		98	a	**(b)**	c	d
49	a	**(b)**	c	d		99	a	b	**(c)**	d
50	a	b	**(c)**	d		100	**(a)**	b	c	d

PROGRESS TEST I (UNITS 1–4)

Tick (√) the best answer.

1 My name ☐ am Rob.
☐ be
☐ are
☐ is

2 I ☐ am 16 years.
☐ have 16 years.
☐ has 16.
☐ am 16.

3 Mr and Mrs Bond ☐ are from Hastings.
☐ is
☐ be
☐ am

4 ☐ They house isn't very big.
☐ Their
☐ Theirs
☐ There

5 Mrs Bond's about 40. ☐ His name's Sue.
☐ Hers
☐ She's
☐ Her

6 Steve is ☐ Rob's father.
☐ the father of Rob.
☐ Robs father.
☐ Robs' father.

7 'How do you do?' ☐ 'Fine thanks.'
☐ 'Very well thank you.'
☐ 'How do you do?'
☐ 'Not too bad.'

8 'I'm sorry I'm late.' ☐ 'That's OK.'
☐ 'Not too bad.'
☐ 'That's nothing.'
☐ 'I'm all right.'

9 ☐ This is your bedroom over there.
☐ These
☐ That
☐ Those

10 ☐ This drawers here are for your clothes.
☐ These
☐ That
☐ Those

11 Hastings is a town in ☐ a south of England.
☐ an
☐ the
☐ ....

12 What's ☐ the name of this book?
☐ a
☐ ....
☐ an

13 'Thanks very much.' ☐ 'All right.'
☐ 'Fine thanks.'
☐ 'You're OK.'
☐ 'You're welcome.'

14 The Bonds ☐ are having two children.
☐ has got
☐ have got
☐ has

15 Rob ☐ hasn't got a moped.
☐ haven't
☐ not has
☐ don't have

16 ☐ Have Dominique a sister?
☐ Has Dominique got a sister?
☐ Has got Dominique a sister?
☐ Does have Dominique a sister?

17 Have the Bonds got a big house? ☐ No, they not.
☐ No, they haven't got.
☐ No, they hasn't.
☐ No, they haven't.

18 Hastings is ☐ an old town.
☐ a
☐ ....
☐ the

19 Dominique ☐ speak good English.
☐ do speak
☐ speaks
☐ speaking

20 Where ☐ do he come from?
☐ does he come from?
☐ is he come from?
☐ does he come from?

21 ☐ 'Do you want to listen to this record?'
☐ 'Want you
☐ 'Does you want
☐ 'Are you want

22 He ☐ don't like the record by Razzmataz.
☐ isn't like
☐ doesn't likes
☐ doesn't like

23 Does he like French pop music? ☐ Yes, he do.
☐ Yes, he likes.
☐ Yes, he does like.
☐ Yes, he does.

24 7.35 is ☐ seven and thirty-five.
☐ thirty-five past seven.
☐ twenty-five to eight.
☐ eight less twenty-five.

25 12.57 is ☐ three minutes to one.
☐ three to one.
☐ three before one.
☐ twelve and fifty-seven.

Tick (√) the best answer.

1 ☐ Never is he late for school.
   ☐ He is never late for school.
   ☐ For school he is never late.
   ☐ He is late for school never.

2 ☐ I sometimes forget my homework.
   ☐ I forget sometimes my homework.
   ☐ My homework sometimes I forget.
   ☐ Sometimes forget I my homework.

3 ☐ What time starts school?
   ☐ What time do school start?
   ☐ What time school start?
   ☐ What time does school start?

4 My sister ☐ wash   her hair three times a week.
            ☐ is washing
            ☐ washes
            ☐ are washing

5 Mike ☐ doesn't like   fish.
        ☐ don't like
        ☐ not like
        ☐ doesn't likes

6 Can I ☐ has   a Coke, please?
         ☐ having
         ☐ have
         ☐ to have

7 'Can I borrow your bike tonight?'
   ☐ 'No, I'm sorry you can.'   ☐ 'Yes, I'm afraid you can.'
   ☐ 'Yes, of course not.'   ☐ 'No, I'm afraid you can't.'

8 'Have you got your passport?'
   ☐ 'Yes, here is it.'   ☐ 'Yes, here we have.'
   ☐ 'Yes, here I have.'   ☐ 'Yes, here you are.'

9 'How much do these jeans cost?'
   ☐ 'It's £25.50.'   ☐ 'They costing £25.50.'
   ☐ 'They're £25.50.'   ☐ 'It costs £25.50.'

10 ☐ Is she got   a boyfriend?
   ☐ Has she got
   ☐ Does she got
   ☐ Have she got

11 ☐ Can he speak English?   ☐ Does he speaks English?
   ☐ Speaks he English?   ☐ Can he English?

12 'Can you play chess?'
   ☐ 'No, I don't can.'   ☐ 'Yes, I can't.'
   ☐ 'Yes, I can.'   ☐ 'No, can't.'

13 ☐ You don't must take photographs here.
   ☐ You mustn't take photographs here.
   ☐ You mustn't to take photographs here.
   ☐ You no must take photographs here.

14 ☐ It rain   again!
   ☐ It rains
   ☐ It's raining
   ☐ It raining

15 Listen! ☐ Is the telephone ringing?
          ☐ Are the telephone ringing?
          ☐ Does the telephone ring?
          ☐ Is ringing the telephone?

16 ☐ I never am speaking   English in Italy.
   ☐ I never is speaking
   ☐ I never speak
   ☐ I never speaking

17 'Can I speak to Tina, please?'
   ☐ 'What's the message?'
   ☐ 'No I'm sorry, she's not in.'
   ☐ 'No, I'll tell her.'
   ☐ 'What's your number?'

18 ☐ Can I take   a message?
   ☐ Can I give
   ☐ Can I tell him
   ☐ Can I have

19 Have you got ☐ some sisters?
               ☐ one sisters?
               ☐ any sisters?
               ☐ sisters?

20 I haven't got ☐ money.
                ☐ some money.
                ☐ a money.
                ☐ any money.

21 He wants ☐ an   information.
            ☐ some
            ☐ any
            ☐ all

22 ☐ There is   two men outside.
   ☐ There are
   ☐ It is
   ☐ They are

23 ☐ Is it   any bread left?
   ☐ There is
   ☐ Are there
   ☐ Is there

24 'Would you like to go for a walk?'
   ☐ 'Yes, all right.'
   ☐ 'Yes, I like.'
   ☐ 'Yes, I'd like.'
   ☐ 'Yes, I do.'

25 ☐ You like to dance?
   ☐ Would you like to dance?
   ☐ Like you to dance?
   ☐ Would you dance?

PROGRESS TEST 3 (UNITS 8–12)

Tick (√) the best answer.

1 ☐ Was | you in bed when I phoned?
   ☐ Were
   ☐ Did
   ☐ Are

2 I | ☐ is | at home at 10 o'clock last night.
      ☐ was
      ☐ are
      ☐ were

3 The film I saw last night | ☐ weren't | very good.
      ☐ didn't be
      ☐ wasn't
      ☐ didn't was

4 ☐ Did you had | a good game of tennis?
   ☐ Have you
   ☐ Did you has
   ☐ Did you have

5 ☐ Did your mother answer the phone?
   ☐ Your mother answered the phone?
   ☐ Did answer the phone your mother?
   ☐ Answered the phone your mother?

6 ☐ I don't go | to the party. I was too tired.
   ☐ I didn't went
   ☐ I didn't go
   ☐ I don't went

7 What time | ☐ do you phone | me yesterday?
      ☐ you phoned
      ☐ you did phone
      ☐ did you phone

8 'Did you see the film last night?' | ☐ 'Yes, I saw.'
      ☐ 'Yes, I did.'
      ☐ 'Yes, I did see.'
      ☐ 'Yes, I do.'

9 ☐ What did you do | last night?
   ☐ What do you do
   ☐ What did you
   ☐ What you did

10 He | ☐ come | to school late this morning.
      ☐ comes
      ☐ came
      ☐ do come

11 I'm bored. | ☐ What do we do?
      ☐ What are we do?
      ☐ What we shall do?
      ☐ What shall we do?

12 I've got an idea. | ☐ Let's go | to the beach.
      ☐ Why we don't go
      ☐ Let's to go
      ☐ Why we not go

13 'Can I help you?' | ☐ 'No, I'm looking only thanks.'
      ☐ 'No, I just look thanks.'
      ☐ 'No, I'm just looking thanks.'
      ☐ 'No, I only look thanks.'

14 Can I | ☐ prove | these jeans please?
      ☐ try on
      ☐ test
      ☐ fit

15 My brother is taller | ☐ as | me.
      ☐ than
      ☐ that
      ☐ ....

16 A mile is | ☐ longer | than a kilometre.
      ☐ more long
      ☐ more longer
      ☐ most long

17 I think maths is | ☐ importanter | than English.
      ☐ more important
      ☐ most important
      ☐ the more important

18 'The' is | ☐ the more commoner | word in English.
      ☐ the most commonest
      ☐ the most common
      ☐ most common

19 My English is | ☐ gooder | than yours.
      ☐ best
      ☐ more good
      ☐ better

20 I think English weather is | ☐ the baddest | in the world!
      ☐ the worst
      ☐ the most bad
      ☐ worst

21 Is it | ☐ fine | if I come home late tonight?
      ☐ well
      ☐ OK
      ☐ good

22 ☐ What are you going | to do tonight?
   ☐ What you are going
   ☐ What you going
   ☐ What are you go

23 I | ☐ going to | have a pizza.
      ☐ go to
      ☐ am going to
      ☐ am going

24 She | ☐ doesn't go | to miss you.
      ☐ not going
      ☐ isn't go
      ☐ isn't going

25 What's the date? | ☐ The eleven of June.
      ☐ June the eleven.
      ☐ The eleventh of June.
      ☐ The eleventh June.

PROGRESS TEST I (UNITS I–4)

I Put the following sentences into the singular.

Example: They're old houses.
            It's an old house.

1 They're difficult questions.
2 They aren't European countries.
3 They're important exams.
4 New cars are expensive.
5 Modern supermarkets are usually very big.
6 Black and white televisions are cheap.
7 Umbrellas are useful in England.
8 Cities are big towns.

2 What are the questions?

Example: Yes, I've got two sisters.
            Have you got any sisters?

1 .... ? My name's Chantal.
2 .... ? I'm 16.
3 .... ? I'm from France.
4 .... ? No, I can't speak Italian but I can speak Spanish.
5 .... ? It's half past three.
6 .... ? I'm fine thanks.
7 .... ? No, I haven't got a computer.
8 .... ? He comes from London.
9 .... ? No, she doesn't like football.
10 .... ? They live in Hastings.

3 Put the following sentences into the plural.

Example: This bag's heavy.
            These bags are heavy.

1 Who's that girl?
2 This question's easy.
3 Whose is this?
4 What's that?
5 That isn't your bag.
6 My brother's got a problem.
7 What does this mean?
8 That doesn't work.

4 Put do / does / don't / doesn't in the gaps in the following sentences.

1 What .... you want?
2 He .... know the answer.
3 .... he speak English?
4 We .... live here, we live in London.
5 Where .... they come from?
6 They .... understand a word of English.
7 What .... this mean?
8 How much .... these cost?
9 Banks .... open on Saturdays.
10 This machine .... work.

PROGRESS TEST 2 (UNITS 5–8)

I Put the words in the following sentences into the right order.

1 late he often is
2 often he does late how home come?
3 always home they at are
4 never I watch television football on
5 brother goes in always my the evening out
6 night usually I go a party to on Saturday
7 hair your often you do wash how?
8 my sometimes forget I homework

2 Put some or any in the gaps in the following sentences.

1 Have you got .... sisters?
2 I haven't got .... money.
3 I need .... new shoes.
4 He wants .... information.
5 I don't want .... sugar in my coffee.
6 Do you know .... English people?
7 There are .... men outside.
8 They don't want .... more.

3 What are the questions?

Example: My name's Enrico.
            What's your name?

1 .... ? No, I'm not French. I'm Italian.
2 .... ? There are six people in my family.
3 .... ? Yes, I've got one brother.
4 .... ? His name's Marco.
5 .... ? No, he can't speak English.
6 .... ? I'm staying in a hotel.
7 .... ? It costs £55 a week.
8 .... ? I usually get up at 7.30.
9 .... ? It starts at 9 o'clock.
10 .... ? I wash my hair twice a week.

4 Complete the following sentences with the correct form of the present simple (*she works*) or present continuous (*she's working*). Use the verbs in brackets.

Example: Go away! I .... (work)
            Go away! *I'm working!*

1 I .... my hair once a week. (wash)
2 My sister .... her hair three times a week. (wash)
3 'The telephone .... Can you answer it please?' (ring)
4 My father .... to bed at the same time every night. (go)
5 'Why .... you .... to bed?' 'Because I'm tired.' (go)
6 I .... to her twice a week. She never .... to me. (write)
7 Listen! I .... to you (talk)
8 It .... again! (rain)
9 'What .... you ....?' 'I'm a teacher.' (do)
10 'What .... Anna ....? She .... a bath.' (do) (have)

1

Put *was/wasn't, were/weren't* in the gaps in the following sentences.

1 Where .... you yesterday?
2 I .... ill.
3 What .... wrong with you?
4 My temperature .... 39.
5 .... you in bed?
6 No, I ....
7 .... your parents at home?
8 No, they ....

2

Answer the questions

Example: What did he buy?
He bought a record.

1 Where did they go?
.... to London.
2 Who did he meet?
.... some friends.
3 What time did it leave?
.... at 11.15.
4 When did they get there?
.... at 12.30.
5 Which train did he catch?
.... the 10.55.
6 What did she say?
.... 'Goodbye'.
7 How much money did he take?
.... £20.
8 Who did he ring?
.... me.
9 How did he come?
.... by train.
10 What did he forget?
.... her telephone number.

3

Put the correct form (comparative or superlative) of the word in brackets in the gaps in the sentences.

Example: Spain is .... than England. (hot)
Spain is _hotter_ than England.

1 Sweden is .... than England and the winters are much .... (cold) (long)
2 Germany is .... than England but it isn't .... country in Europe. (expensive)
3 Spain is .... country in Europe for holidays but it isn't .... (popular) (cheap)
4 English is a .... language than Italian but Italians say that their language is .... than English (useful) (beautiful)
5 For Spanish people, English is .... to learn than Italian. (difficult)
6 A lot of people say that English food is .... in Europe. (bad)
7 French food is definitely .... than English food. (good)
8 French people say their food is .... in the world. (good)

4

Complete these sentences using the *going to* future.

Example: The train/leave/soon.
The train's going to leave soon.

1 We/meet/at 8 o'clock.
2 Which film/you/see?
3 I/not stay/at home this evening.
4 The lesson/finish soon.
5 What time/this programme/end?
6 They/not/pass the exam.
7 I/pass it?
8 The shops/close at 5.30.